Conversations with Susan Sontag

Literary Conversations Series

Peggy Whitman Prenshaw
General Editor

Conversations
with Susan Sontag

Edited by Leland Poague

University Press of Mississippi
Jackson

Copyright © 1995 by the University Press of Mississippi
All rights reserved
Manufactured in the United States of America

98 97 96 95   4 3 2 1

The paper in this book meets the guidelines for permanence and durability of the Committee
on Production Guidelines for Book Longevity of the Council on Library Resources.

Library of Congress Cataloging-in-Publication Data

Sontag, Susan, 1933–
    Conversations with Susan Sontag / edited by Leland Poague.
        p.   cm. — (Literary conversations series)
    Includes index.
    ISBN 0-87805-833-8 (cloth : alk. paper). — ISBN 0-87805-834-6
(paper : alk. paper)
        1. Sontag, Susan, 1933– —Interviews. 2. Women authors,
American—20th century—Interviews. 3. Motion picture producers and
directors—United States—Interviews. 4. Critics—United States—
Interviews. I. Poague, Leland A., 1948– . II. Title.
III. Series.
PS3569.06547Z47   1995
818′.5409—dc20   95-18986
                                                                  CIP

British Library Cataloging-in-Publication data available

Books by Susan Sontag

Sontag's publishing history is very complex. Not only are Sontag's books and essays frequently translated, but in the process they are often considerably repackaged, not always with her knowledge or consent. Many of the essays collected in *Styles of Radical Will,* for example, appear in various European editions of *Against Interpretation;* indeed, there are no French or German editions of the former. Most of Sontag's books are still in print and are available in various paperback editions.

Due to this bibliographic complexity, the following list of books is organized categorically and is generally limited to the original "book" publication of each. (In two cases, *AIDS and Its Metaphors* and *Alice in Bed,* a book-format translation appeared somewhat in advance of the English-language publication; we only list the latter.) In section I are books written by Sontag and published under her direct supervision, chiefly by Farrar, Straus, and Giroux. In section II are books edited and introduced by Sontag. In section III are various European titles. Two are "repacked" collections of Sontag's writings. Another is the Dutch translation of Sontag's 1989 Huizinga-lezing Lecture: "Traditions of the New, or: Must We Be Modern?" The others are book-format translations of various of Sontag's longer essays or stories—"Pilgrimage" published as *Pellegrinaggio,* for example.

I.

The Benefactor. New York: Farrar, Straus and Company, 1963.
Against Interpretation. New York: Farrar, Straus, Giroux, 1966.
Death Kit. New York: Farrar, Straus, Giroux, 1967.
Trip to Hanoi. New York: Farrar, Straus, Giroux, The Noonday Press, 1968.
Styles of Radical Will. New York: Farrar, Straus, Giroux, 1969.
Duet of Cannibals. New York: Farrar, Straus, Giroux, The Noonday Press, 1970.
Brother Carl. New York: Farrar, Straus, Giroux, The Noonday Press, 1974.
On Photography. New York: Farrar, Straus, Giroux, 1977.
Illness as Metaphor. New York: Farrar, Straus, Giroux, 1978.
I, etcetera. New York: Farrar, Straus, Giroux, 1978.
Under the Sign of Saturn. New York: Farrar, Straus, Giroux, 1980.
A Susan Sontag Reader. Introduction by Elizabeth Hardwick. New York: Farrar, Straus, Giroux, 1982.
AIDS and Its Metaphors. New York: Farrar, Straus, Giroux, 1989.
Illness as Metaphor and AIDS and Its Metaphors. New York: Anchor Books, Doubleday, 1990.
The Way We Live Now. With engravings by Howard Hodgkin. London: Jonathan Cape, 1991.
The Volcano Lover: A Romance. New York: Farrar, Straus, Giroux, 1992.
Alice in Bed: A Play in Eight Scenes. New York: Farrar, Straus, Giroux, 1993.

II.

Antonin Artaud: Selected Writings. Edited, and with an introduction, by Susan Sontag. Translated by Helen Weaver. Notes by Sontag and Don Eric Levine. New York: Farrar, Straus, Giroux, 1976.

A Barthes Reader. Edited, and with an introduction, by Susan Sontag. Hill and Wang, 1982.

Selected Stories. By Robert Walser. Edited, and with a foreword, by Susan Sontag. Translated by Christopher Middleton, et al. New York: Farrar, Straus, Giroux, 1982.

The Best American Essays 1992. Edited, and with an introduction, by Susan Sontag. New York: Ticknor & Fields, 1992.

Homo Poeticus: Essays and Interviews. By Danilo Kiš. Edited, and with an introduction, by Susan Sontag. New York: Farrar, Straus, Giroux, 1995.

III.

Pornografien som forestillingsverden. Translated by Aase Rørvik. Oslo: J. W. Cappelen's Forlag A.S, 1971.

A Pusztulás Képei. Edited by Osztovits Levante. Translated by Göncz Árpád, et al. Budapest: Európa Könyvkiadó, 1972.

Bijgedachten over de beurijding van de vrouw. Amsterdam: Wij, Odijk: Sjaloom, 1973.

A la rencontre d'Artaud. Translated by Gérard H. Durand. Paris: Christian Bourgois Éditeur, 1976.

Tanken som lidelse: Essä om Elias Canetti. Translated by Caj Lundgren. Stockholm: Brombergs, 1981.

L'écriture même: à propos de Barthes. Translated by Philippe Blanchard with Susan Sontag. Paris: Christian Bourgois Éditeur, 1982.

Geist als Leidenschaft: Ausgewählte Essays zur modernen Kunst und Kultur. Translated by Gertrud Baruch, et al. Leipzig: Gustav Kiepenheuer Verlag, 1989.

Tradities van het nieuwe, of: Moeten wij modern zijn? Translated by René Kurpershoek. Amsterdam: Uitgeverij Bert Bakker, 1990.

Pellegrinaggio. Translated by Paolo Dilonardo. Milano: Rosellina Archinto, 1995.

Contents

Introduction

It is hard, at the end of the twentieth century in America, *not* to have some picture of Susan Sontag, "That Sontag Woman," already in mind.[1] For some, the picture will be textual; for others, it will be visual. Few intellectuals who came of age in the 1960s or 1970s, for example, are likely to be lacking at least some books by Susan Sontag in their private archives. The books they do have—use-tattered copies of *Against Interpretation* or *Styles of Radical Will* or *On Photography,* I imagine—are probably in paperback and therefore mostly lacking those always elegant, sometimes pensively dignified and self-contained, sometimes smilingly and openly vulnerable photographs that have, over the years, adorned the hard-cover editions of her books. But there is no end of Sontag imagery available from other sources—photographs and cartoons in newspapers and magazines, streak-haired Sontag impersonators on "Saturday Night Live," not to mention those written accounts of her oeuvre that begin, like this one, by reference to Sontag's singular and strikingly time-defying *look,* often by interpreting some *particular* photograph. Thus, for example, Angela McRobbie begins her reappraisal of Sontag in *Postmodernism and Popular Culture* by reference to the cover of the Vintage paperback edition of *I, etcetera* where Sontag "is shown full length, in black trousers, black polo-neck and wearing cowboy boots. She is stretched out on a window-sill with a pile of books and papers under her arm. The seriousness is lightened by the faint flicker of pleasure: this is an image which pleases the author. At home, with books, wearing black."[2]

That America's preeminent critic of photography should be so frequently and hauntingly photographed is only one intriguing complexity among the many on view in *Conversations with Susan Sontag.* Sontag has herself noted the similarity of being photographed and being interviewed—to the extent that both, as she told Charles Simmons in *The New York Times Book Review,* are ambivalently tempting opportunities "to manifest oneself" through the agency of some

other.[3] A second exhibit-in-evidence on these photographic accounts—which I take as exemplifying Sontag's ambivalent relation to
and reception by contemporary culture—is somewhat more complicated than the one discussed by McRobbie. Properly speaking, it is
more than a photograph, though it is profoundly photographic. I have
in mind an ad hoc triptych I once encountered at the Museum of
Modern Art. It is a piece by Robert Heinecken, "Assisted by Jill
Kremetz and Hali Rederer," entitled "The S.S. Copyright Project
'On Photography.' "

The installation's first "panel" is a framed, roughly letter-size
statement comprising a title line, six paragraphs, and a signature/
copyright line. The first two of the six paragraphs establish the entire
piece as a parody of critical discourse on photography—or at least as
a parody of Sontag's view of photography, in light of Heinecken's
dead-pan claim that photography was invented in 1833 and underwent
a "re-discovery" in 1977, the year *On Photography* was published.
And each of the remaining four paragraphs poses a mock question
cued by a four-fold Borgesian distinction among "A. Knowledge, B.
Subject Matter, C. Craft, and D. Distancing." In every case, moreover, the question's answer is specified as a choice between two
pictures, the triptych's other two panels. One of these uses a collage
of differently photocopied pages (some lighter, some darker) from *On
Photography* to construct an outsized simulacrum of a famous Jill
Krementz photo-portrait of Sontag circa 1977. The other panel repli-
cates the same image of Sontag, to the same excessive scale, via the
juxtaposition of several hundred black and white photographs.[4] Hu-
morously enough, the terms in which the questions are posed are
repeatedly reversed, to the point where the two picture panels are
made equivalent when "moving away" is taken as the opposite of
"distancing," an equivalency that is subsequently and literally en-
acted when the beholder steps far enough back from the first panel to
view the "Sontagness" of the other two.[5]

To the best of my knowledge, Sontag has not commented publicly
on Heinecken's MOMA installation. She seldom replies directly to
her critics, in any case, repeatedly describing herself as aversive to
(as embarrassed by) criticism, even when it is complimentary. Indeed,
in discussing the necessity of "visibility" with Charles Ruas—in
response to his observation that "people often refer to you instead of

your work"—she decries the distortions of television and publicity, and in terms that link visual "reflections" with critical reviews. Ruas asks, "Is it terrible having these reflections of your image brought to you again in all these distortions?" To which Sontag replies: "I don't even read what's written about me and still I feel scorched by it," as if images and criticism were indistinguishable, matters alike of hot lights and false impressions.[6]

So avid and prolific a modernist as Sontag no doubt deserves some form of recognition in the Museum of *Modern* Art. But the recognition typically accorded her work is unhappily, often prejudicially, partial, a matter, as in "The S.S. Copyright Project," of tendentious *quotation*. Of course, her aphoristic style is "eminently quotable." But quotation is often *all* that happens. She "is read," that is, "without being debated" (McRobbie 79). Though Sontag has been written about at considerable length, the "tradition" of criticism is oddly static, non-progressive, and not only because most of the words devoted to her appear in book reviews. (Sontag's critics are prone to cite her interviews in lieu of the work of other scholars.)[7] Because Sontag is a freelance intellectual, "without a discipline to define which problems are important," writes Elizabeth Bruss, "Sontag's theorizing has been obliged from the start to raise issues, invent dilemmas, project domains of thought—and to do so in a way that would make her own proposals seem not simply accurate or original but necessary."[8] As a result, the typical response—to Sontag's critical writing, at least—is to "discipline" her, to take whatever is quotable in a given domain with little regard for the role those words might play in the larger drama of her thinking. There are thus multiple "Sontags," as "The S.S. Copyright Project" half-playfully attests, each constructed (as if) from scratch as Sontag shifts genres, topics, hence audiences. In view of her repeated claim that she is, first and foremost, a "writer"—she describes *AIDS and Its Metaphors* to Kenny Fries as "a literary performance" that should be seen more "in relation to what she has written in the past" than to medical research—it is evident that Sontag has found this partiality more than a little frustrating on occasion.

Then again, Sontag is herself drawn to, is therefore a great student and exemplar of, the more frustrating aspects of modern culture and consciousness. Her heroes and heroines—in her essays and inter-

views no less than her fictions—are all "hard cases," "exemplary
sufferers," suicidal philosophers, mad savants, alienated global exiles
or tourists: Simone Weil, Walter Benjamin, Antonin Artaud, Friedrich
Nietzsche, Claude Lévi-Strauss, E. M. Cioran, etc. This breadth of
reference, the range and depth of Sontag's learning and reading in
European languages and literatures, is another token of her multiplicity—and a source as well of something like awe; the *mise-en-scène* of
these conversations is often Sontag's own apartment (usually somewhere in Manhattan), and interviewers are sometimes hard pressed
not to comment, almost reverently, on her extensive private library.

Sontag's writerly style or temperament also evokes the frustrations
of multiplicity in explicitly *formal* terms, in her devotion to the
"fragment" as the basic unit of (modern) thought. In her early
writings, to be sure, fragmentariness is evident in her use of numbered
segments or blocks of text; "Notes on 'Camp' " has 58 of these,
woven intertextually around aphoristic passages from Oscar Wilde;
her semi-autobiographical short story "Project for a Trip to China"
comprises 13 numbered segments, many of which include quotations.
But even her later books and essays—often praised for turning away
from aphorism in the direction of more sustained logical and narrative
continuities—are organized musically, as much "arranged" as "written." (Indeed, individual pieces are often extensively "re-arranged"
in the process of turning an essay into a book chapter.)[9] A claim or
theme is introduced—say, "that illness is *not* a metaphor"—and then
exemplified, historicized, criticized, often by means of extended com-
parisons (of tuberculosis to cancer, say, or of cancer to AIDS) that
confirm the initial claim empirically, historically, culturally.[10] Sontag's
arguments arrive in "waves," as generalizations are advanced, qualified, restated; concepts are adduced, then reformulated (Bruss 244).
"I'm burdensomely aware that there's always more to say," she
avows to Wendy Lesser, in response to a question about her disagree-
ments with herself: "*This,* yes. But also *that*. It's not really disagreement, it's more like turning a prism—to see something from another
point of view." Sontag's rhetoric often circles, looping back in time
from some more-or-less present state of affairs (the redemptive reaction of Watanabe to his cancer in Kurosawa's *Ikiru*) to some newly
relevant historical antecedent (conceptions of disease in Homer's
Iliad and *Odyssey*), thus allowing her to tell the same story over

again, from a new angle, with a new emphasis. Indeed, both *Under the Sign of Saturn* and *The Volcano Lover* share (gloriously) alike in this operatic rhetoric of theme and variation, of return and renewal, of stories told and retold.

Ironically, happily, this lyrical density, this narrative layering, this hypertextual play of voices, means that her essays and books often defy casual recollection.[11] The heretical aphorisms, of course, are unforgettable—"In place of a hermeneutics we need an erotics of art"—but their flavor and force are often quite lost when abstracted from the flow and rhythm of Sontag's carefully nuanced and increasingly self-reflective prose.[12] Sontag avows herself a great rereader: "Most of my reading is rereading," as she told Wendy Lesser. I would argue that Sontag also *writes* to be reread. Indeed, Sontag sometimes praises "quotation"—by ambivalent contrast with "duplication" and "recycling"—for its "directness and assertiveness." "I think the quality of inaccessibility, the mystery, is important," she adds, so "that whatever matters can't be taken in on just one reading or one seeing" (Manion/Simon). No wonder her critics feel enjoined to start from scratch. No wonder her detractors tend to assail her fragmentariness. No wonder she sometimes takes offense at being fragmented, as if duplication, as she argues regarding photography, inevitably drains away context, hence meaning, hence savor. No wonder her more casual readers seize upon her image as a guarantee of coherence or intelligibility: Always the same look. No wonder Sontag has come increasingly to defend "seriousness" and "language"—despite the linguistic skepticism implicit in her attachment to silence and in her critique of metaphor—over and against the ever-rising tide of postmodern televisual imagery. As "The S.S. Copyright Project" makes unhappily, institutionally clear, *see*ing her picture may well blind us to her language.

The character and extent of Sontag's own relationship to language, especially to her *own* language, is a recurrent theme of the interviews collected in the present volume. She repeatedly describes her motive for writing in spiritual rather than psychological terms. "My urge to write," she told Amy Lippman, "is an urge not to self-expression but to self-transcendence." To Wendy Lesser she says: "My work is both bigger and smaller than I am." To Roger Copeland she describes this attenuated relation of self to work in terms of "disburdenment." She has a body of work she "can hardly renounce" (Ruas). But neither is she "interested in hanging on to it," as she told Victoria Schultz: "I do it and it's finished, then I'm interested in what I'm going to do next." "A work of art," she says in the same interview, "is something you make, something you give to other people. It's an object for use, and people can make many different uses of the same work." In a darker mood, Sontag describes her desire for mobility and marginality in terms that link disburdenment to morbidity: "Part of my efforts is to keep myself marginal—to destroy what I've done or to try something else" (Cott). Then again, "as a *reader*, not as the writer of them," Sontag came to the discovery that the stories in *I, etcetera* "have a theme in common—which is the search for self-transcendence, the enterprise of trying to become a different or a better or a nobler or a more moral person" (Cott).

If writing is destruction and reading redemption, then language is an essential medium of experience, of consciousness, of human existence *tout court*. Sontag summarizes this dilemma of necessary mediacy in her short story "Old Complaints Revisited." Her narrator is a translator trying to escape a form of life by writing an accusatory and treasonous letter, eventually specified as the story itself. The writer thus becomes increasingly dependent upon the reader: because only "definite, public, and outrageous acts" are enough to merit expulsion from "the organization" in the first place, and then because a fear of leniency leads to the hope that getting someone *else* to resign will "double" the offense and thereby "guarantee" expulsion. "I feel how verbal we are as I reread what I've written up to now. But I can't see the alternative. If I could be silent, maybe I could walk over my own feet. Maybe I could even fly. But if I'm silent, how can I reason? And if I can't reason, how can I ever find a way out? And if I can't talk, how can I complain, accuse, sum up? I need words for that."[13] This need for words is repeatedly addressed in *Conversations with Susan Sontag*.

Of the key words in the Sontag lexicon, "interpretation" and "modernism" loom largest, with "silence," "camp," "form," and "content" all contending for honors. What most distinguishes *Conversations with Susan Sontag* from other books by her—I will argue that it *is* a book by her—is not its lexicon or agenda so much as the frequency with which Sontag returns, in some cases is reluctantly

*re*turned, to these particular topics. Indeed, the book might as aptly
be titled *A Sontag Rereader* considering how often Sontag is asked to
listen to and comment upon her earlier work. Especially interesting
here is the frequency with which Sontag is asked to recapitulate her
thoughts on the formal "beauty" of Leni Riefenstahl's Nazi-era
filmmaking, especially *Triumph of the Will* and *Olympiad,* though
Sontag's thoughts were already revised in the period between "On
Style" and "Fascinating Fascism" during which she paid increasing
attention to the fact that "the notion of the human body and its beauty
. . . has not been the same, unchanged, throughout all periods"
(Raddatz).

Three discourses of particular significance to Sontag intersect via
the Riefenstahl example: the aesthetic, the political, and the sexual.
To all three she brings her "critical, dialectical, skeptical, desimplifying" intelligence (Bernstein/Boyers). Thus these *Conversations with
Susan Sontag* often turn on questions of usage, on the history
whereby certain terms, especially in these particular realms of
thought, become privileged. We need not linger on the question of
aesthetics, beyond noting the extent to which even Sontag's earliest
pronouncements—*against* interpretation, *on* camp—were carefully
and historically qualified; if always a "besotted aesthete," then always
already an "obsessed moralist" (Bernstein/Boyers). In view of Sontag's public dispute with Adrienne Rich over the Riefenstahl essay, or
in view of the even noisier aftermath of Sontag's 1982 Town Hall
remarks on the relation of communism to fascism, we would do well
to remember the history of Sontag's usage on these sexual and
political accounts too, in which task *Conversations with Susan Sontag*
can be very helpful.

Of course, Sontag has always been, in some sense, a political
writer. Her earliest "interview," not included here, is a report of a
press conference conducted by The Publishers' Publicity Association,
in March of 1966, where she is asked about "The Role of the Writer
as Critic." She construes the task of criticism in terms both political
("The war in Vietnam infects and depresses and corrupts us all") and
literary (William Burroughs, precisely in his difficulty and seriousness, is "one of the most important writers in America in the last 10
years").[14] *Trip to Hanoi,* we might well recall, is less about foreign
policy per se than about the difficult process of recovering some

genuine sense from and use of the already discredited ("unusable, dead, dishonest") language of American political radicalism.[15] A similar concern with political language is on view in her 1975 *Salmagundi* interview, where Sontag expressed significant reservations about the way feminist appropriations "of *gauchisme*" were in danger of perpetuating "philistine characterizations of hierarchy, theory, and intellect" (Bernstein/Boyers).

Thus it should come as no particular surprise that, in the pages of the far left French journal *Tel Quel,* she attacks the binary logic by which being "anti-fascist means to be pro-communist" (Scarpetta). Likewise, though Sontag has been consistent in condemning "sexist stereotypes in the language, behavior, and imagery of our society" (Bernstein/Boyers) in the name of her own freelance feminism—as is evident in her mid-seventies essays on the politics of aging and of beauty—she has also and repeatedly resisted the kind of binarism or essentialism that would "ghettoize" women, especially women writers. In her *Rolling Stone* interview, for instance, even while denying that "sexuality is a metaphor," Sontag still subjects the concept to skeptical critique: "There hardly seems to be anything that is *purely* sexual: it's overloaded with other forms of affirmation and destruction that you are declaring when you engage in a sexual act. We've been instructed that it's the central or only natural activity of our lives. That's nonsense. I mean, it's very hard to imagine what natural sexuality could be. I don't think it's available to any of us." No wonder Sontag repeatedly offers the opinion that a depolarization of sex roles is both probable and highly desirable.

The putative difference between picturing Sontag as a left-leaning apostle of a hedonistic "new sensibility" and picturing her as a cultural cold warrior awkwardly renouncing the party line—apart from its uncanny echoes of the narrator's dilemma in "Old Complaints Revisited"—is thus, in my view, far more apparent than real, certainly to the extent that it underestimates the continuity of Sontag's intellectual commitment to demystification. As Sontag stated the principle to Jonathan Cott: "The intellectual project is inevitably involved with constructing new metaphors, because you have to use them to think, but at least you should be critical and skeptical of the ones you've inherited."

An equal danger, increasingly remarked upon in Sontag's later

interviews, is a failure to inherit language *at all.* I have already
commented on Sontag's critique of television as nihilism. A plaintively
negative view of the situation is the one Sontag gave to Michael
Cronin in response to a question about the "morality of writing" and
the writer's role "as a guardian of language": "I mean by the term
'guardian' the mandate to use the language to its fullest capacity, to
maintain a rich and varied vocabulary. . . . The public language, what
Brodsky would call the 'language of the state,' the language of
television, is language at its lowest common denominator. . . . Every
time you use an adjective which is not one of the 25 adjectives which
most people content themselves with, you are keeping a word alive."[16]
A more positive take on the same situation is evident in Sontag's
conversation with Nadine Gordimer. There Sontag argues that writing
is not a "private activity" because the writer "is always making
something social in standing for excellence, in standing for a certain
hierarchy of values, protecting the language." The writer's "highest
duty," she told Amy Lippman, "is to write well—to leave the language in better rather than worse shape after one's passage." Though
this concern for the health of language is more emphatic in the later
interviews—especially when paired with praise of the literary canon
over and against "the relativist position" (Jonsson)—it is worth
remarking that Sontag has been defending intelligence and the value
of the intellectual life from early on, as is evident in the earliest of the
interviews reprinted here, with Edwin Newman, and in this regard
television is already (circa 1969) a trope for mindlessness, for the
"fundamentally unintelligible." Sontag has not changed her tune on
these cultural accounts anyway near so much as her harsher critics
would have us believe.

Though Sontag occasionally declares herself "suspicious of conversation"—on the Kafkaesque premise that "conversation takes the
importance, the seriousness, the truth out of everything" (Movius)—
she is nevertheless enamored of "voices." In the essay on Paul
Goodman with which she begins *Under the Sign of Saturn,* for
example, Sontag avows: "It was that voice of his which seduced me"
(6). Toward the end of that essay she describes her writerly task as
one of hearing her "own voice" and of discovering what she really
thinks. The value Sontag attaches to voices and their interplay is thus
variously attested to—not only by her experiments with narrative

point of view in her fiction, for instance, nor by her long-standing interests in theater and opera, but also by the great number of interviews she has given over the years, many of which are likely to be unfamiliar to Sontag's more casual readers.

Well over half of the material in this book, for example, appears here in English for the first time, including interviews originally published in German, Italian, French, Polish, Spanish, or Swedish. Though we had English versions of several of these interviews to work from, many of them invite the old complaint that translation is a form of treason in a particularly acute form. The two French interviews, for instance, were both *conducted* in French. To the extent that the French-speaking Sontag and the English-speaking Sontag are different, if not in ideas, then at least in rhythms and habits of expression, this presented an obvious intertextual dilemma. In general, I have urged the translators to take a conservative approach. To eliminate all elements of "strangeness" or difference seemed as inadvisable as ignoring the fact that most of the translated interviews were originally conducted in English; hence the translations published here are often duplicates, translations *of* translations. (A matter of "voice" or voices indeed.)

Perhaps the best evidence I can offer of Sontag's devotion to voice is the fact that, in response to my preliminary table of contents, Sontag expressed the hope that the entire volume would consist of substantial question-and-answer interviews. Except in those few cases where interview coverage of Sontag's activities, especially her more recent ones, was lacking, this was not a problem. *Most* of her books and films are discussed here, often at considerable and satisfying length. The most obvious anomaly on these accounts is the very brief treatment afforded *The Volcano Lover,* by far the most successful of Sontag's more recent books. Indeed, Paula Span's *Washington Post* discussion of *The Volcano Lover* is one of only three "profile" pieces included in *Conversations with Susan Sontag*. (With the exception of Nadine Gordimer's, which appears here slightly revised, interviews previously published in English are reprinted unaltered, though book titles have been italicized and typographical and proofreading errors have been silently corrected. The Newman and Servan-Schreiber interviews—derived alike from verbatim transcripts of television interviews—have been edited for this publication.)

   Though Sontag did no more than express her preference for "conversational" as opposed to "profile" pieces, one result of respecting her wishes has been to cut down on the amount and kind of biographical detail occasionally on view in the "Literary Conversations" series. In fact, many of the interviews in *Conversations with Susan Sontag* do take up the question of autobiography and the extent to which Sontag's life is figured in her work. But the general effect of minimizing the number of profile pieces in the collection is to bring it into accord with Sontag's frequently expressed distaste for "biographical" essays and her even more emphatic rejection of psychoanalytic approaches to literature. Indeed, Sontag frequently associates psychoanalysis with a misguided preference for "realism" in fiction and with a typically American penchant for denying the past. As she tells Edwin Newman in the earliest interview in the book, psychoanalysis is a process "whereby you can go over your past and evaluate it, and then dump it, and remake yourself." (Then again, Sontag has repeatedly declared herself an "American" in exactly this equivocal sense of the term.) Or perhaps, like the narrator of "Old Complaints Revisited," Sontag hopes to avoid providing the kind of personal detail that might tempt readers to a reductive understanding of her project: "I don't want to go into too much detail. I'm afraid of your losing the sense of my problem as a general one" (126).

   I have described Sontag's rhetoric—in her criticism no less than her fiction—as musical or multi-voiced: "*This,* yes. But also *that*" (Lesser). I have also noted how this recursive rhetorical style allows her "to tell the same story over again, from a new angle, with a new emphasis." The rhetoric of *Conversations with Susan Sontag* is similarly polyphonic in that Sontag is repeatedly prompted to revisit her old complaints, to talk not only with her various interlocutors but with earlier versions of herself. One of the most striking aspects of these discussions, especially when they are read sequentially, chronologically, is the extent to which they are, for all their candor and intimacy, for all their revelations and concealments, *essentially* philosophical, expressions of a love for wisdom, for words. It is implicit in the agenda of topics—morality, art, language, etc. It is explicit in Sontag's philosophical reference points: Plato, Aristotle, Hegel, Nietzsche, etc. I now want to say that her love of wisdom, her *philo-*

sophia, is also expressed, as it were, *generically*—in her preference for interviews that take "dialogue" form.

Of course, this claim too involves a return, a recovery of origins. It is hard to read Molly McQuade's first-person recounting of Sontag's experience at the University of Chicago without remarking on the Socratic quality of Sontag's education, which she describes as "a constant dialogue of texts." (Sontag defines literature, in her exchange with Amy Lippman, as "the dialogue among books.") In adding my voice, here, as a supplement to the interviews and voices that follow, I want to say that the primary value of these interviews is not "biographical" or "autobiographical." Not in the sense that seizing on her image, on her story, can render Sontag's writing more intelligible of a sudden. I would rather say that these conversations are, finally, *more* of her writing, a natural extension of the intellectual procedures that have motivated her writing from early on. As such, they fully participate in the dramatistic play of thought and temperament, of subject and meta-subject, of partisanship and alienation, of self and other, which we experience "Under the Sign of Sontag." The voices we hear are alternately seductive and admonitory, engaged and distant, skeptical and spiritual, contentious and generous. Sontag is thus a subject in process, in dialogue with herself and her readers. In that sense, she is always—as in Robert Heinecken's MOMA installation—*beside* herself, always trying to step over her own feet, longing to dance, to sing, to fly.[17] There is pathos here, as of an impossible but endlessly inspiring task: self-transcendence through self-expression. ("My problem is identical with my language," complains the old complainer [142].) But there is also a great and festive passion for words, a passion that is positively, if not Platonically, *erotic.*[18] These *Conversations with Susan Sontag* would not have seen print in the present volume apart from many supplemental conversations that it is my textual pleasure to acknowledge by way of conclusion.

I first began collecting these interviews in the process of compiling a scholarly bibliography of works by and about Susan Sontag. In that regard, thanks for encouragement and (world-historical) patience are owed to my bibliographic editors, William Cain and Phyllis Korper, and to my bibliographic collaborator and Iowa State University colleague, Kathy A. Parsons, of ISU's Parks Library. Abundant thanks are also due to humanities bibliographer Ed Goedeken and the Interlibrary Loan Office staff. Some of the work of collecting material for this volume took place while I enjoyed a Faculty Improvement Leave granted by Iowa State, for which I am especially grateful.

Thanks are also due to my former department chair, Frank Haggard, and to the current chair of the ISU Department of English, Dale Ross, for granting me department-level research support. Colleagues who gave generously of their time and advice include (from the English department) Jamie Stanesa, Rebecca Burnett, Susan Yager, Neil Nakadate, Loring Silet, Nina Miller and (from the Philosophy department) Robert Hollinger, Joseph Kupfer, and David Roochnik; thanks to all. Most of the translations were done by colleagues from ISU's Department of Foreign Languages and Literatures; especial thanks to Kathy Leonard, Peggy Johnson, and Clyde Thogmartin. I am grateful to Stefan Jonsson for providing the English-language text from which his *BLM* interview with Sontag was derived, and to Ingrid Anderson for translating passages that appeared only in the Swedish version of the interview. Monika Jankowiak of Grinnell College provided similar assistance with the Monika Beyer interview, for which I am equally grateful. Marithelma Costa of CUNY is to be thanked for providing a nearly complete text of the English-language interview from which "Susan Sontag: The Passion for Words" derives. Special thanks also to Ann Stapleton, not only for helping with permissions correspondence, but also for transcribing audio-tapes while remaining in remarkably good humor.

My wife, Susan, and our daughters, Amy and Melissa, have all worked at various times on the larger Sontag project of which this book is a part. Their devotion and patience have been my constant companions; their assistance and affections have seen me through. I am happily and forever in their debt. I am also gladly indebted for assistance and support to my former student and colleague Katherine Sotol and to my former research assistants Jennie VeerSteeg, Vida Cross, and Jennifer Quinlan. I have undertaken considerable travel in connection with my Sontag research; I am grateful to Tim Sanford and Lisa Finstrom, to Jimmy Beaumont, and to Jon and Carol Sanford for their hospitality. I am likewise grateful to Bob and Bobbie Nerell for hospitality shown on the occasion of my visit to North Hollywood High in 1991; my cousin Loren Nerell is to be thanked for negotiating the greater Los Angeles freeway system and for assisting my research at various L. A. area libraries. (Special thanks to Dr. Louise Teems of the North Hollywood High School library.)

The contributors named in the table of contents and the copyright owners acknowledged in the headnotes to each interview are also owed my personal thanks, which I tender here. But so too are many people whose names do not appear elsewhere. Victor Bockris, Miriam Berkley, Leslie Garis, Terry Gross, and Erika Munk are all to be thanked for their kindness and encouragement. Thanks to Dana Polan for providing a transcription of the Servan-Schreiber interview. Margaret Marco of the American Association of University Women provided much appreciated assistance while I was researching the chronology. Among the literary and legal professionals who helped, special thanks for special efforts are due to Peter Brooks of NBC, Ilse Schulze of *Die Zeit,* Lily Marx of *L'Espresso,* Donatella Barbieri of Agenzia Litteraria Internazionale, David Bradshaw of BBC Enterprises, and Sonja Singleton of *The Guardian.* Nadine Gordimer, who generously allowed the use of her BBC exchange with Sontag, requested that notice be taken of the miraculous changes that have occurred in South Africa since that interview originally appeared. My University Press of Mississippi editor Seetha A-Srinivasan and her assistant, Anne Stascavage, have always been there when difficult questions needed quick answers. I am deeply grateful to both for their professionalism, and especially to Seetha A-Srinivasan for helping me to find the introduction I wanted to write amidst the introduction I thought I was writing. Thanks also to the series editor, Peggy Whitman Prenshaw, for her enthusiastic support.

Susan Sontag's assistants, Karla Eoff and Miranda Spieler, have been very helpful in providing information and responding to questions. Ms. Sontag herself has been generous with permissions and suggestions, not to mention her time. I am deeply grateful to all three, though especially to Susan Sontag—for her patience and kindness in responding to my inquiries, but above all for the exemplary literary life that the interviews here collected bring so pleasurably and inspiringly to mind.

Though *Conversations with Susan Sontag* is more Sontag's book than my own, however much I am finally responsible for its contents, my editorial last words are words of dedication. This book is for my sisters, Cherise Thompson and Sharlene Poague, and in memory of

our Army Air Corps father, who lived, if not his best life, at least his
last life, in North Hollywood, California.

LP
March 1995

Notes

1. Bruce Bawer, "That Sontag Woman," *The New Criterion* 11.1 (September 1992): 30–37. Though Bawer's title, in alluding to the 1941 Alexander Korda movie about Lord Nelson and Emma Hamilton that is one of the many sources of Sontag's *The Volcano Lover,* is more than a little prejudicial, it is exactly my point that summary characterizations run that risk, mine included.

2. Angela McRobbie, *Postmodernism and Popular Culture* (London: Routledge, 1994): 77. (Cited in-text hereafter.) An earlier version of McRobbie's Sontag chapter appeared as "The Modernist Style of Susan Sontag" in *Feminist Review,* No. 38 (Summer 1991): 1–19.

3. Charles Simmons, "Sontag Talking," *The New York Times Book Review* (18 December 1977): 4.

4. Barbara Long reports that the Krementz photo in question accompanied review copies of *On Photography*. See "Against Photography: Sontag Exposes the Politics of Images," *Politicks & Other Human Interests,* No. 10 (14 March 1978): 25–26.

5. Because my 1988 visit to MOMA was rushed, I relied (aptly, ironically) on what turned out to be an unreliable camera to make a record of the Heinecken installation. Because it failed, I cannot tell for sure which of the two pictures of Sontag is which; their left-to-right order may reverse the one suggested here. Then again, Heinecken substitutes "Jill Kremetz" for "Jill Krementz." Or is this a matter of marking a (textual) difference?

6. Quotations from interviews included in this volume are documented in-text by interviewer or publication venue.

7. This "non-progressive" aspect of Sontag criticism can be seen by comparing the Bawer article cited above to Cary Nelson's "Soliciting Self-Knowledge: The Rhetoric of Susan Sontag's Criticism," *Critical Inquiry* 6.4 (Summer 1980): 707–26. Though Nelson is still the most perceptive and appreciative of Sontag's critics, his description of her rhetorical project is uncannily echoed by Bawer, even if their respective evaluations could hardly be more different. The only book about Sontag to date is Sohnya Sayres, *Susan Sontag: The Elegiac Modernist* (New York: Routledge, 1990). See also Liam Kennedy, "Precocious Archaeology: Susan Sontag and the Criticism of Culture," *Journal of American Studies* 24.1 (April 1990): 23–39.

8. Elizabeth Bruss, *Beautiful Theories: The Spectacle of Discourse in Contemporary Criticism* (Baltimore: Johns Hopkins UP, 1982): 224. (Cited in-text hereafter.)

9. My favorite instance of this rhetorical "rearranging" is that undergone by "Mind as Passion" in its passage from *The New York Review of Books* (25 September 1980): 47–52 to *Under the Sign of Saturn* (New York: Farrar, Straus, Giroux, 1980): 179–204. (Subsequent references to *Under the Sign of Saturn* will be documented in-text by page number.) That Sontag is still an adept of fragmentation is clear from her "Introduction" to *The Best American Essays 1992* (New York: Ticknor & Fields, 1992): xiii–xix.

10. Susan Sontag, *Illness as Metaphor* (New York: Farrar, Straus, Giroux, 1978): 3.

11. Lest this description seem prejudicial, I cite Sontag's own description of E. M. Cioran, whom she praises for exemplifying "a new kind of philosophizing: personal (even autobiographical), aphoristic, lyrical, antisystematic." See " 'Thinking Against Oneself': Reflections in Cioran," in *Styles of Radical Will* (New York: Farrar, Straus, Giroux, 1969): 78. I also recommend Jan Zwicky, *Lyric Philosophy* (Toronto: U of Toronto P, 1992).

12. Susan Sontag, *Against Interpretation* (New York: Farrar, Straus, Giroux, 1966): 14.

13. Susan Sontag, "Old Complaints Revisited," *I, etcetera* (New York: Farrar, Straus, Giroux, 1978): 118, 132, 129–30 respectively (cited hereafter in-text).

14. Susan Sontag, "The Role of the Writer as Critic," *Publishers Weekly* (28 March 1966): 36–37.

15. Susan Sontag, *Trip to Hanoi* (New York: Farrar, Straus, Giroux, 1968): 18.

16. Michael Cronin, "Under the Sign of Sontag," *Graph*, No. 5 (Autumn 1988): 16.

17. On the relation of (the female) "voice" to opera I recommend Catherine Clément, *Opera, or the Undoing of Women,* translated by Betsy Wing (Minneapolis: U of Minnesota P, 1988) and Stanley Cavell, *A Pitch of Philosophy: Autobiographical Exercises* (Cambridge: Harvard UP, 1994). On Sontag's relation to opera and to voice, I recommend her short story "The Letter Scene," *The New Yorker* (18 August 1986): 24–32.

18. On the relation of eros to reason or logos I recommend David Roochnik, *The Tragedy of Reason: Toward a Platonic Conception of Logos* (New York: Routledge, 1990).

Chronology

1933   Susan Lee Rosenblatt is born 16 January in New York City, the first child of Jack Rosenblatt, a fur trader based in Tientsin, China, and Mildred Jacobson Rosenblatt, a teacher. Is left in care of relatives when Mrs. Rosenblatt returns to China.

1936   Sister, Judith, is born 27 February in New York City.

1938   Jack Rosenblatt dies of tuberculosis 19 October in Tientsin, China.

1939   Shows symptoms of asthma; with their Irish Catholic nanny, mother and daughters move, via Miami, to Tucson, Arizona. Skipped to third grade when she starts public school.

1940–44 Discovers the Modern Library in a Tucson stationary store.

1945   Mrs. Rosenblatt marries Army Air Corps Captain Nathan Sontag; after the marriage, daughters Susan and Judith take their stepfather's last name.

1946   The family moves to Canoga Park, California. In their "cozy shuttered cottage with rosebush hedges and three birch trees," Sontag's eighth domicile in her 13 years, she finally gets "a door of [her] own." Discovers the Pickwick bookstore on Hollywood Boulevard "within a month of arriving in Los Angeles." Enrolls at North Hollywood High, a member of the Winter '49 class.

1948   Is editor-in-chief of *Vintage '48,* the North Hollywood High literary magazine. Is elected "Commissioner of Publications" and a Member of Student Council in May; takes over as "W '49" editor of the student newspaper, *The Arcade,* in September.

1949   Graduates from North Hollywood High in January. Attends

University of California at Berkeley in the spring term; transfers to the University of Chicago in the fall.

1950   Marries Philip Rieff in December, though she retains her maiden name. Reviews H. J. Kaplan's novel *The Plenipotentiaries* in the Winter issue of *The Chicago Review*.

1951   Graduates from the University of Chicago with a bachelor's degree; moves to Boston area, where Rieff takes up a teaching appointment at Brandeis.

1952   David Rieff is born 28 September in Boston.

1953   Appointed as an instructor in English at the University of Connecticut for the 1953–54 academic year.

1954   Takes graduate classes in English at Harvard.

1955–56 Begins graduate program in philosophy at Harvard, where she studies with Paul Tillich, among others. Is appointed a Teaching Fellow. Is "ranked first among the nineteen Harvard and Radcliffe doctoral candidates in philosophy" at the time of her preliminary examinations.

1957   Receives a master's degree in philosophy from Harvard (Radcliffe). Receives a fellowship from the American Association of University Women to spend the 1957–58 academic year at St. Anne's College, Oxford, in preparation for writing her dissertation on "the metaphysical presuppositions of ethics." Sontag spends the latter part of her fellowship year at the Sorbonne.

1958   Divorces Philip Rieff soon after her return from Paris.

1959   Arrives New York City, with David, in January and finds work on the editorial staff of *Commentary*. *Freud: The Mind of the Moralist* is published; though often described as a husband-wife collaboration, Sontag's name does not appear, by mutual consent following their divorce, on the title page. Begins teaching appointments in philosophy at both City College of New York and Sarah Lawrence College for 1959–60 academic year.

1960   Begins appointment as an instructor in the Department of Religion at Columbia University (which appointment she holds until 1964); begins publishing book reviews in the literary supplement of *The Columbia Daily Spectator.* Visits Cuba from June through September.

1961   "Dreams of Hippolyte," an early version of a chapter from *The Benefactor,* is published in *Provincetown Review.* "Some Notes on Antonioni and Others" is published, under the pseudonym "Calvin Koff," in *The Columbia Daily Spectator Supplement;* it is the first of her many essays on cinema.

1962   Reviews I. B. Singer's *The Slave* in the Summer issue of *Partisan Review.*

1963   Reviews Simone Weil's *Selected Essays 1934–43* in the first issue of *The New York Review of Books. The Benefactor* is published by Farrar, Straus. Short story "The Dummy" appears in September issue of *Harper's Bazaar;* her 15 September review of Yves Berger's novel *The Garden* begins a long series of pieces in *Book Week.* Her analysis of Claude Lévi-Strauss, arguably the first of her "structuralist" essays, appears in the 28 November issue of *The New York Review of Books.*

1964   Receives *Mademoiselle* magazine Merit Award. "Going to Theater" appears in the Winter number of *Partisan Review,* initiating a series of essays on contemporary drama and performance art. Appointed writer-in-residence at Rutgers University for 1964–65 academic year with support from a Rockefeller Foundation grant. "Notes on 'Camp'" is written in Paris during the summer; is published in the Fall issue of *Partisan Review* and "reviewed" in *Time* magazine (11 December). "Against Interpretation" appears in the December number of *Evergreen Review.*

1965   Receives Merrill Foundation grant. "One Culture and the New Sensibility" is published (as "Opinion, Please, from New York") in April issue of *Mademoiselle.* Reviews John Rublowsky's *Pop Art* and Henry Geldzahler's *American Painting in the Twentieth Century,* her first extended discussion of painting, in the 25 July edition of *Book Week.* "The Imagination of Disaster" appears in the October issue of *Commentary.* "On Style" appears in the Fall number of *Partisan Review.*

1966   *Against Interpretation* is published. Receives a George Polk
          Memorial Award in criticism for providing "valuable new
          directions in the appreciation of the theater, motion pic-
          tures, and literature." Receives Guggenheim Foundation
          Fellowship. "Film and Theatre" appears in the Fall number
          of *Tulane Drama Review.*

1967   "The Pornographic Imagination" appears in the Spring
          issue of *Partisan Review.* Is elected to the executive board
          of the American Center of PEN International. *Death Kit* is
          published. Serves on the awards jury at the Venice Film
          Festival and the selection jury of the New York Film Festi-
          val. "The Aesthetics of Silence" appears in Fall-Winter
          number of *Aspen.*

1968   Is signatory to a letter (dated 1 May) to *The New York Times*
          calling for investigation of Oakland (CA) police in the wake
          of a shootout with members of the Black Panther Party, the
          first of many such editorial-page letters Sontag will sign.
          Visits North Vietnam in early May at the invitation of the
          North Vietnamese. "Godard" is published in the Spring
          issue of *Partisan Review.* While visiting Rome, is called to
          Stockholm by Göran Lindgren of Sandrew Film & Teater
          to discuss making *Duet for Cannibals* in Sweden. Serves as
          "judge" (with others) of essays and criticism included in
          *The American Literary Anthology/1: The First Annual Col-
          lection of the Best from the Literary Magazines* (Farrar,
          Straus, Giroux). "Trip to Hanoi: Notes on the Enemy
          Camp" is published in the December issue of *Esquire. Trip
          to Hanoi* is published.

1969   *Styles of Radical Will* is published. Upon completion of
          Duet for Cannibals, Göran Lindgren agrees to produce
          Sontag's next film. *Duet* premieres at Cannes in May. *Styles
          of Radical Will* is published. *Duet* is shown at the New York
          Film Festival in September.

1970   Returns to Stockholm to shoot *Brother Carl.* The *Duet for
          Cannibals* screenplay is published.

1971   *Brother Carl* is finished in early January; the film premieres
          at the Cannes Film Festival in May. Is one of 60 signatories
          to a letter (published in *Le Monde* and *The New York Times*)

to Fidel Castro protesting Cuba's treatment of the poet Heberto Padilla. Joins the editorial board of the short-lived *Libre,* a Spanish-language journal published in Paris by (mostly) Cuban and Spanish exiles; begins living for extended periods in Paris.

1972   *Brother Carl* is screened at the Museum of Modern Art; opens at the New Yorker Theater in August. Serves on jury selecting European films for the New York Film Festival. "The Double Standard of Aging" appears in the 23 September issue of *Saturday Review.* Visits Vietnam in December.

1973   Begins six-week visit to China in January. "Project for a Trip to China" appears in the April issue of *The Atlantic Monthly.* "Approaching Artaud" appears in 19 May *New Yorker.* "The Third World of Women" (an English version of a piece originally contributed to *Libre*) appears in the Spring *Partisan Review.* "Photography," the first of the essays which eventually make up *On Photography,* appears in 18 October issue of *The New York Review of Books.* Goes to Israel in mid-October to film *Promised Lands,* one week before the Yom Kippur War cease-fire.

1974   Short story "Baby" appears in February *Playboy. Promised Lands* premieres in New York in June. Receives a Rockefeller Foundation grant through PEN American Center. *Brother Carl* screenplay is published.

1975   Is hospitalized for breast cancer. "Fascinating Fascism" appears in 6 February edition of *The New York Review of Books;* Sontag responds to Adrienne Rich's critique in 20 March issue. "A Woman's Beauty: Put Down or Power Source?" appears in the April *Vogue;* "Beauty: How Will It Change Next?" in the May issue. Receives Guggenheim Foundation Fellowship. Appears with Kate Millett and others as part of a televised feminist symposium in Mexico City; the conversation is eventually published in book form as *liberación femenina* (Televisa/Organización Editorial Novaro). Serves on selection committee of the New York Film Festival.

1976   Receives Arts and Letters Award of the American Academy and Institute of Arts and Letters; Brandeis University Creative Arts Award citation; Ingram Merrill Foundation Award in Literature in the field of American Letters. *Antonin Artaud: Selected Writings* is published. Is a founding member of the New York Institute for the Humanities.

1977   *On Photography* is published. "Unguided Tour" appears in 31 October edition of *The New Yorker*.

1978   *On Photography* receives the National Book Critics Circle Award for criticism. *Illness as Metaphor* and *I, etcetera* are published. Appears in Gina Blumenfeld's movie *In Dark Places*.

1979   Elected to American Academy and Institute of Arts and Letters. Directs Pirandello's *As You Desire Me* in Turin, Italy. Receives annual award of the Academy of Science and Literature in Mainz, Germany. Receives New York City Mayor's Award of Honor for Arts and Culture.

1980   *Under the Sign of Saturn* is published. "Mind as Passion" appears in 25 September edition of *The New York Review of Books*. Her production of *As You Desire Me* opens in Florence and Rome in December.

1981   "Dance and Dance Writing" is published in *New Performance* magazine, the first of a series of essays on topics in dance and dance history. *As You Desire Me* opens for a second season at the Teatro Stabile in Turin in May. Attends "The Writer and Human Rights Congress" in Toronto in October (its proceedings are published in 1983 by Anchor/Doubleday as *The Writer and Human Rights*).

1982   Delivers, 6 February, her "Poland and Other Questions: Communism and the Left" remarks at Town Hall, in New York City. "Writing Itself: On Roland Barthes" appears in the 26 April *New Yorker*. Shoots *Unguided Tour* for RAI Three (Italian Television) in Venice in the fall. *A Susan Sontag Reader* and *A Barthes Reader* are published. Walser's *Selected Stories* is published.

1983   *Unguided Tour* is completed and broadcast. Appears (as herself) in Woody Allen's *Zelig*. "The Unseen Alphabet: Kafka's Inner World" appears in July *Vogue;* "Novel into Film: Fassbinder's *Berlin Alexanderplatz*" appears in September *Vanity Fair*.

1984   Appears in *Mauvais Conduite* (Improper Conduct), directed
            by Nestor Almendros and Orlando Jiménez Leal. Named
            "Officier de l'Ordre des Arts et des Lettres." "Model
            Destinations" appears in 22 June edition of *The Times
            Literary Supplement*. Short story "Description (of a De-
            scription)" appears in Autumn number of *Anteus*. Appears
            in *Le Deuxième Sexe,* a four-part series derived from Si-
            mone de Beauvoir's book, on French television, in No-
            vember.

1985   Milan Kundera's *Jacques and His Master* premieres in
            January, under Sontag's direction, at Harvard's American
            Repertory Theatre. "Sontag on Mapplethorpe" appears in
            July *Vanity Fair*.

1986   Short story "The Letter Scene" appears in 18 August *New
            Yorker*; "The Way We Live Now" in 24 November *New
            Yorker*.

1987   Elected President of the PEN American Center in June (her
            term expiring in 1989). "The Way We Live Now" is selected
            for publication in *The Best American Short Stories 1987*
            (Houghton Mifflin). "Wagner's Fluids" appears in 10 De-
            cember *London Review of Books; "*Pilgrimage" in 21 De-
            cember *New Yorker*.

1988   Though opposed to the choice of venue, Sontag leads the
            PEN American Center delegation to the PEN International
            Congress in Seoul, South Korea, in order to protest govern-
            ment persecution of Korean authors. Voices the part of
            Sarah Bernhardt in Edgardo Cozarinsky's documentary film
            Sarah, which premieres in September at the New York Film
            Festival. "AIDS and Its Metaphors" appears in 27 October
            New York Review of Books.

1989   *AIDS and Its Metaphors* is published. Testifies in support
            of Salman Rushdie before the Subcommittee on Interna-
            tional Terrorism of the Senate Foreign Relations Commit-
            tee. Is brought to Berlin by the Deutscher Akademischer
            Austauschdienst (DAAD); starts *The Volcano Lover*. Deliv-
            ers the 18th annual Huizinga-lezing Lecture in Leiden, the
            Netherlands: "Traditions of the New, or: Must We Be
            Modern?"

1990   Receives MacArthur Foundation Fellowship. Returns to
            Berlin at the invitation of DAAD. "The Way We Live Now"
            is selected for publication in *The Best American Short
            Stories of the Eighties* (Houghton Mifflin). "Traditions of
            the New" is published in Dutch as *Tradities van het nieuwe,
            of: Moeten wij modern zijn?* (Uitgeverij Bert Bakker). *Ill-
            ness as Metaphor and AIDS and Its Metaphors* is pub-
            lished.

1991   Receives Elmer Holmes Bobst Award. *The Way We Live
            Now* is published. *Alice in Bed* premieres in Bonn in Sep-
            tember.

1992   *The Volcano Lover* is published. *The Best American Essays
            1992* is published.

1993   Receives an honorary degree from Harvard in June. Directs
            Waiting for Godot in Sarajevo. Robert Wilson's staging of
            Alice in Bed opens in Berlin in September. "Godot Comes
            to Sarajevo" appears in 21 October *New York Review of
            Books*. *Alice in Bed* is published.

1994   *Susan Sontag,* a 43-minute documentary-cum-interview
            movie by Matteo Bellinelli, originally produced by RTSI
            (Radiotelevisione della Svizzera Italiana) Lugano, circa
            1985, is released on video by Films for the Humanities &
            Sciences. Receives the Montblanc de la Culture award in
            recognition of her work in Sarajevo.

1995   *Homo Poeticus* is published.

Conversations with Susan Sontag

Speaking Freely

Edwin Newman / 1969

Mr. Newman: Hello, I'm Edwin Newman. SPEAKING FREELY today is Susan Sontag. Susan Sontag is best described, I think, as a woman of letters, though she might object to the title. She's a critic, an essayist, a novelist, a film-maker. She's one of those people we look to to tell us what our society is doing and where it's going. Miss Sontag, I said you might object to being called a woman of letters because I think you dislike the emphasis on letters—at least I get that impression from your writing.

Miss Sontag: Well, I always just thought of myself as a writer until I started making films. "Woman of letters" is an awkward phrase. But I guess "writer" is probably as good as anything else, since I've only made one film. Not until I make the second one will I really have the nerve to say that I'm a writer and a director and feel comfortable with that.

Mr. Newman: What I had in mind there was that people are still stuck in an age where letters, where writing, where the literary performance, was the most important aspect of art, and you no longer think that.

Miss Sontag: Well, I hate to invoke Marshall McLuhan at this point, but I am reminded of his saying: "I think we're in the age of television, but all I do is read books." I don't identify myself with McLuhan, but my own taste is certainly very much formed by literature and that's mainly what I've done. The film-making is a new enterprise that just began last year when I made my first film in Sweden. I know what you're talking about. (LAUGHS) I'm not going to say I didn't say anything to support your question. But the most I would want to say is that I'm interested in the relationship of all the arts. Some years ago I wrote some essays in which I was very concerned to point out what I thought was the exclusively literature-oriented emphasis of

3

people who wrote about literature. When I read things by critics of dance or painting and sculpture or music, I got the sense that they knew about the other arts, and that that informed and contributed to what they said about the art in which they were most interested. But when I read most people who wrote about literature, I thought that these people didn't know anything—anything serious or comparable in depth—about painting or sculpture or films or so-called nonverbal arts. So it was really to redress or correct an imbalance rather than to say the McLuhanite thing. I don't believe the age of literature is over, but I do believe that a great deal of what is exciting is going on in other art forms, and that literature can't be understood outside of that context.

Mr. Newman: You also believe, don't you, that even within literature—certainly within the other arts—we're moving away from content and toward form, or at any rate that too much emphasis has been placed on content and not enough upon form—at least I take that to be a rather vulgar interpretation which I have made of your essay "Against Interpretation."

Miss Sontag: I was trying to say that certain standards are still being applied to literature which are no longer necessarily applied in the other arts. Not just realistic standards but let's say formalist standards are recognized in other art forms, and they're slowest in coming to be recognized in literature. So I was just asking for people to look at literature from a more sophisticated point of view, such as you find in the attitude toward other art forms because there's a lot you can't deal with except in formalist terms.

Mr. Newman: Well, for my benefit if for nobody else's, may we be more specific about this? You think that interpretation—that is, the compulsion people feel to interpret what they read, to get at the meaning of it—is a hindrance, a nuisance, "a philistinism." Now— let's be elementary, again, for my sake—does not every work of art have content?

Miss Sontag: Yes, certainly. Again, I feel a little uncomfortable, actually, in defending things that I wrote four, five years ago (LAUGHS), or six years ago in the case of that essay. But it's hard for me to just say, well, okay, that's what I believe. Because I believe it in a context in which I think it's being ignored. Obviously, if nobody were paying attention to content or meaning or message, then probably I would be talking about that. Things move so fast in the arts, as in the whole world of commodities in this culture, so that it's not quite as relevant today, as it was even five or six years ago, to make that point.

What I was struck by is a kind of reduction that was being practiced on work whereby the work became what it meant, or its message, and the texture of the work was lost, the formal qualities of the work were lost. This is not to say—though I know many people have thought that's what I meant, and I really don't think even what I wrote then supports it—that I don't think things have any meaning. But I think that the meaning is something "added on to it." I'm very interested in the idea that works of art are open-ended, and have to be understood also not just from a formalist point of view but from a sociological point of view. I think that each generation, different groups of people, different individual minds, invest certain meanings in works of art. And one should be self-conscious about that. So that it isn't that there isn't any meaning, but I think there is a more sophisticated view of what meaning is in a work of art.

For instance, I don't think the author of a work of art is the owner of its meaning. I think that somebody else might have a better idea of what one of my novels means than I do—or my film.

Mr. Newman: Is this idea more readily applicable, let us say, to something abstract than it is to something concrete, something representational?

Miss Sontag: Yes, but I think that the dominant influence in the arts—if you take a very long view—is toward abstraction. It's already a hundred years ago since Flaubert said, when he was writing *Madame Bovary,* "I want to write a novel about nothing at all, a novel that has no meaning, that's pure form." When we read *Madame Bovary* we don't, on the whole, read it that way. We see it as a realistic novel of the provincial bourgeoisie in France in the nineteenth century. Flaubert thought he was making a great move toward abstraction in that novel—and in some sense he did. It's obviously a kind of horizon that we'll never get to, but the tendency has been toward more formalist art, I think, in the last hundred years.

Mr. Newman: I'm correct in supposing that this kind of development is more readily adapted to the movies, for example, than it is to written work?

Miss Sontag: Well, I think that there's a kind of energy going into movie-making which on the whole makes it a more exciting art form than the novel or prose fiction. Most people I know can think of more good movies made every year than novels that they really like. I don't think there's any great historical inevitability in that. I don't think prose fiction is dead. But I do think we're in a period when there's more talent in film than in prose fiction.

Mr. Newman: But why is there more talent? Is it because it is a more nearly contemporary form of art?

Miss Sontag: Well, probably just because it's a new art form. After all, movies are only eighty years old, and probably fifty years old in the sense of very sophisticated kinds of film-making—narrative film-making. And also, I suppose, because it's unlike literature, is genuinely a multiple art form; it's also literature, but I think it's primarily image and it's sound, and it has elements of dance and theatre. It's an art form which is composed of many sub-forms, whereas ultimately literature is language. Some poets and a few prose writers have attempted to do things with typography on the page and make the written word more of a purely visual experience, but in the end we have an alphabet system and not calligraphy, and it's language, and language that we hear with the inner ear. It's not pictures and it's not something for the eye, fundamentally.

Mr. Newman: Miss Sontag, maybe what I should do is abandon *Against Interpretation,* which as you say you wrote some years ago, and come up to a more recent volume of essays, called *Styles of Radical Will,* in which the first essay has to do with what you call the pursuit of silence, an idea somewhat related to the notion that you set out in *Against Interpretation.*

Miss Sontag: ''Against Interpretation'' is just one essay in the first book—the lead essay, if you will. But I didn't want to suggest in that first volume that every other essay was part of some organic argument. Some essays were written before and some after the title essay.

And in the second book, *Styles of Radical Will,* ''The Aesthetics of Silence'' is, in some sense, the main essay, at least so far as it continues from the material in the first book of essays. And I suppose it is, in a way, Against Interpretation Revisited. I think it's a better essay than ''Against Interpretation.'' If ''Against Interpretation'' is about the problems of interpreting anything—it's not to say that you can't interpret anything or that nothing should be interpreted, but it's an attempt to talk about the problems of interpreting works of art—"The Aesthetics of Silence" is about—from within the point of view, not of the person who talks about art or thinks about art, but the person who makes a work of art—the pursuit of silence, about this principle of internal limitation in works of art that's peculiar to the modernistic period—which is kind of an anti-art impulse, where people have been, in a sense, rebelling against the very idea of art itself, or trying to make art do tasks which traditionally in our culture art hasn't done—like transcend itself or cannibalize itself, or even perform a basically religious or spiritual function.

Mr. Newman: Well, specifically, when you say "cannibalize itself," you mean the sort of creation in which you have something that destroys itself—Tanguy's work perhaps?

Miss Sontag: Well, that's a very extreme example, but a leading theme in a lot of modern art is the demonstration of the impossibility of doing what is in fact being done. Beckett is a perfect example, because he writes so much about and within the idea of silence that—you use language, but in a sense it's impossible—the subject of the work of art becomes the impossibility of saying something, or of completing your statement, or of being able to go beyond it. So the end of that is a kind of silence. Of course, it's only a kind of silence, since—unless the artist actually gives up, like Rimbaud, doesn't do anything anymore—he then goes on, refining this statement. I think it's not just true in literature, of course; it's true in painting and many other arts.

Mr. Newman: You seem to think—am I correct in this?—that one of the objects of a work of art might be to bring silence to the person who is looking at it, who is experiencing it.

Miss Sontag: I think it's very hard to say clearly, or systematically, what people intend when they make works of art. This is a very complicated question, and most people deal with it very simply. One of the oldest ideas around is that it's just self-expression, or that it's communication. But I think a lot of so-called modern artists would reject that idea—Jasper Johns and Arnold Schoenberg, I think, would not like to think of their work either as self-expression or communication, but some kind of—

Mr. Newman: Don't they—

Miss Sontag: Don't they want to communicate, or don't they—

Mr. Newman: You must have been asked that before.

Miss Sontag: No, no (LAUGHS), I'm just running ahead. Well yes, they do—but that's not the point, or that's not the value. I suppose the one point that I would like to keep on making, and probably will throughout our conversation, is that these arguments are very much within a context—where something is being emphasized so you want to say, "Well, this is being neglected"—and you can't forget what the context is. If nobody was thinking psychologically at all, then it would be very creative to say, "Yes, but don't you see this as self-expression" and so on. But in a period in which that kind of psychological explanation of why people make art is so pervasive, because psychological explanations are so pervasive throughout our culture, then what gives energy to people is finding a different way of looking at things. It doesn't mean that it's wrong to look at it the other way, but it does mean that it's not very useful, or not very inspiring.

So some people like to ignore or look away from—and I suppose I'm one of those people, at different points of my own work—more realistic psychological approaches. Again, not because they're not true, but because they're not very useful, because they're so obvious. Why not think about it in some other way?

Mr. Newman: You say at one point that it is the characteristic aim of modern art to be unacceptable to the audience. Is that a desirable thing? Or is it sensible even to talk about it as something desirable? Why should an artist want to affect the audience at all?

Miss Sontag: Well, I think everybody's art has some relation to some idea of an audience; there's no doubt about that. To really answer the question, one would have to talk about the society as a whole, and what degree of disruption or alienation of consciousness is in this society. But I think it's true that most of what is serious in our culture is conceived of as antagonistic, or at least challenging. And again that's very complicated, because it has partly to do with the prestige of novelty. It seems as if in Bali or in ancient Egypt an artist didn't feel required to produce something new; it was very nice if you could go on doing even better what people had always done. But since Romanticism, the notion that the artist must produce something new is a very important idea that most people think is just self-evident; it's not self-evident. It's an idea of our period that part of the value of a work of art is that it's new, is that nobody's done that before.

If you follow that idea, of course, you're bound to get into notions like the avant-garde, like moving ahead. If so-and-so did this last year, I must do this this year. Ideas like that are more powerful, for instance, in painting and sculpture than they are in literature. But then how do I get ahead, the artist asks; how do I produce something that hasn't been done? Then you get—this is only part of the explanation—into a kind of antagonistic relation to the audience. The audience likes that, what Jones was doing last year; well I'm going to do something new. It's not necessarily going to be something that people immediately like, except so far as they see it's new.

Mr. Newman: Almost by definition, to find something new you have to find something that the audience is unaccustomed to and will reject.

Miss Sontag: That's right. And there is a rather unhappy analogy that you can draw between the world of art and the world of fashion. Some famous designer—Courrèges or somebody like that—said that high fashion is always ugly, initially; it's always something that people don't like, if it's really high fashion. They don't like it at first, and then they get used to it, and then it becomes fashionable. But to present people with what they like is almost by definition to present them with what they're familiar with. So it's partly bound up with the idea of the search for what's new.

Mr. Newman: If the search for what is new is that strong in our society, and so strong as to differentiate us from societies that went before, is it a devastating idea, Miss Sontag? Does it use up creative energy and talent at a very great rate? And does it cost us something to go on with it?

Miss Sontag: Well of course it burns people out. There are lots of quick careers in this society. And the whole apparatus of promotion cooperates with that, because—not in literature so much, but in the world of the visual arts—people speak of things like the art market, and they're quite right to use that image. And the first showings in the fall in New York, in the galleries, are really like the spring collection in Paris or something. If you can't keep up the pace, you're out. So there's a kind of quick glorification of certain people, and then two years later they are being viciously attacked—which I think is very bad for the artist, both this premature promotion and then the terrible attack that comes very soon after, when some new idol is found.

Mr. Newman: The comment is often made in Europe that the United States produces a great many one-book authors, two-book authors, who don't last for a very long period. Does that have anything to do with this, do you think?

Miss Sontag: Probably everybody gets too much favorable publicity to begin with; and then everybody gets too much negative publicity soon after. I think publicity in general is a very destructive thing, for any artist, working in any medium whatsoever. It always is a problem. Because even if it's good, the extent to which you get all this attention is an extra thing for you to take account of. You start thinking about your work as an outsider—you start being aware of this in relation to that, and what people think of you. And you become self-conscious. You can become either overly complacent or overly critical, but whatever it is, it's taking your attention away from your own business. Imagine if a surgeon got reviews on his operations every time; I think it wouldn't be very pleasant, and would make it much harder to be a good surgeon. In a sense, a writer or painter is perhaps more like a surgeon. I don't know how to stop it, and it's not that I'm recommending that the whole reviewing business be discontinued, but it's as much of a problem as I think it would be if a surgeon had reviews.

Mr. Newman: Does the pace with which we use up talent, then, and the demand we make for new things so much of the time, have anything to do with the extraordinary emphasis that is placed in this country on the young—to the extent that we seem even to have a cult of youth?

Miss Sontag: I'm not sure. I really never have thought of that.

Mr. Newman: If you've never thought of that, I congratulate myself.

Miss Sontag: Maybe the other way around (LAUGHS). Now I'm thinking of it for the first time. What occurs to me right off the top of my head is that, if there is a connection, it would be that there's the same thing behind both phenomena. In other words, youth itself really is an invention, just as art in the modern sense is an invention. In traditional societies, there wasn't a separate period that was youth, with the kind of attention it gets in our society. You were a dependent child and then you were quickly integrated into the adult world in terms of some traditional role. But the notion in this society that there's a whole period of your life which is being young, which has certain values and certain styles and certain demands, is a very interesting phenomenon. But it's part of our society. Youth seems, in our society—adolescence, I guess, is what it used to be called—seems to run from about ten to thirty-five, roughly. The adolescents are much younger—kids ten years old are incredibly sophisticated. And one meets many people who are still adolescent in their early thirties.

Mr. Newman: This has all been accompanied, though, hasn't it, by a decline in the importance of language? At least it seems to me to have been so accompanied. Has perhaps the decline in the importance of language—if you agree with that—made it easier for people to remain adolescents longer? Does it make it easier because precision of expression is not valued very much, and when precision of expression is not valued very much, experience tends to count for less?

Miss Sontag: I'm really not sure there is a decline in the importance of language. I think that certain developments in language which are very curious—like the fact that, among a large section of young people, inarticulateness is prized, and many young people actually control their natural articulateness—

Mr. Newman: You mean they're doing that deliberately?

Miss Sontag: (LAUGHS) I think so. Yes. But I think that's perhaps something rather peculiarly American. Of course I know this country better than others, so maybe I'm harder on this country, too, than others. But I think there is a certain deep anti-intellectual tradition in America—mistrust of the word, of reason, of being too cerebral, a very old-fashioned thing, where you have reason and the verbal arts on one side and on the other side things standing for emotion and feeling and spontaneity. Also action versus thinking, another polarity. I think a lot of American culture is very much bound up in this suspicion of the intellect. In that sense, I suppose language—precision of language—in some way has always been attacked as being a snobbish or a patrician or aristocratic thing. A classical stereotype in movies of twenty or thirty years ago was somebody named Algernon, you know, who spoke very precisely and went to Harvard—that kind of thing.

Mr. Newman: Yes, and he was usually hit before the film ended.

Miss Sontag: (LAUGHS) Yes, and he wore glasses, and he was physically rather a mess. And I think that's still going on, the great

American search for the body and for the spontaneous, which is very often conceived in terms which bypass language. I mean, when D.H. Lawrence was in this country, in the twenties, he sensed this very much, and liked that about America, because he had very American ideas about the difference between the mind and the body.

Mr. Newman: A great belief in the blood.

Miss Sontag: Yes.

Mr. Newman: Perhaps that's something to do with the frontier and its part in American life.

Miss Sontag: Partly that, too.

Mr. Newman: Miss Sontag, in one of your essays you say there has been an "unprecedented change in what rules our environment from the intelligible and visible to that which is only with difficulty intelligible, and is invisible." You recognize that?

Miss Sontag: Yes.

Mr. Newman: You stand by it?

Miss Sontag: Yes. I think that's generally true of what makes the modern experience. That's not particularly American, of course; that's true wherever modernization, industrial society, has really taken hold. But it must be a radically important experience that now, for the first time in the history of the planet, a couple of generations of people have had to deal with things in their everyday life that they don't understand, that they don't know how to handle, that are evident material magic—like the telephone, the television set, the radio. Most of us don't understand anything more complicated than a typewriter or an automobile. And yet, we're watching moon shots, and we're surrounded by an environment in which power resides in things which are fundamentally unintelligible.

Mr. Newman: Well this has some effect, obviously, on the sensibility. Do you think it has a practical effect as well? Does it make people think that control cannot possibly lie in their hands? And, to push it along a bit more, doesn't it lead to a revulsion—aren't we seeing something of that now?

Miss Sontag: Well I think we're all suffering from having a sense of being in societies which are too big and fundamentally unmanageable—especially, I think, when you live in a continental country like the United States or the Soviet Union or China. China obviously is a very special case because there is an attempt in China to give people

a sense of community—whatever you may think of that community
and the values behind it, people feel connected with each other—and
also because, given the low industrial level of China, people are still
largely involved in handicraft operations on a very old-fashioned level.
But in a country like the Soviet Union or the United States, especially
the United States, all sorts of issues come up all the time in which
most people have no competence. You can see it even in New York
City, not to mention a country over 200 million people. Most people
do not understand the issues at stake, and they are not easily intelligible. The psychological experience of people living in these big countries, as Americans do, is very different than if you live in a small
country. Even the difference between, let's say, the United States
and France—and France is a big, relatively modern country with a
population a quarter that of the United States—must make an enormous difference for how connected you feel to the country, and what
sense you can have of what's going on in it. And if you are in a much
smaller country, especially one that's besieged, let's say like Cuba or
Israel or North Vietnam, it's an entirely different psychological experience; you feel you know what's going on, you know people or
you're one step away from people who are making decisions. That's
certainly not true of most people in this country.

Mr. Newman: Does that have an effect, do you think, in the field of
art, in the field of culture?

Miss Sontag: Well I think that a so-called alienated art is much more
likely to grow up in one of these big mass societies. Sure, where
people feel fundamentally estranged from what's going on.

Mr. Newman: May I push on, then, to what might be called a
political application of this kind of thing? You went to North Vietnam,
wrote about it at length, and you are obviously very much struck by
many things in North Vietnam, not only by what you just mentioned,
but by the feeling you had that the people of North Vietnam were
aware of the fact that they lived in the past, the present and the future.
What do we live in in the United States?

Miss Sontag: Well, it's hard to speak for more than myself and my
friends, but most people I know are pretty pessimistic about this
country, for one reason or another. And I think that a lot of other
people are also pessimistic, though I might disagree with them politically. The worry among people now, I think, a very widespread

feeling in this country, is that it's going to get worse, however you define "worse," whether you're on the right or the left or in the middle or whatever. Unfortunately, one of the rules of life is, however bad things are, they can get even worse than that.

To mention another point that's connected with this—you speak of past, present, and future—I think that Americans have a rather weak connection with the past. That's one of the peculiarities of this country. One of the most interesting facts about this country is that it's made up of people from other countries who are breaking with their past. And so Americans, I think, have always had a certain resistance to a historical sense—you know, a frontier spirit again: If you don't like it, move on. You don't necessarily have roots anywhere, and the past doesn't really matter because you can always go and move someplace else and start a new life. That's really the dominant myth in this country. I think, parenthetically, it has a lot to do with the vogue of psychological thinking in this country. Psychoanalysis, for instance, has succeeded in this country in a way that it hasn't anywhere else because it's experienced by people as an instrument for breaking with their past. There is this process available to you in some form or other whereby you can go over your past and evaluate it, and then dump it, and remake yourself, and go on to something new. Freud was a great pessimist, but psychoanalysis has become on the whole an instrument of optimism in this country, a myth that through psychological understanding you can get rid of the past.

Mr. Newman: And yet there is this curious clinging that so many people engage in, to the countries not that they come from necessarily—and usually *not* that they come from—but that their parents come from, or their grandparents come from. And so you get all these so-called hyphenated American groups, which seem if anything to be stronger now, as popular as they've ever been.

Miss Sontag: I don't know if I agree, because my feeling is that that's rather a New York point of view, perhaps because I'm not originally a New Yorker, and was myself surprised when I came to live in New York eleven years ago at how ethnically conscious this city was, and how everybody was a hyphenated something. I don't think it's so true of the rest of the country as it is in New York because New York was the point of entry for immigrants. In that

The King's Library

sense New York is rear-guard. In Arizona and California, where I grew up, there was much less of that kind of consciousness.

Mr. Newman: It seems still to count in elections, or at any rate, we profess to believe that it counts in elections—maybe it counts less than we think it does.

Miss Sontag: Well, again, one has to be careful because we only speak out of our own experience. I mean, the electorate itself is a peculiar sample. I read somewhere recently that the average age of the person who votes in this country is forty-seven—which is not the average age of people in this country. So I rather think that the ethnic self-consciousness is on the way out, even though it's true that it's still being reflected in electoral results, particularly in big cities.

Mr. Newman: Miss Sontag, why did you go to North Vietnam?

Miss Sontag: Well, to answer the question two different ways, on the very practical level I went because I was invited, given the opportunity to go; and to answer a little more interestingly, I went because I felt I couldn't possibly refuse, that I'd been talking and participating in teach-ins and speaking on campuses around the country against the war for some time—I began rather early, I think the end of 1964; it's painful to think that many of us still engage in the same activity and it's almost 1970—but since I had made this commitment and given the anti-war movement my support and some of my time, I felt that I couldn't possibly turn the invitation down. But it was really in that spirit that I went, thinking I had the chance to go and I had to go, not that I'd wanted to go or it was my dream or my aspiration. I didn't really have any idea of what I could find there.

And what I wrote about in that long essay is my surprise at all the thoughts that the experience of being in North Vietnam provoked in me. Of course, I was a special kind of visitor. I wasn't surprised that the country had been devastated by American bombing, because I already knew that. It wasn't a political thing that I found out, because I already was against the war, and I already had a fair idea—because I'd been reading lots of things, including things published in Europe—of the extent of the devastation. But I was surprised at my experience of the people, and my experience of the limitations of my own point of view, once I was there. If I'd gone earlier, of course, I would have written something much more factual, because it would have been more valuable a year or two earlier, just to spread the news

about the bombing. Most of the people in this country didn't know
anything about the bombing until Harrison Salisbury wrote that series
of articles in early 1966. And that I think was a turning point, the first
time, really, when the anti-war movement began to pick up some real
steam. Because the government had been lying and saying only
military targets were hit, and of course Americans are in the habit of
believing the government. I used to believe that government too
(LAUGHS).

Mr. Newman: Miss Sontag, one of the things that struck you in
North Vietnam was what you called the blandness of the culture there
compared with the variety that Western culture brings.

Miss Sontag: Well, bland was only one word which I used in a very
special context. I didn't say the culture was bland; I said I found that
at first the contact with people seemed to have a certain blandness. I
don't know what I expected; I'd never visited a country at war,
and certainly—

Mr. Newman: Possibly language had something to do with it.

Miss Sontag: Yes. I'd never been in a country at war, certainly
never been in a country which was being massacred by my country.
So I guess I expected a certain kind of emotionalism. I was betraying
also my own lack of knowledge of Asian culture altogether, because I
think a great deal of what I saw in Vietnam is Asian, as opposed to
Western—not even specifically Vietnamese. But Asians have a different emotional style. I mean, that wasn't the main point that I wanted
to make, but it was part of my reaction—I wanted to describe
my reaction.

Mr. Newman: What was the main point?

Miss Sontag: Well, it's always hard to do that—the essay's ninety
pages long. I suppose if I try to think of the main thing that I
experienced in the trip, it was that my idea of what people are like,
and of what the possibilities of human society are like, was changed;
that I realized I had been making generalizations about human nature
and the possibility of human society from not only a Western point of
view but from a very particular point of view that's confined to being
middle-class and living in the big cities and knowing really just
Western Europe and the United States and having a kind of disillusion-
ment about the possibilities of community, or even what people are

capable of, that I feel was contradicted by my experience in North Vietnam.

Mr. Newman: Well, when you came back from Vietnam, you spoke about the necessity of a kind of patriotism to save the United States. You said probably no serious radical movement has any future in America unless it can revalidate the tarnished idea of patriotism.

Miss Sontag: Oh, and I feel it ever more strongly today—I know it's not the day our viewers are watching this program, but the day when we're recording it happens to be the Moratorium day, November 14th, and I would like to have carried the American flag. Unfortunately, it doesn't make sense, because it would be misinterpreted. It's the right-wingers or the people who are for the war who are carrying the flag. The people who are against the war have signs like "End the War" or "Moratorium" or whatever—I have a button like that on my coat— but it makes me very mad that in this country patriotism is monopolized by right-wing or reactionary people, and that what it means to affirm this country is to set your mind against all kinds of criticisms which I think are valid. And I think that a serious radical movement in this country, which I would like to be part of, has to be for this country; it has to be for this country being different from what it is. But as long as flag-waving and putting flag decals on your car means something else, it's going to be very difficult.

This is a very old problem, of course. And I think a radical movement in this country has to make connections with American radicalism, of which there is a very real and serious tradition. And that is the primary task, not to find models in other countries, however interesting these models might be.

Mr. Newman: Why do you feel you couldn't carry a flag, for example, in an anti-war, and anti-Vietnam rally—aren't many people doing that?

Miss Sontag: Of course, if I'm in a demonstration, I could (LAUGHS) carry a flag. But you know, if I put the flag on my car—unless I put a little sign underneath it (LAUGHS) explaining in what sense I'm carrying the flag. . . . This is a trivial example; I don't want to pin it on the flag. But it just happens in this country that the symbols have gotten rationed out in that way, and that people say, "America, love it or leave it," you know, and there is this whole idea in this country of being un-American—which is to be critical. I mean, you can be a radical of any persuasion in another country, and people don't say "You're un-French" or "You're un-Cuban" or un-German or something. Even if you are opposed by your fellow citizens, they don't say, "Well then you are not a member of this country, go back where you came from." There's always this idea in America that you chose to come here and therefore you owe a different kind of loyalty. I have friends in the anti-war movement who are five or ten years away from being Mayflower descendants—two people I know quite well whose families came over here in the 1630s, two different people. And they're regularly shouted at (LAUGHS) when they speak at demonstrations—"Oh, go back where you come from" or "You lousy foreigner" or something—because that's the prejudice here. So it demands a whole new way of thinking. I don't, by the way, think that my idea is original. But still there is a problem, especially when one is as critical of this country as I am—and many people I know are critical of what this country is doing, its imperialist role in the world and so on. It takes a certain kind of moral tact to separate out the criticism of the country's policy and investments in the world and the role America's playing in the world today from what one feels about this country. But I don't think you can change this country—I don't think the movement as such can make any headway—without that kind of commitment.

Mr. Newman: You said, very early in the program, that you were pessimistic, and most people you knew were pessimistic. You obviously want to change the United States. Do you think there's any hope of it being changed along the lines that you would prefer?

Miss Sontag: Sure, I think there's hope, which is not to say that I think it's inevitable, but I think one has to believe it's a possibility, and that I don't think is unreasonable, and then do what one can to try to bring it about—which is to involve more and more people. That's my fundamental idea for any radical movement in this country, that its value, its success and its authenticity depend on the numbers of people it involves.

Mr. Newman: Are you a believer in smaller units of government, for example?

Miss Sontag: Absolutely. Absolutely. That's a problem, of course, which is not peculiarly American. But I agree with many of the things Paul Goodman has said about the different possibilities of decentral-

ization in this society. Until people feel they have actual contact with
things—I mean that's what democracy is, not going to the polls every
four years.

Mr. Newman: Doesn't the run of technology make that much
less likely?

Miss Sontag: Well, technology as it exists now, yes, but I don't
think that there is a single style in which we have technology. We now
have a conception of technology and a use of technology which
require greater and greater concentration at the top, but, first of all,
some of that technology may be unnecessary, and simply a diversion
of resources; and secondly, I think there are ways of organizing things
so that people on a local level have much more control. That, by the
way, is a very curious place in which the right and the left come
together in this country. Because the right wing in this country,
though they mean something very different by it, are always talking
about local government and local control. They want it to protect the
status quo, of course, not to make changes—like in the case of school
segregation and so on. But part of their attitude comes out of a very
genuine assessment that there is something wrong in this very heavy
degree of control from the top.

Mr. Newman: To take you out of your role as an essayist and critic
for a moment, let's talk about movies. You made your first movie not
long ago—it's called *Duet for Cannibals*—and you made it in Sweden,
I know, because somebody in Sweden gave you the money to make a
movie. And I suppose if somebody (LAUGHS) provided right here,
you would make it here.

Miss Sontag: Oh, yes, I would much rather make movies here than
in Sweden. But I'm (LAUGHS) very grateful for this Swedish company that had this crazy idea and asked me to come to Sweden and
make a movie there. I've wanted to make movies for years—I suppose
like a lot of people—and I don't think it's unconnected with my work
as a novelist. Insofar as I'm just a writer, I consider my novels much
more important and certainly much more interesting to me than my
essays. Essay writing has been a secondary activity. And the impulse
to make movies, of course, did come partly out of that sense that
there were things I wanted to do with narrative; I didn't want just
language, I wanted something that was primarily visual. Though the
themes in the movie may come out of the same bag of fantasy, the

making of it was a completely different process from writing. And I
like that very much; I like working with people.

Mr. Newman: Since it was done in Swedish with English subtitles
by you, and since I presume you know a little Swedish—how did you
know, as the director, how well the actors, cast members, were
carrying out your desires?

Miss Sontag: (SIGHS) Well, that's a good question. (LAUGHS)
First of all, not only was I director, of course, but I was the author of
the script—and there was a very detailed shooting script which I
wrote before we ever began to make the movie. I couldn't be absolutely sure when it comes to the ultimate nuances that separate
Swedish and English. . . . Of course my Swedish is extremely
limited—I was in the country a total of about seven months and I now
understand Swedish pretty well, but I wouldn't say I have any serious
command of the language—but I was helped first of all by the fact that
Sweden is literally a bilingual country, everybody there speaks English; English was the language of the set. And I knew the script by
heart, in English and Swedish, and I was working with highly professional actors who were extremely good. I couldn't have worked with
non-professionals; I couldn't have done improvisation, obviously, in
a foreign language. So I felt ninety percent sure that they were doing
what I wanted them to do, there's no doubt about that, but the more
important question is whether what I wanted them to do was right for
Swedish. I felt ninety percent sure of that, and then for the ten percent
I just crossed my fingers and left it to their skill.

Mr. Newman: Miss Sontag, as movies go, that one is not what one
would call daring—certainly as movies go these days.

Miss Sontag: Daring in what sense?

Mr. Newman: Well, it's not particularly undressed, put it that way.

Miss Sontag: Oh.

Mr. Newman: But you have made a very considerable study of
pornography, which you think is a perfectly acceptable form of
literature or art, provided it is well done. You don't rule it out simply
because pornography is pornographic. Did you have any such intention in making that movie—I mean, did you wish to excite erotic
desires on the part of the audience?

Miss Sontag: No. No. When you say I made a considerable study,

I'm a little embarrassed. (HE LAUGHS) I wrote an essay—it's rather long, I admit.

Mr. Newman: It's a very interesting one.

Miss Sontag: I was moved to write that essay because I thought that pornography is an interesting sub-genre of literature—let's say like science fiction; I think it's quite related to science fiction.

Mr. Newman: It is so much in the public eye—(LAUGHS) perhaps not the best way to put it.

Miss Sontag: It wasn't so much when I wrote it. Anyway, it doesn't interest me to write pornography or to make films which are basically pornographic. I don't think I have a talent for it. I was interested in validating it as a possible genre—as I say, the way you validate science fiction.

Mr. Newman: I certainly don't want to give the wrong impression about the movie. But what I wanted to lead up to is to ask you if you will, if you feel able to, put into context this outburst of sexuality that we now seem to have on stage, on screen, in books. You have dealt with this subject; you've dealt with the question of whether one should be concerned about this, whether one should be worried about it. You even think that it results from the economic organization of the United States.

Miss Sontag: In the endless search for new commodities (LAUGHS), this is one of the new commodities around, just because it hasn't been. I'm not really very interested in pornography, to tell the truth. And that's, I suppose, why my film isn't—I mean if my film was involved in creating a particular emotion in the audience, it was not erotic excitement, it was anxiety. (HE LAUGHS) If I was trying to make people feel something of a particular emotional kind, I was trying to make them feel anxious. Uneasy.

Mr. Newman: Uneasy, right.

Miss Sontag: The film was always putting, you know, situations off-balance, and reversing expectations. But as for the so-called outburst of pornography in this country, I don't think it's very interesting, but I think it's perfectly understandable. It's the exact other side of hypocritical repression, seems to me slightly better than hypocritical repression, so let's say, in the end, I'm a defender of the new permissiveness, but just within that spirit, that it's better than hypocrisy, or it's better than repression. I'm against censorship. I don't think pornography is valuable in itself, and I certainly don't think it's particularly good for promoting sex, but I think it's just the natural swing in the other direction that's being sold as a kind of commodity, and a very cheap thing, really, for most people. I don't think it's anything to get excited about; I just think we're paying the price for our older attitudes. And what one can hope for is that we'll go through this period and then come, not on a back-swing to the old attitude, which would be a disaster, but to some better attitude which is more relaxed and less voyeuristic.

Mr. Newman: Well, I hate to ask this with less than two minutes to go, but you foresaw something you called a depolarization of the sexes—if you'd (LAUGHS) like to talk about that in one minute.

Miss Sontag: (LAUGHS) Yes. I don't know if I foresaw it, but I think that is a development among young people, and I think it's a good one. Our society's been based on very stereotyped roles of men and women, and I think this is very bad; it's obviously very destructive for women, and in a less obvious way for men too. So that women are afraid of being intellectual and men are afraid of having feelings, and all sorts of distortions like that. So that to the extent to which the roles are being challenged and the clear, stylistic distinctions between the sexes in matters of dress and hair style and so on are being broken down, this—unlike the development of pornography, which I view with a sort of sigh—is I think a really positive development.

Mr. Newman: It's understandable, I suppose, that it makes older people feel so uncomfortable, since it's so great a change for them.

Miss Sontag: Yes, but I think it's really a very good development. I feel a fair amount of confidence that it's a real discovery of young people that they don't have to play these stereotyped sexual roles and repress part of their nature which has become identified with the opposite sex.

Mr. Newman: Thank you, Miss Sontag. Susan Sontag has been SPEAKING FREELY. Edwin Newman, NBC News.

Susan Sontag on Film

Victoria Schultz / 1972

From *Changes* (May 1, 1972), pp. 3–5. Reprinted by permission of Victoria Schultz.

Susan Sontag's penthouse apartment overlooks the Hudson and has the Spartan, uncluttered look of a place you've just moved into. The essential pieces of furniture—couch, comfortable chair, desk, table—have been delivered, the cartons of books have been unpacked and placed on long rows of shelves, and in the kitchen the first things to go up on the walls are the neatly framed black and white stills from thirties and forties Hollywood movies. A bunch of fresh yellow chrysanthemums in the bare living room confirms your daily presence in the new surroundings.

With compelling directness and warmth Sontag discussed her main preoccupation of the moment—film. Our conversation often digressed to concerns of feminism—something that happens all the time nowadays when women talk with each other. Sontag told the photographer, Gosta Peterson, who was admiring the sunny view from the apartment, that she has been living here for the past five years. But most of that time she has been away in Europe fulfilling her dream of making films.

When I met her, she had just returned from Europe with her new film *Brother Carl,* which was shown several weeks ago at the Museum of Modern Art and will be opening at the New Yorker theatre in May. People who still think of Susan Sontag as critic, essayist, and novelist should realize that she has made the difficult transition from writing to film-making and has indeed changed mediums.

Both her first film, *Duet for Cannibals,* and *Brother Carl* were made in Sweden. *Duet for Cannibals,* which is also in Swedish, tells the story of a young man who becomes involved in the life of an eccentric middle-aged couple. Husband and wife play strange games with each other and draw the young man into their charades of false alliances and deceptive appearances. The film is very much in the vein of black humor.

23

Some of the bizarre overtones of *Duet for Cannibals* recur in
Brother Carl, which, however, is more somber and complex. Laurent
Terzieff is brilliant as Carl, the main character around whose mute
"presence" the other three people convulsively act out their passions.
I asked Susan Sontag about the film.

V.S.: The presence of the autistic child and mute Carl in *Brother Carl*
brought to mind some of the preoccupations in your essay on the
aesthetics of silence. Also you seemed to depict madness in a Laingian
fashion as a reaction, a retreat from a hostile world. Did you have any
of these things in mind?

S.S.: I do think it's valid to see those connections, but I didn't have
them in mind. I have very little consciously in mind when I'm actually
doing something. The most I could say about *Brother Carl* or *Duet
for Cannibals* or about the two novels are things I have discovered
after I have finished them, often through other people's comments.
The story of *Brother Carl* was born in two hours. I saw the whole
situation, and I didn't reflect on it at all. Now perhaps I can say that,
yes, something is an obsession of mine or fascinates me or comes into
my work.

V.S.: You mean for instance the use of silence in *Brother Carl?*

S.S.: It isn't for me to say. Apparently it is, since people notice it.
I'm not aware of it, but I certainly wouldn't deny it. In other words
I'm challenging your assumption that a work is done according to a
certain kind of consciousness of what one is doing. I'm not saying
that some people don't work that way, but I don't.

People have pointed out that one of the two main characters in my
second novel, *Death Kit,* is a girl who is blind. One might say that is
an equivalent of someone who doesn't talk. . . . I could say that, but
it would be looking at myself from the outside, and it's not my job to
do that.

V.S.: How do you feel about the comments and interpretations of
your films?

S.S.: I don't mind them at all. I just don't feel that I have to do it.
A work of art is something you make, something you give to other
people. It's an object for use, and people can make many different
uses of the same work. Works of art which people consider really
valuable—especially those that are very old—are the ones that have

proved rich enough to lend themselves to many kinds of readings and many kinds of uses. I don't think there is a privileged reading of a given work of art. There is the reading that a given person makes and a particular generation makes.

In fact I'm rather pleased that people get different things from what I do. What do I get out of it? I don't get anything out of the comments, except some pleasure that people are interested and have had a strong reaction. In any case I'm not very involved with my past work. I'm not interested in hanging on to it. I do it and it's finished, then I'm interested in what I'm going to do next.

V.S.: What's your next film going to be?

S.S.: I'm working on the script now. The next film is very different. First of all, I'm not going to work anymore in Sweden. I have a French producer, so I'll probably be shooting a lot of the film in France. The story takes place in the thirties. It's a period film in the sense that it doesn't take place in either a concretely pictured or an abstract present, as in the case of the two Swedish films. It will demand a whole effort of historical reconstruction with clothes, furniture, and cars. It's film-making on a more ambitious scale, both technically and financially.

Though part of me would like to go on in black and white, the film will be in color, because it will cost a great deal more than the two Swedish films and the producer wants some possibility of recouping the investment. I'm working on the script now and I hope to start shooting at the end of the year.

I'd like to work mainly in France with this film. But the characters in it are English and American, and I'll be using English and American actors, so there won't be this element of accents as in the Swedish films.

V.S.: How did you feel about Swedish actors speaking English in *Brother Carl?*

S.S. You ask it as if they did it, and I had to react to it. I wrote my first film script in English. It was translated into Swedish and then the film was spoken in Swedish. I had mostly Swedish actors, and by that time I understood perfectly well what they were saying, as I knew my own script by heart. The language of the set was English. When the cameras rolled, they said their lines in Swedish and we worked from

two texts, the original English and the Swedish translation. That was
quite all right.

Having had that experience I didn't want to do it again, since I was
going to work once more in Sweden. I started to do something else
with my situation of being a foreigner in a bilingual country, which
was to have the actors act in English and to introduce the problem of
speaking—the question of accents—as one of the formal elements in
the film. The difficulty of speaking, the question of having different
kinds of accents, is an element of the film. It's not something that
happened which I reacted to, it's one of the original ideas of the film.

V.S.: Will the new film include politics?

S.S.: Yes, a great deal. That's another thing that I really look
forward to. I liked the two Swedish films very much, but I know they
are limited. Their limitation is that they work within an imaginary
psychological universe; partly realistic in the sense of everyday psychology and partly a kind of fantastic psychology which I also believe
is true—yet not true on the level of plausibilities of daily life. Although
I think there are many kinds of psychology.

The two films are related in the sense that although the material is
somewhat different they do form a pair. One is a sequel to the other,
not in terms of story but in terms of certain preoccupations. The
relationship of Carl to Martin for instance is a development, or
another aspect, in a completely different emotional register, of the
relationship between the wife, Francesca, and Bauer in *Duet for
Cannibals*. And also between Bauer and Tomas.

Some of the formal elements recombine with different emotional
and moral tones but with some of the same problems of madness (real
or imaginary), domination, exploitation, psychological cruelty. Where
the tone of *Duet for Cannibals* was cool, detached, and comic in a
very black sense, the tone of *Brother Carl* is much closer, more
emotional and not at all detached. The thematic materials in the films
are the same, but the emotional register is different. However, they
go together. They're two stages of the same process of thinking which
is partly inspired by the special conditions of working in Sweden,
being a foreigner and working with very low budgets.

Now with the third film I would like to do something quite different.
I'll be working with a story and with certain national character traits
(the main character for instance is an American) which I understand

very well and I don't have to view from the outside. I understand the psychology of the characters from the inside so that the film can, on one level, be very realistic.

Part of the abstraction of the Swedish films has to do with the fact that I could only work with abstracted material because I could never try to describe, from the inside, the Swedish reality. I would always be a foreigner there. If I work with material where I can be on the inside, which is a certain kind of American, then I can move to themes that are more concrete in a historical sense and do involve politics. The political problems in the film are the problems of the late thirties in the country where the film takes place. There will be concrete historical and sociological detail as well as a direct political theme.

Somebody once said, and I think it's true, that *Duet for Cannibals* is about the psychology of fascism. I didn't think of it when I was making it, but it's true because in a sense all work is political, there is a political dimension to everything you do. I didn't think that's what I was doing. But when I heard this remark I thought, yes it's true.

Bauer is obviously a fascist, he's a study of a fascist temperament. There are all sorts of little clues; he is German and he says "I'm expecting a telephone call from Argentina." It's systematically ambiguous; he's also got that cigarette lighter Brecht gave him. But, you know, he's a very suspicious character. In a sense he's almost a caricature image of a fascist. His relations show a kind of psychological fascism with sadistic and masochistic sides in typical formations. When people used to ask me why the film isn't political, I used to respond rather naively that I couldn't make a political film in Sweden because that world was too alien to me.

You asked me how I feel about comments on my films. Well I'm helped, because I now realize that was a dumb answer on my part and the film is in fact more political than I had understood, not political in the sense that it's about Sweden, but political in dealing with a psychology which connects with a political attitude. The third film will be about a very specific political situation.

V.S.: You've been quoted as saying you didn't like the kind of political films Jean-Luc Godard is doing now.

S.S.: I have been misquoted on that. Someone once asked me a very leading question which I answered without changing it. That was my error. "Do you like what Godard does now as much as what he

did before?'' was the question. And I said no. But I adore all of
Godard's work. And I admire very much this turn he's made, his
refusal to continue giving audiences (including me) what we liked so
much, and his willingness to take risks. I think Godard is really
serious politically and I honor, respect, and admire the sectarian trend
which his film-making has taken, even though I, as an individual
member of the moviegoing audience, don't get the same kind of
pleasure out of these films as I did from the films through *Weekend*.

But what he's doing is marvelous, and I don't see why we should
reproach him or criticize him for not repeating himself. There are so
many different kinds of pleasures you can get. I don't have the kind
of pleasure I had before but I have, let's say, the pleasure of being
puzzled or even of being frustrated. I don't understand everything
that he's doing now, and it's very interesting also not to understand.

I don't want to give the impression that I don't like what he's doing.
Everything he does is important, even his smallest effort is worth the
greatest things most other people are doing now. He's really a model
for taking chances. With a few exceptions most directors do their best
work early. Bergman is an exception. He was a very mediocre filmmaker in the beginning and he's grown and grown and grown. For
most film-makers their first four or five films are their best. After that
they just go on repeating themselves. They get safer and safer. Godard
is a noble example of somebody who wants to grow and take chances.

V.S.: Don't you think his new development came out of the revolutionary politics of the sixties?

S.S.: Yes, but a lot of other people were involved and excited and
went to demonstrations and meetings. But it didn't shake them up the
way it shook up Godard. Most European film-makers are more or less
left-wing and were highly sympathetic to what went on in 1968. Few
people were really ready to raise havoc with their whole careers and
go off in a very special direction.

V.S.: Why did you start working in film in Europe?

S.S.: I am sure, looking back on it, that one of the reasons it
seemed to me quite natural to start working in Europe was that I
knew a woman director was more acceptable there than here. And in
fact it is the case. Now there are a couple of women directors, like
Shirley Clarke in the independent cinema, but she's had a very
difficult time making films, and Elaine May, who works on more or

less Hollywood terms. Even in Hollywood there's been one woman director in every generation. But still a woman director is a freak in this country. It's perhaps changing now.

In Europe there are a couple of women directors in every country, and there have been for some time. It's just easier. Backward as the Europeans may be in the sense that they don't talk, as some people do here, in women's liberation terms, you don't get that kind of question you get here that, well, how does it feel to be a woman and a director. I mean it's not surprising to people. Of course you're in a small minority. In France there is Agnès Varda and Nelly Kaplan right now. The most interesting of all the Czech directors happened to be a woman, Věra Chytilová. Her films were the ones I liked best of all the Czech New Wave films in the sixties. At any rate the woman director has been visibly around for ten or fifteen years in Europe.

V.S.: Did you attempt to make films here or did you steer instinctively elsewhere?

S.S.: No, no, I never tried. It was just an instinctive feeling in the late sixties that it would be easier to work there. Not only for that reason. Far more important was my sense that the European film industry was still much less industrialized, much less bureaucratized, that there was much more chance of an outsider getting in. There was also a precedent for writers becoming directors. Marguerite Duras, Robbe-Grillet, Pasolini, were all pretty well known writers before they directed their first films. I liked the European conditions of film-making, with lower budgets, smaller crews, the tradition of independence, and the possibilities of controlling the film from beginning to end.

V.S.: Didn't the independent film-making here interest you?

S.S.: To be quite honest I didn't know how one did that. I'm very bad at asking people for money. I wouldn't have known how to go about getting the money since I have no money myself except what I've earned through my writing. The only way I understood was that you got some kind of orthodox producer to back you. I thought in America that meant Hollywood money and then you had to be part of some kind of set-up. I was a complete outsider with that nasty label of being an intellectual. It just didn't occur to me to work in the independent cinema. It just seemed to me that in Europe there was a precedent for my kind of person getting into film-making and here there wasn't.

So I didn't even try. I just hung around a lot in Europe. I know a lot of directors and actors and I just felt around without knowing exactly where I wanted to work or how it would happen. Finally I got a very lucky break. A Swedish producer who had heard indirectly that I wanted to make films called me up and asked me if I'd like to come to Sweden. I went to Sweden and stayed for almost two years. And now I have found a French producer.

I'm going on with this series of accidents, but I would very much like to work here. In the two Swedish films I had to work with this very special aesthetic point of view of having to deal head on with the problem of accents and choosing therefore to incorporate it as a major formal element in the film. For the third film, though most of it is going to be shot in France, the story mainly concerns American and English people. I'll be working with material closer to home. In an imaginative sense I'm creeping back, but since English is an international language and Americans are everywhere, obviously I could go on working in Europe for some time.

The only language besides English that I do speak well is French and I have lived a lot in France. I think perhaps it is the one foreign country where I could make a film and feel somewhat at home. I can't say I know France well, but I know Paris very well and the world in which I live in Paris. I live there now most of the time, and my world is completely French. I don't know foreigners in Paris. I live in a world of French people, I'm the only American they know. So I've been lucky in that way. It's not so easy. It took me a long time. I've been spending a lot of time in Paris for over a decade before I've finally started moving in a really French world. But I crossed the barrier, that terrible barrier.

Paris is one of the most difficult cities in the world in which to get to know people. But now I'm in a French world and I have a second country. Of course it's never going to be my first country, I'm always going to be a foreigner, but I think it's perhaps the one other country where I could work from the inside. It's not this third film that I'm going to do in that way, of course, but perhaps I could make a French film. And for the rest, I don't know.

V.S.: And you're not confronted with sexism there?

S.S.: No, it's really acceptable. There's a woman director named Nelly Kaplan who is making thoroughly commercial films. Up to now the woman director has been more or less associated with the art film, the avant-garde film, the small audience film, but Kaplan is doing absolutely commercial work, comedies, thrillers for big audiences. Needless to say, however, the women directors are a minority.

I wouldn't say the French have very enlightened attitudes in general. They're extremely sexist in many ways. But there are more women in different professional activities in France than there are here. That's not the problem. The problem is in daily life, because one gets very angry at having to deal with sex stereotypes constantly.

V.S.: Do you feel the same kind of pressure here?

S.S.: No, what one feels, of course, is the injustice of the fact that a few women make it and most can't. I've been in the situation of the exceptional woman, the nigger in a room full of whites. All my life in most work situations I've been the only woman. I've been accepted because there's always room for an exception, and a few women are accepted. A small tiny minority is allowed to enter the professional world which is totally dominated by men.

I've been stubborn and refused even to pay attention to sexist stereotypes. I think I've spent my whole life just pretending they didn't exist and not listening when people patronized me or put me down. I've had such an intransigent attitude all my life that I got away with a lot because I didn't get angry or embarrassed. I just pretended I didn't notice that anyone was putting me down. I just insisted on doing what I wanted to do. So I can't say that, personally, I've been held back in any way. On the contrary, I probably had certain advantages from the situation of being a woman.

V.S.: When did you start being aware that women are oppressed?

S.S.: There was a particular moment more than twenty years ago when I became very militant and very conscious. It was when I read *The Second Sex* by Simone de Beauvoir in 1951. That's the moment I really became militant. I feel I've had these ideas on a conscious level for twenty years and unconsciously all my life. I tried as much as I could always to put them into practice in my own life.

For instance I was married for seven years and I never used my husband's name. When I divorced my husband I refused alimony. I'm very much against women changing their names and I'm very much against alimony.

V.S.: How do you view marriage now?

S.S.: I'm not against people making a legal contract in and of itself. Why not? I think most marriages are very oppressive—to men too, but in more obvious ways to women. The nuclear family is a disaster, for the husband, the wife, and the children who are brought up as the property of their parents.

V.S.: You seem to stress that in the family situation in *Brother Carl*.

S.S.: Oh, the nuclear family is a disaster. The freedom of women and therefore men depends on a big change in family life toward many different kinds of families and groupings, extended families. Mommy and daddy and the two kids locked up in an apartment is just hell. And women are not going to fundamentally change their situation until that fundamental family system is changed.

Day care centers and equal pay for equal work still don't go to the heart of the question as long as you have these family cells with this immense duplication of domestic labor in which, essentially, when the woman comes home from a job she still has to take care of the children and do the housework. That's why it isn't much better in the Soviet Union than it is here. It's true, of course, that women there are much more active in the professional world and in public life, but the family set up is just the same.

I would like to deal with some of these questions in films. One film project that interests me very much is to make a film about women, but that's not the next thing I'm going to do. However, the main woman character in the new film is a doctor. I will try to show some of the contradictions in her situation. It's a story of a couple, and it's very important for me that the woman have a profession. This is a story of people in a certain period with certain prejudices and many ideological limitations. I would like to deal with the change that occurs in the woman's consciousness.

It's also implicit in *Brother Carl* but I would like to take it further. There are two women in *Brother Carl;* one is a working woman who is very independent but, in fact, a complete slave in her attachment to this bastard of a man she wants to get back with. So that for all her independence, she is still in a hopeless emotional situation. And the other woman is a bored, discontented, middle-class housewife with nothing to do.

V.S.: Have you read any of the recent books that have come out of the movement here?

S.S.: I've read almost all of them. I like them all because the main thing is to make a fuss. There are some books I prefer to others. But I think it's good that more and more voices are added and that peoples' heads are in many different places. For instance, I consider Germaine Greer's book to be essentially reactionary, though it has some very good descriptive passages. Early on in the book there's a whole passage about the imagery of the woman's body which is brilliant, a very good phenomenological description of the situation of women and their relation to their bodies. Then the book takes off in quite another direction which I think is ultimately very reactionary—to cite a book which is not one of my favorites.

Still I would not criticize the book in the sense that it is a very good experience for some people and will move them from this place to that, which is an advance in their consciousness. It's not a book that helped me, but for a lot of people it could probably be very helpful. The Kate Millett book has also tremendous limitations, but for some people I am sure it was very good. And, anyway, what's wrong with it is certainly not the same thing that's wrong with the Greer book.

I don't think it's a question of having the correct analysis, but of piling on the pressure on every level and knowing that anything people can do can be of help to someone. Naturally, I'm more sympathetic to more radical positions, because I want to push my own consciousness and go beyond what I've understood all my life. But I think it would be wrong to judge the literature or the activities of the movement from where I am, because I'm in a place which is very different from a lot of other people.

V.S.: Would you make a special effort to have women work on your films, for instance using a camerawoman?

S.S.: Yes, I would say I am certainly prejudiced in favor of using women. Given a man and a woman of equal talent I would prefer to employ the woman for the obvious reason that women have to get experience and their numbers in the professions have to increase. And I like very much working with women. My French producer for instance happens to be a woman, Nicole Stéphane. She is one of the two women producers in France. It gives me a lot of pleasure that my producer is a woman. And I think it's good for our side. Obviously I wouldn't refuse to work with men. But every time I find a woman who is really good, I'm proud. I feel a sense of solidarity with women who do things, and I went to help.

V.S.: What do you think about feminist art?

S.S.: I think anything that makes people aware of the fact that women have done a lot of things is good. I don't think women should ghetto-ize themselves, but there is a hidden history of women. Pascal had two brilliant mathematician sisters. Nobody has ever heard about Pascal's sisters. There is a hidden history of the work of women which has been suppressed and if that work becomes more public that's good.

But I'm not in favor of ghettoizing women. I feel personally a loyalty to women as women, but I don't feel there is a specific women's culture. The works of women aren't essentially different from the works of men. I don't feel that as a woman I am going to make films differently from a man as such. My work might be more related to some male director than to some female director in terms of my own temperament, interest or style.

But any form of insisting is good. I don't think women should be polite about the situation anymore. Women are so afraid of asserting themselves, because that is labeled aggressive or castrating or unfeminine. Women are afraid of getting angry. What is just normal, active, enterprising behavior in a man is considered tough, aggressive and mean on the part of women. They just have to get over that.

Susan Sontag
Joe David Bellamy / 1972

From *The New Fiction: Interviews with Innovative American Writers* (Urbana: University of Illinois Press, 1974), pp. 113–129. © 1974 by the Board of Trustees of the University of Illinois. Used with permission of the University of Illinois Press.

I had met Susan Sontag once, seven years before, at Antioch, where she blew great clouds of cigarette smoke above her head during her lecture describing "the new sensibility." She had nothing but scorn for American fiction of that particular moment, an unsettling message, coming from so obviously formidable a person, for my virgin ears and brain.

Author of *Against Interpretation* (1966), probably the most controversial and provocative collection of aesthetic and critical statements of the last decade in the U.S., Susan Sontag has published two novels, *The Benefactor* (1963) and *Death Kit* (1967), and a second collection of essays, *Styles of Radical Will* (1969), and she has written and directed two films, *Duet for Cannibals* and *Brother Carl*. Her stories, reviews, and essays have appeared in numerous magazines such as *Harper's Bazaar, Harper's, Partisan Review, The Nation, The New York Review of Books,* and *Commentary*.

When the opportunity for this interview presented itself, I was frankly apprehensive, remembering her Antioch appearance. But my worries were groundless; no one could have been more charming and cooperative. "I was hoping it would be you," she said, just off the plane, standing out under the awning at the arrival gate in her wraparound sheepskin collar, suede skirt, and boots, just removing a pair of blue-lens sunglasses—just that direct and unpretentious. At lunch, she laughed easily; she seemed playful, almost girlish.

During the interview, conducted later (on March 2, 1972), mostly in Mansfield, Pennsylvania, where she had come to lecture, she was a pleasure to watch—intensely serious, intellectually aggressive, sensitive, precise. The interview was completed on several pitch-black back roads that night during a long detour past rising flood waters surrounding the Chemung County airport, and it was later revised and condensed by Sontag.

Joe David Bellamy: In your essay "Against Interpretation" (1964) you said that the sense of what might be done with form in fiction written by Americans was "rudimentary, uninspired and stagnant." Do you think this is still true eight years later?

Susan Sontag: No. At the time I wrote "Against Interpretation" the new American writer who interested me most was Burroughs. He was the only writer who seemed to me to have broken some of the "realist" stereotypes that limited American fiction. But since 1964 there has been a kind of explosion in prose fiction.

Bellamy: What do you think is responsible for the new climate of the last eight years?

Sontag: That's like asking what created the 1960s. Everything got more interesting didn't it? Look at films. Look at popular music. Even fiction, that sluggish art, couldn't resist certain influences from other arts. And there has been more sophistication, more awareness of what is going on in other places. In the immediate postwar period American writers became very provincial. In the twenties and thirties I think that American writers were much more international. Many of them spent time abroad and came in contact particularly with French literature, and writers like Joyce were very important here. But after the war there were no longer writers who were continuing even the kind of very moderate experiments of a Dos Passos or a Nathanael West—not to mention Gertrude Stein, who was simply a figure of fun and seemed to stand totally outside American literature, or Djuna Barnes, or the still undiscovered fiction that Laura Riding wrote in the 1930s. The aims of the postwar period reverted to a kind of moral, sociological reportage in the tradition of the nineteenth century.

Then in the sixties, after I wrote that essay, people got more international again. And certain foreign writers began to have a real impact here. Borges, for instance, has mattered a lot. And older writers like Joyce, who had become college classics but who never influenced writers in the postwar period, were rediscovered.

Exactly the same thing was going on in England in that period, too, and there the novel has remained extremely conservative. A writer like Iris Murdoch was, at least at the beginning of her career, considered to be far out; and genuinely experimental writers like Virginia Woolf and Ivy Compton-Burnett had no influence whatever. What I said about American prose fiction still pretty much applies to what is going on in England—but less and less to what is happening here.

Bellamy: Why do you think this change has come about? Is it a refusal to see reality in the same banal ways as the nineteenth-century novel saw it? A realer kind of realism? Is it the result of writers accepting the fact that thinking or fantasy is *part* of reality and is worthy of consideration (obviously that realization has an effect upon form), or is it something beyond that?

Sontag: Partly it was the influence of other forms, I think. And partly it was the competition of other forms, like journalism, which has gotten much livelier, and TV. The form of the novel that was dominant here in that postwar period (that lasted about twenty years) was one that crystallized in the late nineteenth century before the advent of other media. But just as painting changed when photography came in, and the painter could no longer feel that his job was so self-evidently to give an image, the novel has slowly changed under pressure of tasks that are now shared in other forms.

Bellamy: So, the novel, you would say, is having to resort to those things it can do best, those things that other forms can't do as well?

Sontag: Well, I feel a little hesitant in talking about the novel as if it were one thing. The novels that are most popular are still in the older mold, the so-called realistic form of writing that gives what most people expect from prose fiction, a strong, clear story suggesting a certain amount of sociological and psychological information about an exotic world. The writer reports on a world you don't know: airport control towers, the Mafia, the secret life of a small town, the Hollywood movie colony, and so on.

But the relationship between more difficult fiction, which has a smaller audience, and the popular forms is still pretty close. You can see how popular fiction imitates or parodies certain formulas which began as advanced or experimental fiction. Look at the influence of Hemingway, whose stylistic mannerisms became incorporated into the most commercial kind of fiction. I think that the general public always follows the limited public, exactly as you see in the movies, where forms of film narration which only ten or fifteen years ago were to be found in avant-garde films, underground films, European art films, are now the common language of Hollywood.

Bellamy: You see it in television too—certain film-cutting techniques.

Sontag: And in advertising. The visual language of advertising has moved very rapidly, and has been even more directly influenced by advanced techniques from feature films.

Bellamy: I hadn't thought about that in quite that way. I've generally been persuaded by the argument that television has influenced form in fiction, especially because of the swiftness of the image and the rapidity with which scenes and persons change. That is, even if you watch an hour series, every ten minutes you get six commercials, so you are whisked away to some faraway place. One of the conventions that seems to be growing in some experimental fiction is the use of a lot of space, a lot more space *breaks,* and that could be attributed to what is happening in television. But, of course, what's happening on television, I suppose, is either accidental or comes about from copying advanced film techniques.

Sontag: I think it comes more from films, and that's an old influence. Faulkner and Dos Passos, for instance, were both strongly influenced by film narrative techniques, and some devices in *U.S.A.* are a direct imitation of feature film and newsreel kinds of cutting. People are learning to deal with more information at the same time, and certain kinds of exposition have come to seem less necessary, even boring. Most young readers—high school and college students—will tell you that they find older novels too long. They find it hard to read Dickens or James or Tolstoy or Proust. They want something that's faster and less descriptive.

Bellamy: Do you think the novel is headed in a new direction?

Sontag: I think prose fiction is going to be more and more open to the influence of other media, whether that be journalism, lithography, song, or painting. It's very difficult for the novel to maintain its purity—and there's no reason why it should.

Bellamy: Toward the end of your essay "Nathalie Sarraute and the Novel" you said you saw Sarraute's argument as basically a realist argument; that is, you point out that in getting rid of hard character and psychological explorations and the omniscient author she was actually asking for a more complex awareness of human behavior and therefore a deeper psychology and a deeper realism. Then you said that this was really a weakness in her theorizing, because the idea that the novel should approximate life is a banal idea and should be dispensed with for a while. What I'd like to ask then is: If the main purpose of the novel is *not* to imitate life, whether it's life at a fantasy or intracranial level or the level of ideas or a sociological level, what are the alternatives?

Sontag: Intracranial?

Bellamy: Inside of the head.

Sontag: What isn't inside the head?

Bellamy: Well, you know. The old epistemological distinctions—the idea of external reality as something we can all agree upon versus the idea of the individual vision which assumes that subjective reality is all there is and that yours and mine are quite different from each other.

Sontag: I think the amount of external reality that people could actually agree on is so small, so banal, that any description involves a tremendous amount of interpretation and subjectivity. The concept of external reality as an object to be reproduced in words is very dubious. It's perfectly true that people using the same language will respond with the same words when asked to identify certain objects, certain sensory impressions. Everybody using the English language who would be considered psychologically normal would call what you're doing "sitting in a rocking chair." But there are an infinite number of ways to describe that rocking chair and you sitting in it. It's really just *naming* that we agree on, naming on a very simple level. I think the distinction between the inner and outer is not useful or interesting. And there aren't, really, any "facts." Or if there are facts, they are so primitive they're hardly worth mentioning; they're the things that everybody agrees on.

About Nathalie Sarraute—I was too hard on her. There is a real inconsistency between the theoretical program she subscribed to and what she actually was doing. But I was too severe in my emphasis on that inconsistency. So okay, she was inconsistent—because her novels are basically psychological novels. What is interesting in Sarraute is her attempt to do it all through the voice, through dialogue and inner speech and subspeech. She gives the voices one after another, what they are saying and also what they are not saying, what they are thinking. She doesn't describe how people look or what they are wearing. The method comes partly out of Joyce and also from late Virginia Woolf. *Between the Acts* is the clearest model of that kind of writing. One of the principal directions of modern literature is toward the oral, toward the recording of different kinds of human voices. The conventions of dealing with people's physical appearance that were developed through the so-called realistic novel became flat. They lost their power to enlarge people's sensibilities.

Bellamy: All right. But still, as you are going along, it seems to me that you are adhering to a realist argument yourself. That is, you seem to be talking about the validity of finding new ways to approximate experience. You mention that Sarraute's achievement seems to be in that direction, but you also said in that essay on Sarraute that you wish the metaphor of the novel, as something that tries to approximate experience, would be retired for a while. If the novel did not try to approximate experience at some level, what else could it do?

Sontag: I would talk in terms of creating experience. Art manipulates images that people have about their own and other people's experience, but where the notion of experience comes in, I think, is not "imitation" or "approximation" but "creation" of experience.

Bellamy: It sounds to me as if you are describing a position that Oscar Wilde took, which was that nature imitates art. External reality is the result of the workings of our imaginations. Imagination is a faculty of perception. We make nature. That is—the inverse of Plato's notion that art copies nature.

Sontag: Yes, I think nature imitates art more than art imitates nature, though we operate under the illusion that we are imitating nature. Artists are spokesmen of what in our sensibility is changing, and they choose among a number of possible different ways of rendering experience.

I don't think there is one way of rendering experience which is correct. I believe in a plurality of experience. I don't believe there *is* such a thing as "human experience." There are different kinds of sensibility, different kinds of demands made on art, different self-conceptions of what the artist is. And what the artist has thought it necessary to do for some time is to give people new shapes of experience, to be the cutting edge for some kind of critical or reactive change. This is hardly the only possible definition of the artist, but it's the one that has persisted in this society for well over a hundred years. The artist is someone challenging accepted notions of experience or giving people *other* information about experience or other interpretations. The artist says, "There is this cliché about this kind of experience, or this misinformation; now I will show you what it's *really* like, or I will show you *another* way of looking at it." And that is why the arts now proceed by a very rapid succession of stylistic changes, because it seems as if certain devices or forms of sensibility get used up. Once they become too widely known, too widely practiced, there is a demand for another way of looking at things. But none of this fits into any definition of art as basically realistic.

Realism is a convention. You know the marvelous book by Auerbach, *Mimesis?* What he does is examine a series of passages in which something is being described—the first is from *The Odyssey* and the last is from *Mrs. Dalloway*—to give a history of the notion of realism in European literature that spans almost three thousand years. Homer thought he was being realistic. So did Virginia Woolf. Every writer works with the idea that this is how it *really* is. Auerbach shows how the conventions of describing something have changed.

Bellamy: Pursuing this same direction a bit further, in your essay "On Style" you said, "Every style embodies an epistemological decision, an interpretation of how and what we perceive." I take that to mean that every fiction writer makes a statement about perception and about the relationship between fiction and life. But if that's true, how can any writer escape the realist argument?

Sontag: If *realism* is a word that applies to every writer, or at least to every writer's inner conviction about what he's doing, then it has no value at all. I think one escapes it, if you want to talk about escaping it, precisely by showing that everyone operates under the aegis of some kind of realism. Since everyone operates under it, it doesn't essentially distinguish one group of writers from another. Burroughs is as realistic as Thackeray or Arnold Bennett. It's another realism. I would never argue that people don't think they're talking about something that exists. What I was arguing against was the privileged position of a *certain* kind of realism.

Bellamy: I think you resolved my problem.

Sontag: When I said, "Every style embodies an epistemological decision," I didn't mean that everybody has an idea of the relation of fiction to life. I think that everybody has implicitly an idea about what is most interesting to talk about, to emphasize—because any description, any narration, any discourse, is a very radical selection of certain elements to the exclusion of many other elements. There is no total discourse. There are only partial discourses.

Bellamy: I would like to ask you some questions about *Death*

Kit—to see if there is an ideal way to understand it or what your ideal way would be. My reading of "Against Interpretation," if I may summarize that, is that you are asking for readers (or partakers of an art experience of any kind) to respond to a work of art as an aesthetic experience rather than as an intellectual experience primarily, and you complain of the tendency of criticism to push people toward an overly intellectualized response. So you want the experience of the art object to be more sensual and pleasurable and aesthetically oriented.

Sontag: Many readers, many people who are involved in the arts as consumers, have been programmed to look for certain things in works of art—and to lie to themselves about what they actually were experiencing. They have been taught to reduce their experience to certain forms of talking about it, the most notable of these being "what it means." Confronting some art form, you say to yourself, "Well, there's this element in a painting, in a film, in a poem," and then you ask yourself, "What does it mean?" You are, in fact, changing the experience; a process of translation takes place, a false intellectualizing. But I do not view the intellectual experience as opposed to the aesthetic experience, which I felt you were doing when you reformulated my position. I think the aesthetic experience *is* a form of intelligence, and that a great deal of what people call intellectual activity is aesthetic experience.

Bellamy: You are saying then that aesthetic experience and intellectual experience can be compatible and not necessarily at war with each other?

Sontag: They're two parts of the same thing. And, in a sense, everything is an aesthetic experience. Our ideas about what constitute works of art have been highly conventional. We can consider anything as a work of art. Discussions go on all the time about whether to include such-and-such in the category of art or art experience. For a while, people argued about whether films were an art form. More recently there was a lot of discussion about whether the new popular music was art. This is a type of argument that goes on all the time, as certain experiences or objects are included or excluded. For instance, it's quite plausible to speak of nature as an aesthetic category. As soon as you talk about getting pleasure out of the contemplation of trees and mountains and valleys and sunsets, you're treating nature as an art work or form. There was a certain point at which people in this culture started to think of nature as beautiful—before which they didn't look at nature aesthetically. Art is that conventional area where people make objects for aesthetic consumption, and the objects are so designated in advance by the context. But anything can be put into or withdrawn from that context.

Bellamy: What is the relation of your essays to your two novels? Do you mind if readers "interpret" your novels?

Sontag: I wrote a series of essays between roughly 1963 and 1967— between the first novel, *The Benefactor,* and the second novel, *Death Kit*—which were based on responses which I was having as a reader, as a moviegoer, as someone moving around and coming into contact with a lot of new work that was making me rethink my own assumptions and my own tastes. Almost all those essays, as I said, were written between the first and second novel. And I don't do that kind of essay writing anymore. Unlike Nathalie Sarraute and Robbe-Grillet, I never thought that I was formulating a program for myself as a writer of fiction. I was formulating reactions and generalizations based on my experience as a reader. And I doubt that there is a very clear relation between those opinions I expressed about other people's work in literature and film and what I have done myself as a writer of fiction and as a film maker. I was not, in what I said about the novel, building an aesthetic for my own novels. I was giving my reactions as a reader. In the essays I wrote about film, I wasn't preparing the way for my own work as a film maker. I was writing as a passionate moviegoer. I feel uncomfortable when certain ideas, like the attack on one type of interpretation, are returned to me as notions which I ought to embody in my own work or as slogans which I should be reacting to in terms of what critics say about my work. I'm not against "reading," against multiple readings, against analysis.

Bellamy: How do you feel about Theodore Solotaroff's reading of *Death Kit* in his essay "Interpreting Susan Sontag," according to which Diddy's suicide attempt in the beginning is, in fact, not an attempt but a successful suicide?

Sontag: *Death Kit,* like *The Benefactor,* is a linear narrative which contains certain systematically obscure elements. These elements are systematically obscure because I *want* to leave several possible readings open.

Bellamy: But could the narrative read then as the contents of his final coma?

Sontag: Yes. One clue that supports that reading is the presence of the black orderly in the white uniform at the very beginning and at the end.

Bellamy: So who are Hester and Incardona? Are they figments of his imagination?

Sontag: Yes. In that reading this is a world of death that Diddy enters into, a fictional world in which he reprovokes his death through a series of events which he undergoes so that in the end he does die because he has collected or assembled the elements of his death. It's a second death, a second story of dying that is encapsulated through the original suicide, which was provoked by his wife leaving him.

But I like the idea that *Death Kit* can be read in that way and that it can also be read as a straight narrative in which certain magical events take place on exactly the same level as those events which are convincing in terms of everyday life.

I want the novel to have the same kind of believability that a film has. In a film, everything that you see is *there,* even if you understand that it's a flashback or it's a dream or a fantasy. Still, it fills the screen and what you see is the only reality at the moment that you see it. So, for me, it's both. It can be read in this way if you want a reading that explains how magical and conventionally realistic elements can coexist in the same life. You can say it's all a dream. But at the same time, it should be felt as an experience that was actually happening. I don't want the reader to conclude that that's what *Death Kit* is really about. I want the book to exist on both levels of reading. And it's the same for *The Benefactor,* and for the two films.

Bellamy: Solotaroff feels that you *have* demonstrated a great deal of consistency between what you've done in this novel and your theoretical premises—as stated in your essays. He says that the "intense formalism of the novel—each detail held in place by the pattern, each event shaped by the underlying logic of Diddy's intentions—is . . . another demonstration of Miss Sontag's faith in the hegemony of form. . . ."

Sontag: There is the same temperament in the two films and in the two novels, and there are some of the same obsessions, some of the same thematic material. Of course, I'm the same person; I'm the

same sensibility. But what interests me most now is the difference
between novels and films. I know that I would never have made films
out of the stories of *The Benefactor* or *Death Kit*. And I would never
have made novellas or novels out of the stories for *Duet for Cannibals*
or *Brother Carl*. In each case, it was clear to me: That's a novel;
that's a film. I'm not the kind of writer turned film maker, like Pasolini
or Marguerite Duras, who can make a novel and a play and a film out
of the same material.

Bellamy: Do you think film has become the more interesting form
for you then? Have you left the novel? I hope not.

Sontag: No.

Bellamy: Are you working now on a novel?

Sontag: Yes. And on another film. Film is certainly the more
demanding form in terms of time. You can't do it at your leisure. You
work with a schedule and under considerable pressure from other
people—because you can't do it alone. And then work that goes into
preparing a film is very time consuming.

What interests me in each form is going beyond what I've done
before. I think *Death Kit* is better than *The Benefactor* and that
Brother Carl is better than *Duet for Cannibals*.

Bellamy: Do you think *Brother Carl* is better than *Death Kit* or
vice versa?

Sontag: No, I don't compare them. Both *The Benefactor* and *Death
Kit* were born as language in my head. I started to hear words in my
head, a tone, a voice. A certain kind of language, a certain kind of
rhythm, but words—I heard words and somebody talking. In the case
of *The Benefactor* it was a first-person voice. In the case of *Death Kit*
it was a third-person voice, which is really a disguised first person.
The two films were born as images. A film is not simply images. It is
image and sound. But the first elements of the narrative I possessed
were images. The dialogue seemed much less important. So perhaps
the explanation of why some material becomes film and other becomes fiction is as simple as that.

Bellamy: One observation that one might make about your fiction
(and your films, too) is that if there is decipherable autobiographical
material it's more oblique than with the average writer. It's more
disguised or not there. Do you think autobiographical material is

irrelevant to either form, or is its absence just an accidental circumstance of your own work, or am I wrong?

Sontag: No, you're not wrong at all. I have never been tempted to write about my own life. Most writers consciously recount and transform their own experience. But the way in which I found freedom as a writer, and then as a film maker, was to invent. Lately I have begun to think about why that's so—if it wouldn't be possible to crack this barrier. Would I be able to go someplace where I hadn't been because of it? Is it a question of inhibition or modesty or timidity? I'm not sure.

There are so many lives. All lives are possible. In the end, one does bring one's self to every character, but nothing I have written or related in film is autobiographical in the sense that it is an incident from my life.

I remember when I first started writing I wrote a long story about my best friend. I worked very hard on it, and I think it was rather good. But afterwards I felt a revulsion about the way in which I had used him, made him into an object and in that sense made myself superior to him.

Bellamy: That's interesting because it seems just the opposite of Joyce Carol Oates's attitude. She has an amazing ability to get herself "into" people and do them, do their personalities. And her attitude is that she hopes people don't see that as vampiristic. But she feels that so many people are inarticulate and their lives need to be articulated in some way that she feels a need to do that for other people.

Sontag: I think it is vampiristic. What would you do with your friends after you've put them in your novels? Of course, I know people don't usually resent it. I have friends who have told me with obvious pleasure that they figure in barely disguised form in novels or films. But I have a temperamental revulsion against doing that.

Bellamy: Do you think the concept of character which comes to us from the nineteenth-century novel, that people are hardened types, is really a dangerous fallacy? We seem to be moving to a point where some writers assume that character is much more amorphous, that each person is a locus of consciousness and is much less hardened. There have even been some formal attempts to dramatize that aspect of character.

Sontag: I think all the theories are plausible. It depends on what you do with them. There are some novels that don't have characters at all—that have different kinds of voices which you perhaps can associate with characters if you want to, but not characters in the traditional sense. There are some kinds of fiction in which people are viewed behavioristically, and there's no attempt at all to get inside them, inside what they're feeling. For instance, Borges, in his short fictions, locates people in a historical way, but there's no exploration of character. There are some kinds of fiction that work with stereotypes in which people are identified by certain exaggerated qualities they possess, and the argument of the fiction is the interplay of these different humors or types. I don't think there is any theory about character that I would want to subscribe to. The question of character: "Should character develop?" and "Is it wrong to have static or flat characters as opposed to round characters?"—the Forster distinction—is impossible to answer without a context. Either of these possibilities works.

I am most interested in kinds of fiction which are in the very broadest sense "science fiction," fiction which moves back and forth between imaginary or fantastic worlds and the so-called real world. That's what Donald Barthelme, Leonard Michaels, Ishmael Reed— many writers are doing now.

Bellamy: How about the direction of myth—some of the things that Barth has done, or Coover?

Sontag: If you understand the mythical allusions, then it's another level on which fiction may be pleasurable. To grasp the parallels and allusions and the play with *The Odyssey* when you read Joyce's *Ulysses* adds to your pleasure. It's another level of reading, another aesthetic game. But *Ulysses* certainly stands on its own without that knowledge. Yet it's not "better" than some other way of doing things. We live in a time of radically diversified, broken culture in which even myths are literary artifacts and not the property of people in a naïve sense. And we also live surrounded by works of art reproduced and distributed on a scale unknown since the beginning of history, where we have access to and are confronted with kinds of art of all different schools, periods, and cultures.

Bellamy: That kind of historical burden has led some writers to end up resorting to parody.

Sontag: Exactly.

Bellamy: Do you see that as a valid response to the history of, let's say, fiction?

Sontag: I think it's a dead-end response, a decadent response, that is often very creative as long as it lasts. But it can't last very long. Decadence has its pleasures and wisdom. But it's not an answer. It's a response. The glut of cultural goods creates a kind of fatigue—having too many models, too many stimuli. And parody is one way of handling the problem and copping out at the same time. If by "valid" you mean does it answer a real need, yes, it does. It's harder and harder to take things straight. Everything seems to come in quotation marks with its own built-in ironies. But I'm not sure that that situation is going to go on very long.

Bellamy: How do you get beyond parody? What comes next? Something new? I mean, something new which is beyond anything done before? That starts to sound like an idea of progress.

Sontag: No, I don't think there's any progress in the arts in that sense, but I think that this sort of autodestructive mechanism in the arts will come to an end, at least for a while. I don't think the arts can go on indefinitely raping themselves, eating up styles, getting more self-conscious. That's a certain period of sensibility, and people will get tired of it. There are rhythms of activity which are where people move very fast and then lie fallow for a while, and certain kinds of simplifications come to seem more desirable than that kind of sophisticated irony.

Of course, in a large part of the world all this is irrelevant. The whole discussion we've been having assumes the complicated and very privileged situation of the artist—in all forms, including the novel—in Western Europe and North America. These are special notions which prevail in societies where art is a commodity, in a kind of free market, and where the artist is rewarded even if he's a critic of his society and is some kind of outsider. There are many people in this world, in Africa, in Asia, in Latin America, who wouldn't at all agree that this is the direction of the novel or this is the problem of the artist—and who don't feel the need to parody anything and who don't worry about exhaustion and cultural glut and the relation of image and reality. It's important to remember that the discussion we're having has to do with where *we* are politically and morally, and is limited by *who* we are sociologically and historically.

An Interview with Susan Sontag

Geoffrey Movius / 1975

From *New Boston Review*, Vol. 1, No. 1 (June 1975), pp. 12–13.
Reprinted by permission of Geoffrey Movius.

Geoffrey Movius: In one of your recent essays on photography in the *New York Review of Books,* you write that "no work of imaginative literature can have the same authenticity as a document," and that there is "a rancorous suspicion in America of anything that seems literary." Do you think that imaginative literature is on the way out? Is the printed word on the way out?

Susan Sontag: Fiction writers have been made very nervous by a problem of credibility. Many don't feel comfortable about doing it straight, and try to give fiction the character of nonfiction. A recent example is Philip Roth's *My Life as a Man,* a book consisting of three novellas: the first two are purportedly written by the first-person narrator of the third one. That a document of the writer's own character and experience seems to have more authority than an invented fiction is perhaps more widespread in this country than elsewhere and reflects the triumph of psychological ways of looking at everything. I have friends who tell me that the only books by writers of fiction that really interest them are their letters and diaries.

Movius: Do you think that is happening because people feel a need to get in touch with the past—their own or other people's?

Sontag: I think it has more to do with their lack of connection with the past than with being interested in the past. Many people don't believe that one can give an account of the world, of society, but only of the self—"how I saw it." They assume that what writers do is testify, if not confess, and a work is about how *you* see the world and put *yourself* on the line. Fiction is supposed to be "true." Like photographs.

Movius: *The Benefactor* and *Death Kit* aren't autobiographical.

Sontag: In my two novels, invented material was more compelling than autobiographical material. Some recent stories, such as "Project for a Trip to China" in the April 1973 *Atlantic Monthly,* do draw on

my own life. But I haven't meant to suggest that the taste for personal
testimony and for confessions, real and fictitious, is the principal one
that moves readers and ambitious writers. The taste for futurology, or
prophecy, is of at least equal importance. But this taste also confirms
the prevailing unreality of the real historical past. Some novels which
are situated in the past, like the work of Thomas Pynchon, are really
works of science fiction.

Movius: Your contrast between autobiographical writers and the
science-fiction writers reminds me of a passage in one of the *New
York Review* essays, in which you write that some photographers set
themselves up as scientists, others as moralists. The scientists "make
an inventory of the world," whereas the moralists "concentrate on
hard cases." What sort of cases do you think the moralist-photogra-
phers should be concentrating on at this point?

Sontag: I'm reluctant to make prescriptive statements about what
people ought to be doing, since I hope they will always be doing many
different things. The main interest of the photographer as moralist has
been war, poverty, natural catastrophes, accidents—disaster and decay. When photojournalists report that "there was nothing to photograph," what this usually means is that there was nothing *terrible*
to photograph.

Movius: And the scientists?

Sontag: I suppose the main tradition in photography is the one that
implies that anything can be interesting if you take a photograph of it.
It consists in discovering beauty, a beauty that can exist anywhere
but is assumed to reside particularly in the random and the banal.
Photography conflates the notions of the "beautiful" and the "interesting." It's a way of aestheticizing the whole world.

Movius: Why did you decide to write about photography?

Sontag: Because I've had the experience of being obsessed by
photographs. And because virtually all the important aesthetic, moral,
and political problems—the question of "modernity" itself and of
"modernist" taste—are played out in photography's relatively brief
history. William K. Ivins has called the camera the most important
invention since the printing press. For the evolution of sensibility, the
invention of the camera is perhaps even more important. It is, of
course, the uses to which photography is put in our culture, in the
consumer society, that make photography so interesting and so po-

tent. In the People's Republic of China, people don't see "photographically." The Chinese take pictures of each other and of famous sites
and monuments, as we do. But they're baffled by the foreigner who
will rush to take a picture of an old, battered, peeling farmhouse door.
They don't have our idea of the "picturesque." They don't understand photography as a method of appropriating and transforming
reality—in pieces—which denies the very existence of inappropriate
or unworthy subject matter. As a current ad for the Polaroid SX-70
puts it: "It won't let you stop. Suddenly you see a picture everywhere
you look."

Movius: How does photography change the world?

Sontag: By giving us an immense amount of experience that "normally" is not our experience. And by making a selection of experience
which is very tendentious, ideological. While there appears to be
nothing that photography can't devour, whatever can't be photographed becomes less important. Malraux's idea of the museum-
without-walls is an idea about the consequences of photography: our
way of looking at painting and sculpture is now determined by
photographs. Not only do we know the world of art, the history of
art, primarily through photographs, we know them in a way that no
one could have known them before. When I was in Orvieto for the
first time several months ago, I spent hours looking at the facade of
the cathedral; but only when I bought a book on the cathedral a week
later did I really see it, in the modern sense of seeing. The photographs
enabled me to see in a way that my "naked" eye could not possibly
see the "real" cathedral.

Movius: This shows how it is possible for photography literally to
create an entire way of seeing.

Sontag: Photographs convert works of art into items of information.
They do this by making parts and wholes equivalent. When I was in
Orvieto, I could see the whole facade by standing back, but then I
couldn't see the details. Then I could move close and see the detail of
whatever was not higher than, say, eight feet, but there was no way
whereby my eye could blot out the whole. The camera elevates the
fragment to a privileged position. As Malraux points out, a photograph
can show a piece of sculpture—a head, a hand—which looks superb
by itself, and this may be reproduced alongside another object which
might be ten times bigger but, in the format of the book, occupies the

same amount of space. In this way, photography annihilates our sense of scale.

It also does queer things to our sense of time. Never before in human history did people have any idea of what they looked like as children. The rich commissioned portraits of their children, but the conventions of portraiture from the Renaissance through the nineteenth century were thoroughly determined by ideas about class and didn't give people a very reliable idea of what they had looked like.

Movius: Sometimes the portrait might consist of somebody else's body with your head on it.

Sontag: Right. And the vast majority of people, those who could not afford to have a portrait painted, had no record of what they looked like as children. Today, we all have photographs in which we can see ourselves at age six, our faces already intimating what they were to become. We have similar information about our parents and grandparents. And there's a great poignancy in these photographs; they make you realize that these people really were children once. To be able to see oneself and one's parents as children is an experience unique to our time. The camera has brought people a new, and essentially pathetic, relation to themselves, to their physical appearance, to aging, to their own mortality. It is a kind of pathos which never existed before.

Movius: But there's something about what you say which contradicts the idea that photography distances us from historical events. From Anthony Lewis' column in the *New York Times* this morning I jotted down this quote by Alexander Woodside, a specialist in Sino-Vietnamese studies at Harvard. He said: "Vietnam is probably one of the contemporary world's purest examples of a history-dependent, history-obsessed society. . . . The U.S. is probably the contemporary world's purest example of a society which is perpetually trying to abolish history, to avoid thinking in historical terms, to associate dynamism with premeditated amnesia." It struck me that, in your essays, you too are asserting about America that we are deracinated—we are not in possession of our past. Perhaps there is a redemptive impulse in our keeping photographic records.

Sontag: The contrast between America and Vietnam couldn't be more striking. In *Trip to Hanoi*, the short book I wrote after my first trip to North Vietnam, in 1968, I described how struck I was by the

Vietnamese taste for making historical connections and analogies, however crude or simple we might find them. Talking about the American aggression, the Vietnamese would cite something that happened during the thousands of years of invasions from China. The Vietnamese situate themselves in an historical continuum. That continuum contains repetitions. Americans, if they ever think about the past, are not interested in repetition. Major events like the American Revolution, the Civil War, the Depression are treated as unique, extraordinary, and discrete. It's a different relation to experience: there is no sense of repetition. Americans have a completely linear sense of history—insofar as they have one at all.

Movius: And what would the role of photographs be in all this?

Sontag: The essential American relation to the past is not to carry too much of it. The past impedes action, saps energy. It's a burden because it modifies or contradicts optimism. If photographs are our connection with the past, it's a very peculiar, fragile, sentimental connection. You take a photograph before you destroy something. The photograph is its posthumous existence.

Movius: Why do you think Americans feel that the past is a burden?

Sontag: Because unlike Vietnam, this isn't a "real" country but a made-up, willed country, a meta-country. Most Americans are the children or grandchildren of immigrants, whose decision to come here had, to begin with, a great deal to do with cutting their losses. If immigrants retained a tie with their country or culture of origin, it was very selective. The main impulse was to forget. I once asked my father's mother, who died when I was seven, where she came from. She said, "Europe." Even at six I knew that wasn't a very good answer. I said, "But where, Grandma?" She repeated, testily, "Europe." And so to this day, I don't know from what country my paternal grandparents came. But I have photographs of them, which I cherish, which are like mysterious tokens of all that I don't know about them.

Movius: You talk about photographs as being strong, manageable, discrete, "neat" slices of time. Do you think that we retain a single frame more fully than we retain moving images?

Sontag: Yes.

Movius: Why do you think we remember the single photograph better?

Sontag: I think it has to do with the nature of visual memory. Not only do I remember photographs better than I remember moving images, but what I remember of a movie amounts to an anthology of single shots. I can recall the story, lines of dialogue, the rhythm, but what I remember visually are selected moments that I have, in effect, reduced to stills. It's the same for one's own life. Each memory from one's childhood, or from any period that's not in the immediate past, is like a still photograph rather than a strip of film. And photography has objectified this way of seeing and remembering.

Movius: Do you see "photographically"?

Sontag: Of course.

Movius: Do you take photographs?

Sontag: I don't own a camera. I'm a photograph junkie, but I don't want to take them.

Movius: Why?

Sontag: Perhaps I might really get hooked.

Movius: Would that be bad? Would that mean that one had moved from being a writer to being something else?

Sontag: I do think that the photograph's orientation to the world is in competition with the writer's way of seeing.

Movius: How are they different?

Sontag: Writers ask more questions. It's hard for the writer to work on the assumption that just anything can be interesting. Many people experience their lives as if they had cameras. But while they can see it, they can't say it. When they report an interesting event, their accounts frequently peter out in the statement, "I wish I had had my camera." There is a general breakdown in narrative skills, and few people tell stories well anymore.

Movius: Do you think that this breakdown is coincidental with the rise of photography or do you think there is some direct causal relationship?

Sontag: Narration is linear. Photography is antilinear. People now have a very developed feeling for process and transience, but they don't understand any more what constitutes a beginning, middle, and end. Endings or conclusions are discredited. Every narrative, like every psychotherapy, seems potentially interminable. So any ending seems arbitrary and becomes self-conscious, and the form of understanding with which we are comfortable is when things are treated as a slice or piece of something larger, potentially infinite. I think this sensibility is related to the lack of a sense of history that we were talking about earlier. I am astonished and disheartened by the very subjective view of the world that most people have, whereby they reduce everything to their own personal concerns and involvements. But perhaps, once again, that's particularly American.

Movius: All of this also relates to your reluctance to rely principally on your own experience in your fiction.

Sontag: To write mainly about myself seems to me a rather indirect route to what I want to write about. Though my evolution as a writer has been toward more freedom with the "I," and more use of my private experience, I have never been convinced that my tastes, my fortunes and misfortunes, have any particularly exemplary character. My life is my capital, the capital of my imagination. I like to colonize.

Movius: Are you aware of these questions when you're writing?

Sontag: Not at all when I write. When I talk about writing, yes. Writing is a mysterious activity. One has to be at different stages of conception and execution, in a state of extreme alertness and con- sciousness and in a state of great naivete and ignorance. Although this is probably true of the practice of any art, it may be more true of writing because the writer—unlike the painter or composer—works in a medium that one employs all the time, throughout one's waking life. Kafka said: "Conversation takes the importance, the seriousness, the truth out of everything I think." I would guess that most writers are suspicious of conversation, of what goes out in the ordinary uses of language. People deal with this in different ways. Some hardly talk at all. Others play games of concealment and avowal, as I am, no doubt, playing with you. There is only so much revealing one can do. For every self-revelation, there has to be a self-concealment. A life-long commitment to writing involves a balancing of these incompatible needs. But I do think that the model of writing as self-expression is much too crude. If I thought that what I'm doing when I write is expressing myself, I'd junk my typewriter. It wouldn't be liveable with. Writing is a much more complicated activity than that.

Movius: Doesn't this bring us back to your own ambivalence about photography? You're fascinated by it, but you find it dangerously simple.

Sontag: I don't think the problem with photography is that it's too simple but that it's too imperious a way of seeing. Its balance between being "present" and being "absent" is facile, when generalized as an attitude—which it is now in our culture. But I'm not against simplicity, as such. There is a dialectical exchange between simplicity and complexity, like the one between self-revelation and self-concealment. The first truth is that every situation is extremely complicated, and that anything one thinks about thereby becomes more complicated. The main mistake people make when thinking about something, whether an historical event or one in their private lives, is that they don't see just how complicated it is. The second truth is that one cannot live out all the complexities one perceives, and that to be able to act intelligently, decently, efficiently, and compassionately demands a great deal of simplification. So there are times when one has to forget—repress, transcend—a complex perception that one has.

Women, the Arts, & the Politics of Culture:
An Interview with Susan Sontag

Maxine Bernstein and Robert Boyers / 1975

From *Salmagundi*, Nos. 31–32 (Fall 1975/Winter 1976), pp. 29–48. Reprinted by permission.

R.B. In the mid '60s, when I was coming of age, and you were yourself a very young writer, it seemed the most eagerly anticipated of literary "events" was the publication of a new essay by Susan Sontag, usually in *Partisan Review*. The essay didn't have to be as timely as "Notes on 'Camp' " or the piece on science fiction—it might dwell on moral sententiousness in Camus, or on the aspect of disinterestedness involved in an appreciation of style. Those of us who went through those years, awaiting expectantly your new work, are delighted that you are once again writing speculative essays on a more or less regular basis. Word of your return, in this sense, to the intellectual scene, had been circulated for some time, and with the publication of the recent essay on Leni Riefenstahl in *The New York Review of Books* there can be few serious readers who do not know how important that return can be. Did you anticipate the interest that the Riefenstahl essay would generate?

Sontag: It's always agreeable to be welcomed back, though I don't think I've been away. What seemed to you like an absence was for me a going on. After the mid '60s, I wrote a second novel *(Death Kit),* then made two movies; in the last two years I've published five smaller fictions, made a third film *(Promised Lands),* and been tunneling through a third novel. As for essays, I never stopped writing them but I did decide to write fewer. The ones that have appeared recently in *The New York Review* are another go at the same problems that I've been stalking for years—the idea of "modernity," the relation between moral and aesthetic ideas—but, maybe because I'm no longer "a very young writer," the problems seem more and more complex. And I'm still only interested in writing about hard cases. Lately I've been using some ideas I've had about the careers of photographed images to get at these problems in another way. The Riefenstahl essay is not part of the photography series (which will come out as a book early next year), although it was her book of photographs, *The Last of the Nuba,* that supplied me with a pretext for discussing her work as a whole and for reopening the subject of fascist aesthetics. I did expect the essay to matter, because the campaign underway since the '60s to rehabilitate Riefenstahl—minimizing her official connection with the Nazi regime, obfuscating what is explicit in her work—had been so successful.

M.B.: In your essay "On Style," written in 1965 and included in *Against Interpretation,* you state:

> To call Leni Riefenstahl's *The Triumph of the Will* and *The Olympiad* masterpieces is not to gloss over Nazi propaganda with aesthetic len- ience. The Nazi propaganda is there. But something else is there, too, which we reject at our loss. Because they project the complex move- ments of intelligence and grace and sensuousness, these two films of Riefenstahl (unique among works of Nazi artists) transcend the catego- ries of propaganda or even reportage. And we find ourselves—to be sure, rather uncomfortably—seeing "Hitler" and not Hitler, the "1936 Olympics" and not the 1936 Olympics. Through Riefenstahl's genius as a film-maker, the "content" has—let us even assume, against her intentions—come to play a purely formal role.

And, you continue:

> A work of art, so far as it is a work of art, cannot—whatever the artist's personal intention—advocate anything at all.

Yet, in *The New York Review* in February 1975, you seem to be denying that earlier critical evaluation of Riefenstahl's work. There you refer to *Triumph of the Will* as

> . . . the most successfully, most purely propagandistic film ever made, whose very conception negates the possibility of the filmmaker's having an aesthetic or visual conception independent of propaganda.

I assume, in the context of these very separate approaches to evaluat- ing Riefenstahl, that there has been a change of large dimensions in your approach to criticism. Do you agree with me? Or do you see a continuity between these two essays which you could perhaps clarify here?

Sontag: A continuity, to be sure, in that both statements illustrate the richness of the form-content distinction, as long as one is careful always to use it against itself. My point in 1965 was about the formal implications of content, while the recent essay examines the content implicit in certain ideas of form. One of the main assertions of "On Style" is that the formalist and the historicist approaches are not in competition with each other, but are complementary—and equally indispensable. That's where Riefenstahl comes in. Because her work speaks for values that have received an official seal of disapproval, it offers a vivid test of the exchanges between form and content. Knowing that *Triumph of the Will* and *Olympiad* might be considered exceptions to the general argument I was making about the ways in which content functions as form, it seemed necessary to point out that even those films also illustrate the process whereby—as in any other bold and complex work of art—content functions as form. I wasn't discussing the complementary process, how form functions as content. When I set out, early this year, to treat Riefenstahl's work at some length, and with *that* approach, I arrived at an analysis that was simply more interesting, as well as more concrete—and that rather overwhelms the summary as well as formalist use I had made of her work in 1965. The paragraph about Riefenstahl in "On Style" is correct—as far as it goes. It just doesn't go very far. While it is true that her films in some sense "transcend" the propaganda for which they are the vehicle, their specific qualities show how their aestheticizing conception is itself identical with a certain brand of propaganda.

I'm still working with the thesis about the relation of art to the moral sense that is advanced in "On Style." But my understanding of the moral services that works of art perform is less abstract than it was in 1965. And I know more about totalitarianism and about the aesthetics with which it is compatible, which it actually generates, than I did then. One of the experiences that made me more interested in the, so to speak, "contentual" implications of form (without lessening my interest in the formal implications of content) was seeing—three years after I wrote "On Style"—several of the mass spectacle films made in China in the 1960s. One film led to another, inside my head—from *The East Is Red* to, say, Eisenstein's *Alexander Nevsky,* Walt Disney's *Fantasia,* the choreographed patterning of bodies as objects in Busby Berkeley musicals, Kubrick's *2001.* What these films exemplify is a major form of the modern aesthetic imagination which—as I've learned since the Riefenstahl essay was published—Siegfried Kracauer had explored as early as 1927, in an essay called "The Mass Ornament," and Walter Benjamin had summed up a few years later, when he described fascism as an aestheticization of political life.

It's not enough to say that an aesthetics is, or eventually becomes, a politics. What aesthetics? What politics? The key to understanding "fascist aesthetics," I think, is seeing that a "communist aesthetics" is probably a contradiction in terms. Hence, the mediocrity and staleness of the art promoted in communist countries. And when official art in the Soviet Union and China isn't resolutely old-fashioned, it is, objectively, fascist. Unlike the ideal communist society, which is totally didactic—turning every institution into a school—the fascist ideal is to mobilize everybody into a kind of national *gesamtkunstwerk:* making the whole society into a theatre. This is the most far-reaching way in which aesthetics becomes a politics. It becomes a politics of the lie. As Nietzsche said, "To experience a thing as beautiful means: to experience it necessarily wrongly." In the 19th century, ideologues of provocation and transvaluation like Nietzsche and Wilde expounded on "the aesthetic view of the world," one of whose superiorities was that it was supposed to be the most generous and large-spirited view, a form of civility, beyond politics. The evolution of fascism in the 20th century has taught us that they were wrong. As it turns out, "the aesthetic view of the world" is extremely hospitable to many of the uncivilized ideas and dissociated yearnings that were made explicit in fascism, and which also have great currency in our consumer culture. Yet it is clear—China has made it very clear—that the moralism of *serious* communist societies not only wipes out the autonomy of the aesthetic, but makes it impossible to produce art (in the modern sense) at all. A six-week trip to China in 1973 convinced me—if I needed convincing—that the autonomy of the aesthetic is something to be protected, and cherished, as indispensable nourishment to intelligence. But a decade-long residence in the 1960s, with its inexorable conversion of moral and political radical-isms into "style," has convinced me of the perils of overgeneralizing the aesthetic view of the world.

I would still argue that a work of art, *qua* work of art, cannot advocate anything. But since no work of art is in fact only a work of art, it's often more complicated than that. In "On Style" I was trying to recast the truths expressed in Wilde's calculatedly outrageous Preface to *The Picture of Dorian Gray* and Ortega y Gasset's more sober overstatement of the same polemic against philistinism in *The Dehumanization of Art*—by not tacitly separating or actually opposing—as Wilde and Ortega do—aesthetic and moral response. Ten years after "On Style," this is still the position I write from. But I have more historical flesh on my bones now. Though I continue to be as besotted an aesthete and as obsessed a moralist as I ever was, I've come to appreciate the limitations—and the indiscretion—of generalizing either the aesthete's or the moralist's view of the world without a much denser notion of historical context. Since you've been quoting me to myself, let me quote myself back to you. I say in that essay of 1965 that "awareness of style as a problematic and isolable element in a work of art has emerged in the audience for art only at certain historical moments—as a front behind which other issues, ultimately ethical and political, are being debated." The essays I've been writing recently are attempts to take that point further, to make it concrete—as it applies to my own work, as well as to that of others.

M.B.: In response to Adrienne Rich's criticism of your essay (*The New York Review,* March 20, 1975), you state:

> Most of history, alas, is "patriarchal history." So distinctions will have to be made, and it is not possible to keep the feminist thread running through the explanations all the time.

I would like to ask you to address the interesting question of distinctions. They are certainly important, often glossed over with "patriarchy" used as an explanation, which, as you suggest, explains less the more it is used. I would also agree that certain works lend themselves more readily to feminist criticism than others. You say, in response to Rich, ". . . if the point is to have meaning some of the time, it can't be made all the time." What would be the times when that point should be made? And are there certain events, or "movements," or works of art that are more reasonable subjects for feminist criticism? When is it misapplied? When is it appropriate? Or is there a better way that feminist goals can be critically served?

Sontag: I want armies of women and men to be pointing out the omnipresence of sexist stereotypes in the language, behavior, and imagery of our society. If that's what you mean by feminist criticism, then whenever it's practiced—and however coarsely—it's always of *some* value. But I'd like to see a few platoons of intellectuals who are also feminists doing their bit in the war against misogyny in their own way, letting the feminist implications be residual or implicit in their work, without risking being charged by their sisters with desertion. I don't like party lines. They make for intellectual monotony and bad prose. Let me put it very simply, though not—I hope—too plaintively. There are many intellectual tasks, and different levels of discourse. If there *is* a question of appropriateness, it's not because some events or works of art are more "reasonable" targets, but because people who reason in public have—and ought to exercise—options about how many and how complex are the points they want to make. And where, in what form, and to what audience they make them. Rich complained that I had failed to say that Nazi Germany was, after all, the culmination of a sexist and patriarchal society. She was assuming, of course, that the values of Riefenstahl's films were Nazi values. So was I. That's why I wanted to discuss the question: in *what* sense does Riefenstahl's work embody Nazi values? *Why* are these films— and *The Last of the Nuba*—interesting and persuasive? I think it was permissible to assume that the audience for whom I wrote my essay is aware of the derogation of women not only in Nazi ideology, so explicitly proclaimed in the documents of the Nazi era, but in the main tradition of German letters and thought from Luther to Nietzsche to Freud and Jung.

It's not the appropriateness of feminist criticism which needs to be rethought, but its level—its demands for intellectual simplicity, advanced in the name of ethical solidarity. These demands have convinced many women that it is undemocratic to raise questions about "quality"—the quality of feminist discourse, if it is sufficiently militant, and the quality of works of art, if these are sufficiently warm-hearted and self-revealing. Hatred of the intellect is one of the recurrent themes of modernist protest in art and in morals. Though it is actually quite inimical to effective political action, it seems like a political statement. Both avant-garde art and feminism have made large use of, and sometimes seem to be parodies of, the languages of failed political movements. As advanced art, in the 1910s, inherited the rhetoric of Anarchism (and baptised it Futurism), feminism, in the late 1960s, inherited another political rhetoric on the wane, that of *gauchisme*. One common denominator of New Left polemics was its zeal for pitting hierarchy against equality, theory against practice, intellect (cold) against feeling (warm). Feminists have tended to perpetuate these philistine characterizations of hierarchy, theory, and intellect. What was denounced in the 1960s as bourgeois, repressive, and elitist was discovered to be phallocratic, too. That kind of second-hand militancy may appear to serve feminist goals in the short run. But it means a surrender to callow notions of art and of thought and the encouragement of a genuinely repressive moralism.

R.B.: In 1967 you wrote a stunning essay on Bergman's *Persona,* included in *Styles of Radical Will.* Now Bergman has come under heavy fire from a number of quarters, some critics complaining that he is a technically reactionary force in world cinema, that his camera-dynamics are relatively old-fashioned; other critics complaining that he really detests mature women, no matter what he claims to feel, and that his films regularly project "negative" images of women which promise no useful encouragement to people in need of positive identity images. I ask you to address Bergman and his work here because attacks on Bergman amply describe the kind of approaches routinely taken by many people in academic life and especially by a new generation of feminist critics. What, in particular, of approaches such as those which indict Bergman in the terms described above: as a reactionary artist, both aesthetically and politically?

Sontag: I am extremely reluctant to attack anyone as a "reactionary artist." That's the weapon of repressive and ignorant officialdom in you-know-which countries, where "reactionary" is also associated with a kind of pessimistic content or (using the phrase you cite) with not providing "positive images." Being very attached to the benefits of pluralism in the arts and of factionalism in politics, I've grown allergic to the words "reactionary" and "progressive." Such judgments always support ideological conformity, encourage intolerance—even if they aren't originally formulated to do that. As for

Bergman, I'd say that anyone who reduces his work to its neo-Strindbergian views of women has jettisoned the idea of art and of complex standards of judgment. (If correctness of attitude counted most, Abram Room's *Bed and Sofa,* full of appealing feminist intu-itions, would be a greater film than Pudovkin's macho epic *Storm Over Asia.*)

The harsh indictment of Bergman simply inverts the slack standards that prevail in much of feminist criticism. To those critics who rate films according to whether they make moral reparations, it must seem snobbish to cavil about the low quality of most recent movies made by women which do convey positive images. And what's happening when an attack on someone for not supplying "useful encouragement to people" is bolstered by calling him "technically reactionary" and "old-fashioned"? (Presumably, this is how these critics hope to show they are not behaving like stodgy cultural commissars.) I wouldn't call Bergman old-fashioned. But, despite some brilliant narrative inventions in his two best films, *The Silence* and *Persona,* his work doesn't suggest any fruitful development. He is an obsessional artist, the worst kind to imitate. Like Stein and Bacon and Jancsó, Bergman is one of those oppressively memorable geniuses of the artistic dead-end, who go very far with a limited material—refining it when they are inspired, repeating it and parodying themselves when they aren't.

R.B.: Your own view of art, and of particular works of art, has always stressed the indissoluble relation between form and content, a relation to which other critics have paid lip service while persistently violating its premise. In this way you have been able to preserve respect for a given artist's sentiment of being, his particular attach-ment to the object world and to his own appointed place in it, and for those principles of style or form which enable him to structure and evoke that sentiment. Now many people have observed the "scandal-ous" fact that the sentiment of being for most great writers has been decidedly conservative, even reactionary, that their attachment to the given has been ever so much more passionate than their feeling for things yet to be. Is there something about works of art which almost demands that their creators have a preservative or reactionary relation to the world in which they live? That they be, in fact, conservative even when "committed" to this or that "radical" policy?

Sontag: "Reactionary," again! This feels like another version of the same question, so I'll try to answer in a different way. I doubt that there is anything more "conservative" or "reactionary" about artists than there is about people. And why shouldn't people be naturally conservative? That the past necessarily weighs more on the axis of human consciousness is perhaps a greater liability to the individual than to society, but how could it be otherwise? Where is the scandal? To be scandalized by the normal is always demagogic. And it is only normal that we are aware of ourselves as persons in an historical continuum, with indefinite thicknesses of past behind us, the present a razor's edge, and the future—well, problematic is one damp word for it. Dividing time into Past, Present & Future suggests that reality is distributed equally among three parts, but in fact the past is the most real of all. The future is, inevitably, an accumulation of loss, and dying is something we do all our lives. If artists are memory specialists, professional curators of consciousness, they are only practicing—willfully, obsessionally—a prototypical devoutness. There is a tilt in the very experience of living which always gives memory an advantage over amnesia.

To reproach artists for having an insufficiently radical relation to the world has to be a complaint about art as such. And to reproach art is, in more than one way, like reproaching consciousness itself for being a burden. For consciousness can be conscious of itself, as Hegelians quaintly say, only through its sense of the past. And art is the most general condition of The Past in the present. To become "past" is, in one version, to become "art." (The arts that most literally illustrate this mutation are architecture and photography.) The pathos that all works of art reek of comes from their historicity. From the way they are overtaken by physical decay and stylistic obsolescence. And from whatever is mysterious, partly (and forever) veiled about them. And simply from our awareness, with each work, that no one would or could ever do exactly *that* again. Perhaps no work of art *is* art. It can only *become* art, when it is part of the past. In this normative sense, a "contemporary" work of art would be a contradiction—except so far as we can, in the present, assimilate the present to the past.

R.B.: And yet I think you'd agree that a great many contemporary liberationists, radicals of various kinds, have demanded that works of art be new, that they cut loose from the inherited props and furnish-

ings of the familiar material world. And this cutting loose is precisely
what most artists of genuine stature have been unable to manage,
despite their personal commitment to programs espoused by radicals.

Sontag: Cutting oneself loose from the inherited props and furniture
of the world, as you put it—wouldn't that be like peeling off one's
own skin? And doesn't demanding that artists throw away their
toys—that is, the world—mean wanting them not to be artists any
more? Such a talent for jettisoning everything has to be extremely
rare. And its promised benefits have yet to be demonstrated. The
clean sweep being proposed as a goal for radical therapy as well as art
(and, by extension, for politics) suggests that "liberation" can be
very confining. That is, it seems regressive in relation to the full range
of our possibilities—among which civilization tries, to almost everyone's dissatisfaction, to arbitrate. The price we would pay for liberation in that undialectical sense is at least as steep as the price we've
been paying for civilization. If we are indeed going to be forced to
choose between defensive fantasies of liberation and ruling corrup-
tions of civilization, let's work fast to soften the harshness of that
choice. It's sobering to realize that both options seemed just as
morally defective a century ago when Henry James made his pre-
scient, melancholy analysis of our post-1960s cultural dilemmas in
The Princess Casamassima, with imaginary London anarchists antici-
pating American New Left and countercultural ideologues.

You seem to be talking about a politicized version of the classic
modernist demand on Art (Making It New), but then the only difference between the Poundian demand and the more recent imperatives
is a radical politics, and I'm not sure that the language in which this
politics is declared should be taken at face value. Question the self-
designated radicals who appear to be calling for a cultural *tabula rasa,*
and I think you'd find that they are seldom as modernist as their
rhetoric would imply. The way you've formulated their protest seems
to me to confuse a moralistic political radicalism (assumed to be a
Good Thing) with an amoral revolt against the inherited past that is in
full complicity with the status quo. Much of radical dissent is animated
by a kind of restorationism—the wish to reconstitute communal
pleasures and civic virtues that have been wiped out to make possible
the very real *tabula rasa* of our consumer society. A radical in the
sense you describe would be Andy Warhol, the dandy prince and

ideally passive avatar of an economy in which everything of the past is scheduled to be traded in for newer goods.

R.B.: In 1966 Philip Rieff published an important book entitled *The Triumph of the Therapeutic: Uses of Faith After Freud*. What do you make of this:

> Never before has there been such a general shifting of sides as now among intellectuals in the United States and England. Many have gone over to the enemy without realizing that they, self-considered the cultural elite, have actually become spokesmen for what Freud called the instinctual [mass].

Insofar as some of your own work in the mid '60s attempted to legitimate an easier relation between popular culture and the elite that Rieff describes, would you say that you had "gone over to the enemy"?

Sontag: [Laughter]

R.B.: What?

Sontag: Of course I wouldn't say that.

R.B.: Do you think it is useful to draw a distinction between "the cultural elite" and "the instinctual mass"?

Sontag: No. I think the distinction is a vulgar one. By ignoring the difference between the descriptive and prescriptive senses of culture, it can't give a properly specific meaning to either. There are several senses in which "culture" doesn't equal "elite." (Anyway, there are elites—not one, but many.) And I don't think that "instinctual" and "mass" go together—even if Le Bon and Freud did say so. The distinction suggests a contempt for the instincts, a facile pessimism about people, and a lack of passion for the arts (as distinct from ideas) that is not confirmed by my own instincts, pessimism, passions.

Intellectuals who want to defend our poor sick culture should resist the all-too-understandable temptation to fume about the unlettered masses and accuse other intellectuals of joining the enemy. If I'm leery of talking about a "cultural elite," it's not because I don't care about culture but because I think the notion is virtually unusable and should be retired. For instance, it doesn't explain anything about the cultural mix I was writing about in the mid '60s—a particularly vivid moment in a century-long set of exchanges between different levels of culture, different elites. Early modernists like Rimbaud, Stravinsky, Apollinaire, Joyce, and Eliot had showed how "high culture" could assimilate shards of "low culture." (*The Waste Land, Ulysses,* etc. etc.) By the 1960s the popular arts, notably film and rock music, had taken up the abrasive themes and some of the "difficult" techniques (like collage) that had hitherto been the fare of a restricted cultural elite, if you will—the university-educated, museum-going, cosmopolitan audience for the avant-garde or experimental arts. That "low culture" was an important ingredient in the modernist takeover of "high culture," that the modernist sensibility had created new boundaries for popular culture, and was eventually incorporated into it— these are subjects that nobody who has cared for culture can ignore or should fail to treat with high seriousness. Is trying to understand something—in this instance, a process that had been going on at least since Baudelaire—legitimizing it? It hardly needed me to offer that legitimacy. And the 1960s seems rather late to stop identifying culture with some Masterpiece Theatre of World History and to respond—on the basis of contemporary experience, and moved by pleasure rather than resentment—to how complex the destiny of "high culture" has become since Matthew Arnold whistled in the dark on Dover Beach. The notion of culture implied by Rieff's distinction seems to me awfully middlebrow, and plausible only to someone who has never been really immersed in or gotten intense pleasure from contemporary poetry and music and painting. Does culture here mean art? (And what art?) Does it mean thought? They're not the same, and culture isn't exactly synonymous with either. Toryish labels like cultural elite and instinctual mass do not tell us anything useful about how to protect that endangered species, "high" standards. Diagnoses of cultural sickness made in such general and self-congratulatory terms become a symptom of the problem, not part of the answer.

    M.B.: You state in the famous essay "Notes on 'Camp,' " which you wrote in 1964: "I am strongly drawn to Camp, and almost as strongly offended by it. That is why I want to talk about it, and why I can." You then say, "To name a sensibility, to draw its contours and to recount its history, requires a deep sympathy modified by revulsion." Could you share with us that dual set of attitudes—sympathy/ revulsion—particularly in relation to what you describe as "the corny

flamboyance of femaleness" embodied in certain actresses; and go on
to relate those attitudes to your own feminist sensibility?

Sontag: Like the recent essays on photography, "Notes on
'Camp' " grew out of speculations of a rather general order. How "to
name a sensibility," how "to draw its contours, to recount its history"—that was the problem I started from, and then looked for an
example, a model. And it seemed more interesting not to pick Sensibility X from among those heaped with ethical or aesthetic laurels,
and to evoke instead a sensibility that was exotic and in obvious ways
minor, even despised—as the rather quirky notion of a "sensibility"
had itself been slighted, in favor of that tidier fiction, an "idea."

Morbidity was my first choice. I stayed with that for a while,
attempting to systematize a long-term fascination with mortuary
sculpture, architecture, inscriptions and other such wistful lore that
eventually found an unsystematic place in *Death Kit* and *Promised
Lands*. But the material was too detailed, and cumbersome to describe, so I switched to camp, which had the advantage of being
familiar as well as marginal, and could be illustrated in a more rapid
and comprehensible way. Camp, I knew, was a sensibility that many
people were tuned into, although they might have no name for it. As
for myself: by deciding to write "Notes on 'Camp' " instead of
"Notes on Death," I was choosing to humor the part of my seriousness that was being zapped and loosened up and made more sociable
by camp wit rather than to fortify the part of my wit that got regularly
choked off by seizures of morbidity. Compared to morbidity, camp
was hard to pin down. It was, in fact, a rich example of how a
sensibility can have divergent meanings, can have a latent content
that is more complex than—and often different from—its manifest
one.

Which brings me to the question of ambivalence. I've dawdled in
the culture graveyard, enjoying what camp taste could effect in the
way of ironic resurrections, just as I've stopped to pay my respects to
real death, in real cemeteries, off the country roads and in the cities
of three continents. And it is in the nature of such detours that some
sights fascinate, while others repell. The theme you single out—the
parodistic rendering of women—usually left me cold. But I can't say
that I was simply offended. For I was often amused and, so far as I
needed to be, liberated. I think that the camp taste for the theatrically

feminine did help undermine the credibility of certain stereotyped femininities—by exaggerating them, by putting them between quotation marks. Making something corny of femaleness is one way of creating distance from the stereotype. Camp's extremely sentimental relation to beauty is no help to women, but its irony is: ironizing about the sexes is one small step toward depolarizing them. In this sense the diffusion of camp taste in the early '60s should probably be credited with a considerable if inadvertent role in the upsurge of feminist consciousness in the late 1960s.

M.B.: What about women like Mae West, an old-style sex queen who didn't, apparently, strike audiences the way you suggest? Why didn't she have the effect you describe?

Sontag: I think she did. Whether or not she started with the oldest of blandishments, her glory was as a new-style sex queen, that is, the impersonator of one. Unlike Sarah Bernhardt's style, which audiences at a certain moment stopped being able to take straight, Mae West's was appreciated from the beginning as a sort of parody. Letting oneself, self-consciously, be beguiled by such robust, shrill, vulgar parody is the last step in a century-long evolution—and progressive democratization—of the aestheticism whose broader history and implications are sketched in "Notes on 'Camp,' " but which has had its most knowing reception from the milieu in which the word "camp" appeared some fifty years ago. (Although scholars of slang disagree as much about the origin of "camp" as they do about "O.K.," I would assume that it derives from *camper*—which the Oxford French Dictionary translates as "to posture boldly.") And it was in the 1920s that a kind of de-construction of the stereotypes of femininity gets underway, a mocking challenge to sexism that complements the moralistic call for justice and reparations to women that had found its voice in the 1890s in, say, Shaw's essays and George Gissing's novel, *The Odd Women.* What I am arguing is that today's feminist consciousness has a long and complicated history, of which the diffusion of male homosexual taste is a part—including its sometimes witless putdowns of and delirious homage to the "feminine." Feminists have been less quick at seeing this than some of their opponents—for example, Wyndham Lewis, whose novel-diatribe *The Childermass,* written in the late '20s, contains a long speech about how the naturally feminine and the masculine are being subverted jointly by homosexuals and by suffragettes. (Contemporary homosexuality is denounced as "a branch of the Feminist Revolution.") And Lewis was not wrong to link them.

M.B.: In your excellent essay, "The Pornographic Imagination," written in 1967 and included in *Styles of Radical Will,* you describe the heroine of *Story of O* as a woman who "progresses simultaneously toward her own extinction as a human being and her fulfillment as a sexual being." You then wonder "how anyone would ascertain whether there exists, truly, empirically, anything in 'nature' or human consciousness that supports such a split." It seems to me that that event (the loss of self in exchange for sexual fulfillment) can be viewed as an allegory of the new feminist awareness of the dilemma that many women are confronting today. That is, in exchange for our "fulfillment as women" (not sexually, but within the confines of cultural expectations) we have often given up our identities as individuals of free will and have willingly participated in our extinction as separate human beings. Assuming that you agree with this, would you be willing to say that there might be more to *Story of O* than you saw in 1967? Could that book be considered a peculiarly political work whose meaning could be enriched by the feminist perspective?

Sontag: Though I'd agree that one can extract useful lessons from all sorts of unpromising material, O's destiny seems to me an unlikely allegory of either feminist awareness or, simply, the age-old subjection of women. My interest in *Story of O* was, still would be, in its candor about the demonic side of sexual fantasy. The violence of the imagination that it consecrates—and does not at all deplore—cannot be confined within the optimistic and rationalist perceptions of mainstream feminism. Pornography's form of utopistic thinking is, like most of science fiction, a negative utopia. Since the writers who have insisted on how fierce, disruptive, and antinomian an energy sexuality (potentially, ideally) is, are mostly men, it's commonly supposed that this form of the imagination must discriminate against women. I don't think it does, necessarily. (It could discriminate against men, as in Monique Wittig's celebrations of unfettered sexual energy.)

What distinguishes the work of "the pornographic imagination" from other accounts of the erotic life is that it treats sexuality as an extreme situation. That means that what pornography depicts is, in one obvious sense, quite unrealistic. Sexual energy is not endlessly renewable; sexual acts cannot be tirelessly repeated. But in another sense pornography is rudely accurate about important realities of desire. That voluptuousness does mean surrender, and that sexual surrender pursued imaginatively enough, experienced immoderately enough, does erode pride of individuality and mocks the notion that the will could ever be free—these are truths about sexuality itself and what it may, naturally, become. Because it is such an *ascesis* to live completely for voluptuousness, only a few women and men ever do pursue pleasure to this terminal extreme. The fantasy of sexual apocalypse is common enough, however—indisputably, a means for intensifying sexual pleasure. And what that tells us about the inhuman, as it were, character of intense pleasure is still being slighted by the humanist "revisionist" Freudianism that most feminists feel comfortable with, which minimizes the intractable powers of unconscious or irrational feeling.

You propose a political view of the book in place of my tentative idea about something "in 'nature,' or in human consciousness." But I would still reaffirm that speculation. There seems to be something inherently defective or self-frustrating in the way the sexual impulse works in human beings—for instance, an essential (i.e. normal), not accidental (i.e. neurotic), link between sexual energy and obsession. It appears likely that the full development of our sexual being does clash with the full development of our consciousness. Instead of supposing that *all* our sexual discontent is part of a tax sexuality pays for being civilized, it may be more correct to assume that we are, first of all, sick by nature—and that it is our being, to begin with, what Nietzsche called "sick animals," that makes us civilization-producing animals.

It is the innate incongruence between important achievements in the realms of sexual fulfillment and of individual consciousness that is exacerbated by the enlarged use to which sexuality has been put in modern, secular culture. As the credibility of religious experience has declined, erotic experience has not only gotten an inflated, even grandiose significance, but is itself now subjected to standards of credibility (thereby attaching a whole new sort of anxiety to sexual performance). In particular, the quest for the experience of complete psychic surrender now no longer enclosed within traditional religious forms has become increasingly, and restlessly, attached to the mind-blowing character of the orgasm. The myths of total sexual fulfillment dramatized in *Story of O* concern that peculiarly modern *via negativa*. Evidence about the feelings and sexual tastes in our culture before it was wholly secularized, and in other cultures past and present, suggests that voluptuousness was rarely pursued in this way, as the organon to transcend individual consciousness. Perhaps only when sexuality is invested with that ideological burden, as it is now, does it also become a real, and not just a potential, danger to person-hood and to individuation.

R.B.: Philip Rieff writes in *Fellow Teachers:*

> True criticism is constituted, first, by repeating what is already known. The great teacher is he who, because he carries in himself what is already known, can transfer it to his student; that inwardness is his absolute and irreducible authority. If a student fails to re-cognize that authority, then he is not a student.

What do you take Rieff to mean when he speaks of authoritative knowing—it has of course nothing to do with the expertise of the specialist. Would you agree that, according to Rieff's definition, there are very few students in our institutions of higher learning?

Sontag: Precious few students, according to that definition—yes. But perhaps still more than enough, since—again following Rieff's definition—there are probably *no* professors. The authority of the professoriat being invoked here goes no further back than Wilhelmine Germany. That there are very few "students" (prescriptive sense: devoted, talented lovers of learning) is surely as well known as that there are many more "students" (descriptive sense: bodies in class-rooms), liberal arts education having assumed those functions which, precisely, make it harder than it was a generation ago to assign so-called difficult books and to expound complex ideas without backtalk from students. But Rieff does not make his case against mass education more convincing by overstating it. When in Western intellectual history did the college teacher have "an absolute and irreducible authority"? Even in the great ages of faith, which one might suppose well-stocked with models for the pedagogue as dictator, a closer look discloses a reassuring ferment of dissent, of heterodoxy, of questioning what was "already known." Fiat cannot restore to the office of the teacher (now irrevocably secular, transmitting a plurality of "traditions") an absolute authority which both the teacher and what is being taught do not have—if they ever did.

The genuine historical pressures to lower the standards for "higher learning" that do exist aren't weakened by declaring what words *ought* to mean—defining a teacher as one who teaches authoritatively, a student as one who accepts the authority of the teacher. But perhaps one should take Rieff's definitions as evidence that the fight to maintain the highest standards really is a lost cause. If the decline of first-rate teaching in universities really is irreversible, as it probably is, then one should expect exactly such a defense of the ancient regime as is projected by these empty definitions of great teacher and great student. Making a virtue of its own historical inappropriateness to the late 20th century, Rieff's authoritarian theory of the university parallels the authoritarian theory of the bourgeois state advanced in Germany and France in the late 19th and early 20th centuries. The substance and the sociological moorings of the teacher's authority having been eroded, only its form remains. Authority itself ("that inwardness") is made the defining characteristic of the great teacher. Perhaps one only stakes out such a large, truculent claim to authority when one doesn't, can't possibly, have it. Even in the Maoist conception of the relation between leaders and masses, the authority of the Great Teacher does not derive, tautologically, from his authority, but from his wisdom—a much-advertised part of which consists in overturning "what is already known." Though Rieff's notion of the teacher has more in common with the Maoist pedagogic conception than with the main tradition of Western activity and high culture which he thinks he's defending—against barbarous students—it is formulated in a fashion more dismissive of independence of thought than Maoism.

To define a teacher primarily in terms of the idea of authority seems to me grossly inadequate to the standards of that elite education for which Rieff is proselytizing. That the definition encourages wishful thinking and licenses personal arrogance is relatively unimportant. What is important is that it leaves out virtually all the teacherly virtues. Wisdom, as I've already mentioned. And the Socratic pedagogic eros. Forget about humility—if that is too radical, or it sounds mawkish. But what about skepticism?

A little skepticism about what one "carries" in oneself, if one is well-educated, might be especially useful—to balance the temptations of self-righteousness. As someone who, like Philip Rieff, had the good fortune to do undergraduate work in the most ambitious and the most successful authoritarian program of education ever devised in this country—the Hutchins-era College of the University of Chicago—I remain as much as he, I would think, a partisan of the non-elective curriculum. But I'm aware that all such forms of consensus about "great" books and "perennial" problems, once stabilized, tend to deteriorate eventually into something philistine. The real life of the mind is always at the frontiers of "what is already known." Those great books don't only need custodians and transmitters. To stay alive, they also need adversaries. The most interesting ideas, after all, are heresies.

M.B.: I would like to link "The Pornographic Imagination" with your essay on Riefenstahl, where you discuss the aesthetics of totalitarian art. To what extent is *Story of O* a totalitarian work, or an ironic commentary upon such work? And is there, then, a connection between this tale of total female submission to the doctrines and advantages of others and Riefenstahl's work, with its focus on obeisance to an all-powerful leader?

Sontag: I don't find *Story of O* ironic, either about totalitarianism or about the Sadean literary tradition of which it is a self-conscious but exquisitely limited modernization. Is it a totalitarian work? The connection that could be drawn between *Story of O* and the eroticized politics of Nazism seems a fortuitous one—and extraneous to the book and the intentions of the elderly French mandarin (male) who wrote it, pseudonymously—however easily it springs to mind now, especially since the sado-masochistic dramaturgy started going in for Nazi drag. And there is still another difference worth noting, the one between the eroticism of a political event (real or, say, in a film) and the eroticism of a private life (real or fictional). Hitler, when he used sexual metaphors to express the authority of leaders and the obeisance of masses, in characterizing leadership as violation, could only *compare* the masses to a woman. (But "O" *is* one woman, and the book is about an individual salvation, through the erotic, which is profoundly anti-political, as all forms of mysticism and neo-mysticism are.) Measured against submission and fulfillment in a real erotic situation, the eroticism of Hitler's notion of leadership (as rape) and of followership (as surrender) is a cheat, a fake.

As there is a difference between an idea, mediated by a metaphor, and an experience (real or fictional), the metaphors used by the modern regimes that have sought to create total ideological consensus have different degrees of closeness to or distance from practical reality. In the communist view of how leaders lead masses, the metaphor is not one of sexual domination but of teachership: the teacher who has authority and the masses who are students of the teacher. Although this metaphor makes Maoist rhetoric very attractive, almost as attractive as Nazi rhetoric is repellent, its result is probably a much more total system of control over minds and bodies. While the eroticized politics of fascism is, after all, a pseudo-eroticism, the pedagogic politics of communism is a real and effective process of teaching.

R.B.: One last question. In 1984, you wrote an essay on science fiction films called "The Imagination of Disaster," included in *Against Interpretation.* Have you reflected more about science fiction since—for example, about the idea of intelligence proposed in Arthur Clarke's *Childhood's End?* Can you make a connection between "the imagination of disaster" and "the pornographic imagination"? And between leaders and followers in fascist aesthetics?

Sontag: That essay, among others, could be seen as one phase of an argument about modes of authoritarian feeling and perception. (And the argument isn't only to be found in my essays. For instance, *Duet for Cannibals* and *Brother Carl,* the two films I made in Sweden, and two recent stories, "Old Complaints Revisited" and "Doctor Jekyll," are fictional treatments of the private lives of leaders and followers.) Science fiction—about which I hope to write a better essay some day—is full of authoritarian ideas, ideas that have much in common with those developed in other contemporary contexts (like pornography), illustrating typical forms of the authoritarian imagination. Clarke's fable is one of the abler examples of science fiction's characteristic polemic on behalf of an authoritarian ideal of intelligence. The romantic protest against the assassin mind, a leading theme of art and thought since the early 19th century, gradually became a self-fulfilling prophecy as, in the 20th century, technocratic, purely instrumental ideas of the mind took over, which made intelligence seem hopelessly inadequate to a social and psychological disorder experienced as more menacing than ever. Science fiction promotes the idea of a superior or "higher" intelligence that will impose order on human affairs and messy emotions and, thereby, end childhood—that is, history. Pornography, like the fascist mass-spectacle, looks to the abolition of mind (in an ideal choreography of bodies, of dominators and the dominated).

We live in a culture in which intelligence is denied relevance altogether, in a search for radical innocence, or is defended as an instrument of authority and repression. In my view, the only intelligence worth defending is critical, dialectical, skeptical, desimplifying. An intelligence which aims at the definitive resolution (that is, suppression) of conflict, which justifies manipulation—always, of course, for other people's good, as in the argument brilliantly made by Dostoyevsky's Grand Inquisitor, which haunts the main tradition of science fiction—is not *my* normative idea of intelligence. Not surprisingly, contempt for intelligence goes with the contempt for history. And history is, yes, tragic. But I'm not able to support any idea of intelligence which aims at bringing history to an end—substituting for the tragedy that makes civilization at least possible the nightmare or the Good Dream of eternal barbarism.

I am assuming that the defense of civilization implies the defense of an intelligence that is not authoritarian. But all contemporary defenders of civilization must be aware—though I don't think it helps to say it often—that this civilization, already so far overtaken by barbarism, *is* at an end, and nothing we do will put it back together again. So in the culture of transition out of which we can try to make sense, fighting off the twin afflictions of hyperaesthesia and passivity, no position can be a comfortable one or should be completely held. Perhaps the most instructive discussion of the questions of intelligence and innocence, civilization and barbarism, responsibility to the truth and responsibility to people's needs is in the libretto of Schönberg's *Moses and Aaron*. Dostoyevsky does not let Jesus answer the Grand Inquisitor's monologue, although the whole novel is supposed to give us, does give us, the material to construe that answer. But Moses and Aaron do answer each other's arguments. And although Schönberg uses both dramaturgy and music to stack the whole opera against the view Aaron represents, and for Moses' Word, in the actual debate between them he set their arguments at parity. So the debate is unresolved, as it really is, for these questions are fiercely complicated. "Moses" and "Aaron" are both right. And any serious argument about culture—which has to be, finally, an argument about truth— must honor that complexity.

Interview: Susan Sontag:
On Art and Consciousness

Performing Arts Journal / 1977

From *Performing Arts Journal,* Vol. 2, No. 2 (1977), pp. 25–32.
Reprinted by permission.

Susan Sontag is the author of *Against Interpretation* and *Styles
of Radical Will.* In addition to numerous essays on literature
and the arts, she has published two novels and made three films.
Recently she edited and wrote the introduction to *Antonin
Artaud: Selected Writings.* Susan Sontag's *On Photography* will
be published this Winter. This interview was taped by the
Editors in February 1977.

PAJ: What performances in the last few years have you felt were
worthwhile experiences?

Susan Sontag: Lucian Pintilie's *Turandot.* Robert Anton's puppet
theatre. Merce Cunningham. Peter Brook's *The Ik.* Beckett's Berlin
staging of *Waiting for Godot.* Plisetskaya doing Ravel's *Bolero.* Watergate. Franz Salieri's *La Grand Eugene* (the original Paris production,
not the one that went on tour). Strehler's production of *The Cherry
Orchard.* The invented Act Three of the Met's recent production of
Lulu. Maria Irene Fornes's staging of her play *Fefu and Her
Friends.* . . . Shall I go on?

PAJ: Why haven't you written about these events?

SS: I'm writing other things. Mostly fiction.

PAJ: Don't you want to go on writing criticism?

SS: I don't consider that I ever was a critic. I had ideas, and I
attached them to works of art that I admired. Now I attach them to
other things.

PAJ: How do you view the current critical scene?

SS: You mean monitoring productions and giving out grades—the
kind of consumer reporting that decides whether something is good
or not good, well performed or not well performed?

PAJ: If that is what people are satisfied with, isn't it due to the lack of a new critical vocabulary with which to treat the new theatre?

SS: I don't expect ideas from critics. They come from poets and painters and novelists and even playwrights—doing a stint of writing about the theatre. And from directors who found their own theatres.

PAJ: But the current experimental theatre is such a radical break from our theatrical past, not part of a developing American tradition. No one seems to know quite how to deal with it.

SS: I think the problem is that the more than sixty-year-old international tradition of modernism has bequeathed us a surfeit of critical perspectives—Constructivism, Futurism, Brecht, Artaud, Grotowski, *et al.* And that we give an open-ended but increasingly limited credence to them all. It's not lack of familiarity with experimental theatre that explains the critical vacuum. It's the mounting disenchantment—partly justified, partly shallow and philistine—with modernism. And a widespread boredom with high culture itself.

PAJ: You mentioned Artaud and Grotowski. Their theories—which go back to the origins of theatre in ritual and ceremony—seem to be a negation of everything that's transpired in Western culture. Isn't that a regression? And doesn't their kind of theatre remove one from the immediacy of the moment?

SS: There's no opposition between the archaic and the immediate.

PAJ: I see such theatre as a form of hermeticism, a withdrawal into a world that we have no contact with whatsoever.

SS: Well, I've no objection to art that is hermetic. (Some art *should* be hermetic, I think.) But, far from being hermetic, the theatre influenced by Artaud and by Grotowski is very much about immediate, present experience. The difference is that both Artaud and Grotowski believed in the reality of evil—the reality treated superficially, or denied by, so-called realistic theatre.

PAJ: Why do you emphasize evil?

SS: First of all, because it exists. And because an awareness of the reality of evil is the best defense against artistic trivialization and vulgarity.

PAJ: The modern attack on "dialogue" or realistic theatre seems to have taken two directions. One, represented by Artaud and Grotowski, explores feelings. The other, represented by Foreman, is more interested in exploring the thinking process and modes of perception.

SS: Perception in and for itself?

PAJ: Yes. In order to perceive better.

SS: Perceive *what* better? Doesn't the material offered for perception have to be trivial, precisely so that the audience can't be distracted by it and can concentrate on the process of perceiving? If you are invited to consider the relationship between a chair and a grapefruit—that is, what's on the stage is a chair and a grapefruit and a string connecting them—then you will indeed perceive something about how they are alike and how they differ. But it's no more than an interesting perceptual problem (and that largely because it's a problem one does not ordinarily consider).

PAJ: You don't think being interesting is enough?

SS: I used to think so. But I don't any more. You know, that notion has a history—a rather brief one. To apply the word "interesting" to a work of art was an invention of the Romantic writers of the late eighteenth and early nineteenth centuries, and one that seemed very peculiar at first. (Hegel, for example, thought it was *not* a compliment to say that something was "interesting.") The notion of "the interesting" is approximately as old as the notion of "the boring." Indeed, it seems to me that "the interesting" presupposes "the boring," and vice versa. One of the proudest claims of the modernist theatre is that it is antipsychological. But "the interesting" and "the boring" are psychological categories, nothing more. They are feelings, assumed to be of limited duration, and to be capable of mutating into each other—categories of the solipsistic, narcissistic world view. (They replace "the beautiful" and "the ugly," which are attributes—hypostasized, quasi-objective, assumed to be permanent.) An "interesting" object has an arresting quality: It seizes our attention, we take cognizance of it, and then let it go. An "interesting" experience is one that has no lasting effect. The notion of "the interesting" arises when art is no longer conceived of as connected with truth. (When truth comes to be reserved for science, for so-called rational inquiry.) In continuing to consider something to be valuable—valuable enough—because it is interesting, we perpetuate a romantic attitude that needs reexamining.

PAJ: Foreman's theatre is about thinking, about the-being-consciously-aware at the theatre event of the working of the mind in the theatre. I can't think of another kind of theatre where one feels so consciously in the present. It's Foreman's attempt to actively engage the audience that is important.

SS: I don't agree that consciousness-as-such is Foreman's subject. Or, if it could be—and I don't think consciousness-as-such is really a subject at all—that it could be very engaging.

PAJ: What about Beckett?

SS: Beckett is dealing with emotions, however abstractly, and there is a progress from one emotion to the next that feels inevitable. Not only are his plays narrative but, as Joe Chaikin once observed, Beckett has actually discovered a new dramatic subject. Normally people on the stage reflect on the macrostructure of action. What am I going to do this year? Tomorrow? Tonight? They ask: Am I going mad? Will I ever get to Moscow? Should I leave my husband? Do I have to murder my uncle? My mother? These are the sorts of large projects which have traditionally concerned a play's leading characters. Beckett is the first writer to dramatize the microstructure of action. What am I going to do one minute from now? In the next second? Weep? Take out my comb? Stand up? Sigh? Sit? Be silent? Tell a joke? Understand something? His plays are built on reflections leading to decisions, which impart to his dramas a real narrative push. Lessing was right about the irreducible difference between spatial and temporal arts. A play—or a novel, or a film—can be non-narrative in the sense that it need not tell a story. But it has to be linear or sequential, I think. A succession of images, or of aphorisms, is not enough to give a play the linear cohesiveness proper to the temporal arts.

PAJ: Do you feel the same way about Peter Handke's works—his *Sprechstucke,* particularly, which resemble Foreman's plays in the lack of dialogue, in the attempt at consciousness-raising, in the dialectical relationship of the stage and the audience?

SS: No, because Handke's plays are about specific ideas or problems (not about consciousness or perception as such), dramatized in a sequential form. The ideas matter dramatically.

PAJ: In Foreman's recent *Rhoda in Potatoland,* there are many quotations—from Breton's *Nadja,* from Wittgenstein, etc.—allusions to paintings, and so forth. How can the contemporary artist cope with the radical strides made in art in this century without alluding to them in his work?

SS: Modernist self-consciousness can take many forms. Painters like to quote other painters. But one can't imagine Beckett quoting anybody or making allusions to predecessors and models—as Wittgenstein didn't. The demands of purity and the demands of piety may be, ultimately, incompatible.

PAJ: Consciousness is the principal subject of modern art. Is that in some way a dangerous tradition?

SS: It seems to me that its biggest limitation is the value placed on consciousness conceived of as a wholly *private* activity. Modernist art has given the central place to asocial, private fantasy and, in effect, denied the notion that some intentions are more valid than others. . . . It's hardly surprising that so many modernist artists have been fascinated by the diseases of consciousness—that an art committed to solipsism would recapitulate the gestures of the *pathology* of solipsism. If you start from an asocial notion of perception or consciousness, you must inevitably end up with the poetry of mental illness and mental deficiency. With autistic silence. With the autistic's use of language: compulsive repetition and variation. With an obsession with circles. With an abstract or distended notion of time.

PAJ: Are you thinking of the work of Robert Wilson?

SS: Of Wilson, for one. More generally, of the long *faux naif* tradition in modernist art, one of whose great figures is Gertrude Stein. (What *Four Saints in Three Acts* started, *Letter to Queen Victoria* and *Einstein on the Beach* continue. . . .) But the symptomology of mental deficiency recurs in most of the really seductive productions I've seen recently: Pintilie's *Turandot, The Ik,* Carmelo Bene's *Faust* fantasy, Patrice Chereau's production of Marivaux's *La Dispute.* . . .

PAJ: Twelve years ago, in "One Culture and the New Sensibility," you advanced an argument which anticipates Foreman's—that the function of art is to extend and educate consciousness. You seem now to have moved away from the ideas expressed in that essay.

SS: I don't disagree with what I wrote then. But to assert that art is an exploration of consciousness is vacuous, unless one understands that consciousness has a structure, a thematics, a history. The choice of materials is never accidental or extraneous.

PAJ: Is that what you were arguing in your essay in the *New York*

Review of Books (February 6, 1975) on Leni Riefenstahl and fascist aesthetics?

SS: Yes, that's one assumption behind the essay. It seemed to me all too easy to say that Riefenstahl's work is beautiful. The question is: What kind of beauty? In the service of what ideas, what forms of consciousness, what emotions? Not only ideas but emotions—joy, fear, whatever—have a history. There is such a thing as fascist emotions, a fascist aesthetic impulse.

PAJ: How do you feel about Adrienne Rich's attack in the *New York Review of Books* (March 20, 1975) on your Riefenstahl piece for its "unwillingness" to discuss Riefenstahl as a product of a patriarchal society? Do you feel put upon by feminists who demand that you take another "line" in your writing?

SS: Since I'm a feminist too, the situation can hardly be described as a difficulty between me and "them." As for Rich's argument, I said what I thought about that in my reply (in the same issue of the *NYRB*) to her letter—that it's not as if Nazi Germany were a patriarchal society and other societies aren't. What society is *not* patriarchal? Riefenstahl's work is explained by Nazism, not by the attitudes of Nazis toward women.

PAJ: Yet many people see Riefenstahl's work as purely aesthetic, beautiful films.

SS: There is no such thing as an "aesthetic" work of art—as there is no such thing as the engagement or exploration of consciousness as such. Neither consciousness nor the aesthetic are something abstract. We're not being honest about our experience if we ignore the iconography of consciousness. You can't look at the Rembrandt self-portraits and see them just as an arrangement of forms, as studies in Brown. There's a face there.

PAJ: Isn't this way of looking at art radically different from the one you espoused in "Against Interpretation"?

SS: No. I never argued that all art should be looked at *abstractly;* I argued for the intellectual importance of its being experienced *sensuously.* "Against Interpretation" was a polemic against one reductive way of accounting for art, much more common a decade ago: treating a work as if it were equivalent to the account that could be given of its "meaning." This practice seemed to me misguided—first of all, because a great deal of art doesn't mean very much, in any nontautological sense of meaning. (Of course, a work may not have a "meaning" and still contain "referents" outside itself, to the world.) And because it weakens and corrupts our direct appreciation of a work's "thingness." Instead of relying so much on questions about what elements in a work of art mean, I thought we could rely more on questions about how they function—concretely, sensuously, and formally—in the work.

PAJ: I categorically refuse not to see meaning in a work. Otherwise it doesn't pay for me to go to see something. I have to approach the problem that is put before me and make it worthwhile for my own experiences.

SS: I categorically refuse to ask art to "pay for me." Nor does it have to touch me personally, as people say. Isn't pleasure "worthwhile"? Among other things, art is an instrument of pleasure—and one doesn't have *that* much pleasure in life. And pleasure can be quite impersonal. And complex.

PAJ: Are you positing a hierarchy of art—the kind that gives pleasure and the kind that makes you think? Are they mutually exclusive?

SS: Hardly—since thinking is one kind of pleasure, both solemn and playful. But I don't want to minimize the fact that the role of pleasure in art raises all sorts of serious questions. I find it impossible to keep moral feelings out of my desire for pleasure. That is, part of my *experience* of pleasure is that there are facile pleasures, as there are facile ideas. Since art is a form of flattery, I find myself also responding to the quality of an artist's refusal. The history of art is not only part of the history of pleasure. It is also a series of renunciations.

PAJ: Why should art have to renounce anything?

SS: Because every leading idea—every leading style—needs a corrective. As Oscar Wilde said, "A truth in art is that whose contrary is also true." And a truth *about* art is one whose contrary is also true.

PAJ: What do you hope for when you go to the theatre?

SS: Passion. Intelligence. Intensity. Lyricism. Theatre—and poetry and music—supply a lyricism not to be found in life.

PAJ: Why not?

SS: Because life is too long. For life to be like *Tristan and Isolde,*

the average human life should last two months instead of seventy
years.

PAJ: Is intensity the same as pleasure?

SS: It's better. Sexier, more profound. As you see, I'm an incorrigi-
ble puritan.

PAJ: You seem to be excluding humor.

SS: I'm not. But I get restless when the treatment of the emotions
in art takes second place—it does in so much of modernist theatre—to
the dramaturgy of surprise, to a negative desire, the desire to avoid
the expected.

PAJ: Are you suggesting that surprise is not a worthy element in
the performing arts?

SS: After a century and a half of surprises in the arts—during which
time the ante has been upped steadily, so that people are harder and
harder to surprise—it seems to have gotten much less satisfying. Most
instances of outrage or shock now are gags.

PAJ: You have written in one essay that "the history of art is a
series of successful transgressions." If, as you say, the ante of shock
and surprise is always being upped, what is left to transgress?

SS: The idea of transgression, perhaps. . . . Transgression presupposes successful notions of order. But transgressions have been so
successful that the idea of transgression has become normative for
the arts—which is a self-contradiction. Modern art wished to be—
maybe even was, for a brief time—in an intractable, adversary relation
to the established high culture. Now it is identical with high culture,
supported by a vast bureaucracy of museums, universities, and state
and private foundations. And the reason for this success story is that
there is a close fit between many of the values promoted by modernism
and the larger values of our capitalist consumer society. This makes
it difficult, to say the least, to continue thinking of modernist art as
adversary art. And that's part of what lies behind the disenchantment
with modernism I spoke of earlier.

PAJ: You seem discouraged by this situation.

SS: Yes and no. Rebellion does not seem to me a value in itself,
as—say—truth is. There's no inherent value in transgression. As there
is no inherent value to being interesting. My loyalty is not to the
transgression but to the truth behind it. That the forms of life in this
society, having become increasingly permissive, corrupt, vulgar, and

disgusting, thereby deprive artists of the taboos against which they can, comfortably, heroically, rebel—that seems far less dismaying than the fact that this society itself is based on lies, on untruths, on hallucination.

PAJ: What should artists do now?

SS: In a society which works and enriches itself by means of organized hallucination, be less devoted to creating new forms of hallucination. And more devoted to piercing through the hallucinations that nowadays pass for reality.

Does a Photograph of the Krupp Works Say Anything about the Krupp Works?

Fritz J. Raddatz / 1978

From *Die Zeit* (February 3, 1978), pp. 37–38. Translated from the German by Margaret S. Johnson. Reprinted by permission of Fritz J. Raddatz.

"Coffee's coming right up, I'll be right there," shouts the invisible hostess with a strong, dark voice out of some sort of dungeon. Meanwhile, I am allowed to climb up a dangerous ladder into the "atelier"—a tiny finished Mansard room stuffed full of books, newspapers, LP records, scarcely room enough to "have a seat"—that's Susan Sontag's "pied-à-terre" in Paris; to be sure an impressive address (Baron Empain was kidnapped last week just outside her door), but as lodging rather Spartan though pleasant. Her books and films are intellectual successes throughout the entire world (available in German are, among others, *Kunst und AntiKunst* ["Art and Anti-art," the augmented German-language edition of *Against Interpretation*], *The Benefactor,* and, soon to follow, *On Photography*). "Notes on 'Camp,' " the cultural manuscript of the 60s, defined an era—but Susan Sontag is not a "popular writer."

In sweater and trousers, with a beaming smile, constantly brushing back her loose hair, she greets her guest as though she had just left him the evening before. The conversation begins without digression and without pause. If I had to apply the word "intellectual" to a single person, only she would come to mind. She has a lightening-like joy, an inexhaustible curiosity about events and processes even of the most remote type: "Tell me about the new novel by Grass" is as important as "Did Jimmy Baldwin's boyfriend really leave him?" About the *Tel Quel* group or an incorrect Groddeck translation or her distrust of Handke's writings—then quickly, in the middle of that: "Is he separated from Moreau?" A hunger for the world. No cocktail party chatter; behind each word, every comment, is an observation, experience. "Earn? No, I do nothing to earn a living, actually—but I wouldn't for any prize in the world change my way of living, of working." In New York she even has to change apartments because the rent is so high. In all of what this beautiful young woman says, there is not only grace but dignity. Her serious cancer illness has probably made her even more earnest—and has produced an essay. The essay, "Illness as Metaphor," is the breeziest, the most unusual thing that has been written to date on the theme of illness, cancer and death; the first printing caused the circulation of the *New York Review of Books* to increase by ten thousand copies. "My honorarium for three months' work? $600—but let's get to work."

F.J.R.: To begin with, a comment rather than a question: Last week, when I was reading your new book, *On Photography,* on an airplane, a young woman who was sitting next to me admitted later that she had secretly been reading along with me. She asked: Is that a dissertation or a book for specialists? In any case, it's apparently very difficult to read, although she was a student and was just getting interested in the subject of photography and design. If it is a nonfiction book, do you, while writing, have in mind a particular audience?

Susan Sontag: Not really. I would find that fatal as a writer. When I work on a book, I don't think of anything else except how I can best formulate my thoughts and ideas.

F.J.R.: That sounds more like the answer of a novelist than of an essayist.

Sontag: No, it is just as true for an author of essays. And by the way, I don't consider my book to be so complicated, particularly not for a German audience when I think of how thoroughly I concern myself with Walter Benjamin.

F.J.R.: May I just turn my question around? In this new work, two key words play a prominent role: *consciousness* and *conscience,* that is to say, *Bewußtsein und Gewissen.* Those are aesthetic/philosophical as well as political concepts, and you deal with them throughout in their dialectical unity when you say that photography can only be understood as an image of reality, that is to say, can produce consciousness, if on the other hand there is already consciousness of reality. Isn't there a contradiction there: Consciousness is supposed to be awakened, but it is a presupposition?

Sontag: The two words are typically separated in English, but in French are one concept. Actually, in my work I attempt to some extent to encompass only one concept, namely that of moral conscience. In a broader understanding, art of course claims to develop beyond mere images, but in this book my interest is, above all, in photography as its own art medium. It is its own language, a language that alters the status of art. Actually, photography is for me only a pretext—in order to talk about something entirely different.

F.J.R.: About precisely what?

Sontag: About the problems of our modern society, about complicated differences between our thought and a superficial ability to perceive, about the sequence of experience and the capacity to judge this experience. This new possibility—new for a few generations now—of producing an image and thereby making a picture in a double sense of the word can resolve central problems of modern art as well as of politics. It gives us, so to speak, help in making decisions in order for us to find our way around in our world of capitalism and a consumer society.

F.J.R.: You say experience. Experience is another word for reality. Can photography really do more than reflect this reality? Can it only analyze or explain in an approximate way that which fine arts or literature can analyze without question? You yourself cite in one place Brecht's dictum that a photograph of the Krupp works does not demonstrate the reality of the Krupp works.

Sontag: Yes and no. We mustn't forget that persons nowadays experience reality and its images differently than in eras in which other image-systems were offered to them. Certainly, the photograph of the Krupp works says nothing about the Krupp works—but a painting would say just as little. A photograph of Guernica would already say something—Picasso's picture certainly says more. But why? Photography is in a certain way on the brink, on the knife's edge. It produces its own system of images, and it reproduces them at the same time; it can and claim to be art and can and claim at the same time to be very transient, very transparent. It accumulates reality.

F.J.R.: It is not coincidental that accumulation is a very mathematical concept. One would have to translate: Photography adds experience, while art creates its own experience.

Sontag: We are back to conscience and consciousness. I think that photography contains also a moral detonator [*Sprengsatz*]. For example, one can take something into possession, can "overcome" or "overpower" it, while one is photographing it. Often even more intensively than through verbal art. When you mentioned beforehand the difficulty of the young student in the airplane—presumably she would have more easily understood a volume of photographs, would have understood the passing of time and the development even of the social reality which surrounds it. Look here behind my desk at the great photograph of Marlene Dietrich. It could have been just a picture, of course. But the photograph shows much more clearly the glamour, beauty and transitoriness of the life of such an actress; it even elucidates, by the power of its own medium, that it was the meaning of this life, so to speak, to produce images. This life *was* an image.

F.J.R.: Doesn't this photograph collect, instead of sum up? You yourself state, in another part of your book, that summing up is possible only for art.

Sontag: For me, however, in contrast to you, collecting is not a mathematical concept. It comprises even much more this feeling of acquisition, mastering, indeed using up. Recently a prominent colleague in American television, who ostensibly had read my book but obviously not understood it, told me how much she liked it—she also loved photographs, she owned over two thousand photographs of herself. So this woman understood herself as a "collection." It was proof to her that she exists. For many people photography or collecting is also obviously a struggle against time, destruction and transitoriness.

F.J.R.: When I think, for example, about the set of drawings with which Matisse portrayed Aragon, in connection with the catch words time and transitoriness—don't they render much more emphatically change, development, and decline?

Sontag: Without question. But what Matisse's drawings do not render, as a built-in quality of the product, is the product-ness itself, the possibility of use. Think of Warhol's attempts, or look again at the wonderful photograph of Marlene, a conservative product, presented by means of a conserving product.

F.J.R.: Therefore the Dorian Gray likeness of Marlene Dietrich?

Sontag: Exactly. That ought to have occurred to me. Photographs make us all Dorian Grays.

F.J.R.: It seems to me that there lies a danger precisely in this detached notion of photography. Presumably you know the American sociologist Daniel Boorstin and his book *The Image* in which he analyzes an anecdote that is more than an anecdote. He meets an acquaintance with her baby in a supermarket and says: What a pretty child. And she says: Yes, but you ought to see the photographs.

Sontag: I'm investigating this very danger. I have described a similar example, in one of my essays, where a woman whose house I am admiring shows me pictures of the house, while I am *in* the house, in order to convince me even more of its beauty.

F.J.R.: Pardon my stubbornness, but doesn't that all say that photography doesn't bring about its own consciousness, nor its own possibility of recognition, especially not politically? Literature or painting can and does both.

Sontag: Correct. When Goya represents one of the horrors of the Napoleonic invasions of Spain, then that is like its own discovery of political and human experience. A photograph is completely neutral. Unless one has a capacity to interpret it or can interpret it with help from the photograph itself. If a certain consciousness is not there, then the experience isn't even photographed. Therefore, for example, there are no photos from the Korean War which would be comparable to those from the Vietnam War—simply because the consciousness changed.

F.J.R.: I have to contradict myself, so to speak, when I remind you what you reported about your own experiences with photos of Auschwitz and Dachau: that they taught you, a young girl in America, your first lesson in horror and thereby an understanding of fascism.

Sontag: Again, simultaneously yes and no. You mustn't forget that there was already a pre-understanding awakened, if only through unspeakably bad Hollywood films. Of course, they did not have the intensity of a photograph of a room full of hair or eyeglasses or shoes. For that reason my yes and no: One saw, comprehended—and still one needed to have someone to explain it.

F.J.R.: Well, then, interpretation, to pick up on the key word of one of your most important essays.

Sontag: Yes. In order to identify itself, it also needs interpretation.

One or the other. Nevertheless, photography is a means of bringing strange, otherwise not attainable experience close to a person.

F.J.R.: But which can be smoothed out and made aesthetic? If I may recall your essay about Leni Riefenstahl: Many persons right in America, but without this pre-understanding, found and find her films pretty and otherwise nothing more. The bad thing is: Her Films *are* beautiful.

Sontag: A delicate area. In the case of the photographs of Auschwitz or Dachau, even without historical memory, it would probably not be possible to say "beautiful." I think the sentence "This is a better picture" would not be possible in this context. But at the same time there is the danger, particularly with the work of Leni Riefenstahl, of—as you say—smoothing out, making aesthetic.

F.J.R.: Precisely. It's done with the same cinematic bravado and brilliance as the films of Pudovkin or Eisenstein. The technical medium of film is value free. I think that, with the word, such is not the case. There is no great fascist poem. One cannot turn around, so to speak, Celan's "Todesfuge"; one cannot make a poem *in favor of* Auschwitz.

Sontag: The Celan poem is a striking example. I would even hesitate to call it "beautiful"; it is a *great* poem. Not only because it refutes the famous quotation by Adorno, often taken out of context, that after Auschwitz one could no longer write poetry. Celan not only wrote *after* Auschwitz, but rather even a poem *about* Auschwitz, that is, about an indescribable subject that seemed to be beyond any poetic balance. But that it was able to treat this subject, at all adequately, was made possible by the structure of the poem. It is very important that it deals with two persons. That the ashen hair belongs to one person and the golden hair to another.

F.J.R.: Through which the possibility of identification is offered . . .

Sontag: Yes, in that way there arises not only a fracture, but also a movement. To be sure, not only an architectonic one, but also an emotional one. Sulamith and Margarete—they could not have been banished to the same plateau. They were not living in the same reality.

F.J.R.: Again my objection—the autonomy of art which can create its own reality versus the mere mirror effect of photography.

Sontag: Certainly, you are right; photography can only be a fragment, a mirror shard, an excerpt. It has *eo ipso* a fragmentary character as does much in modern art. Think of John Cage. The principle is that of collage.

F.J.R.: Excuse me, but I must immediately take hold of that word. It is indeed not a coincidence that you choose it, because the greatest photographic collages, for example John Heartfield's, are no longer pure photography, but rather they are "manipulated."

Sontag: Right, they are in a certain way an extension of painting techniques, a kind of multimedia-painting that uses photographic elements just as much as those of painting. Heartfield could have placed Sulamith next to Margarete.

F.J.R.: That is what you call in another place a surrealistic moment in photography. In the case of pure photography, there is nothing surrealistic. In order to formulate it in an apparent paradox: Only truly surrealistic art can be truly realistic art.

Sontag: Nevertheless, I insist that even photography clarifies for humans an element of the fantastic, the unreal, in everyone's everyday life. But on one point you are right; interpretation or consciousness is also a part of it. Every intellectual activity is also interpretation.

F.J.R.: Does that mean that interpreter is a synonym for intellectual?

Sontag: No, not in my concept of it. Intellectuals distinguish themselves from other people in that by constant reflection or interpretation they leaven reality. But what I was attacking at that time in my essay and what I would continue to attack is interpretation in a much narrower sense—namely interpreting away the facts of a case by means of words. Released by my cancer illness, I have concerned myself in a newer, longer work with how words and concepts cover the reality of sickness (it used to be TB, now it's cancer). Actually, it's been clear to me for only three weeks that my essay about cancer is a different version of "Against Interpretation." It is in this way that one has to understand my attack and it is in this way also that my analysis of Leni Riefenstahl is to be seen. What does "beautiful" mean anyway? The concept is not applicable without thinking about the history of certain ideals of beauty. Then one discovers, you know, that there is such a thing as fascist aesthetics, that the word "beautiful" cannot simply be released from its particular historical context, that this or that was considered beautiful in a quite definite historical context that we reject today and is for us ugly instead. The notion of the human body and its beauty, for example, has not been the same, unchanged, throughout all periods. If you want to call that interpretation, I agree, although it expands the notion.

F.J.R.: This historical dimension is of course simultaneously a political one.

Sontag: Quite so. I won't go so far as to say that the works of Leni Riefenstahl are not beautiful; I only say there is something else. I say that this beauty includes also a specific political content. One could just as well draw in, instead of her works, those of Walt Disney—who, by the way, was a great admirer of Leni Riefenstahl. One cannot call him the product of an official fascist culture, but the social impulse for his work was without question the same.

F.J.R.: Now you are injecting other concepts, political, social, historical. Can one say that your entire work—whether it is concerned with the analysis of works by Lévi-Strauss, or your book about Vietnam, or various literary interpretations or now this book about photography—aren't they all, in the final analysis, meant to be political? Still, you took a long-term political stand, in the USA, namely during the Vietnam War.

Sontag: I think it is more complicated. So little do I have literary or other models, so little can I imagine narrow, specific goals. Of course, I talk with people, take on their problems, and people force me to think about my own work. But I couldn't say that I have a precise notion of my work. I probably follow more my own direct interests.

F.J.R.: A somewhat private, not to say narcissistic, answer.

Sontag: Not at all. But I do want to tell you, quite frankly, it's getting a bit boring for me to have to define my position and my goals. To the work of the writer there also belongs quite a goodly amount of innocence, of undefinability. Certainly strong activity is an assumption, but I cannot find it narcissistic if I don't serve some sort of creed, an ideology or even a political movement. The free creative writer acts as a kind of freely suspended conscience. Whenever I sit down at the typewriter, it is always discovery work too. I don't sit down simply to write down what I have just thought out. It is much more a new and ever developing, previously unknown, dialogue, whether with living or dead persons or even with the structures of the world in which I now live.

F.J.R.: An idea to which others are opposed. You frequently mention Walter Benjamin and very seldom Bertolt Brecht, who down to the naming of his dramatic works—didactic pieces—had a precise didactic idea of his goal.

Sontag: The one doesn't have to exclude the other. Of course I would like to influence people, whether on the one hand with a book about Vietnam or with this new book about photography. Behind all of these works, there is a bit of aggression, opposition that is concealed as energy.

F.J.R.: What is it in the new book that goes against the grain?

Sontag: It is in truth an extended political essay. Much more than about art. It is an extended study of our consumer world, about our experiences and the distortions by which consumerism threatens our world. It is very radical, as is every book that takes itself seriously.

Susan Sontag: Dissidence as Seen from the USA

Guy Scarpetta / 1978

From *Tel Quel,* No. 76 (Summer 1978), pp. 28–37. Translated from the French by Clyde Thogmartin. Reprinted by permission.

Susan Sontag, what was the meaning of your presence at the Venice Biennale? What struck you the most there?

I came first of all to listen, to learn things. I didn't speak up about dissidence. I didn't think that I had particularly interesting things to say. What struck me the most is rather the reactions of European intellectuals and those of my own compatriots. But there were few Americans attending, so I've tried to better understand the situation of ideas in Western Europe. In the first place, I was astonished, like many people, with the lack of attendance from Italy. I talked about it right after my arrival with Moravia, who told me right away that he was practically the only Italian intellectual present. And I read that, three days before the opening of the biennale, the communist party decided to boycott it—and it worked, and had a decisive influence on the attitude of Italian intellectuals, even noncommunists. The situation is such that they cannot, they don't feel free to challenge a decision like that one. And on the other hand, on the part of American professors, many of whom are not at all politically committed and who are very happy to go to the Soviet Union from time to time for their work, there was the fear of not getting a visa for the Soviet Union if they participate in the biennale. I learned that right away.

How do you evaluate these pressures, this embarrassment of Western intellectuals about just going to listen *to the testimony of dissidents?*

It's obviously deplorable, something that must be changed. But this discomfort is something very difficult to modify because there is in the West a tendency to "excuse" what is happening in the East. To want to believe the *best* about everything that happens under the flag

97

of communism or Marxism. One hears disagreeable things about the camps, the prisons, the psychiatric hospitals. Right away one tries to find an interpretation that will excuse that—their situation is difficult, they're surrounded, besieged, they started out from a "backward" situation. They have to repress, to put people in prison, etc.

I think that there is a long history, on our side, of this tendency to "find excuses." We are pitiless about situations that are officially described as fascist, and very indulgent about anything that calls itself "socialist" or "communist." That is the real background of this discomfort. Of course there was also this prohibition which came from the Italian communist party, a communist party whose prestige is unsurpassed in comparison to other countries in the West. I remember meeting Visconti in the sixties and I asked him, "How can you, who are a Duke, a billionaire, and so on, vote as a communist? How is it in your best interest to vote against yourself?" And he answered, "I am what I am, but the communists are the good guys."

Exactly, when you see people who come from hell, from the camps, from a universe of implacable repression, and you see a party boycotting their very testimony, can't you say that it's just the opposite of "the good guys"? Isn't there, through this submissiveness of intellectuals before communist "prestige," a totalitarian danger which also threatens the West?

Absolutely. All the more so because we are all "under censorship." You know, the prestige of communism was first of all created by its adversaries. If fascism flew the flag of anti-communism, as in general people think in "binary" or "polarized" terms, then to be anti-fascist means to be pro-communist. This is the logic that has influenced people's minds for the last fifty years and it is this "binary" reasoning that must be abandoned.

What strikes me is that, despite this logic, *information* about the horrors in the Eastern countries has been available for the last forty or forty-five years. And at every moment, there are people who withdraw support, who refuse to identify themselves with what is going on in the Soviet Union and who are treated like shit by the conformist intelligentsia. Look at Gide, on his second return from the Soviet Union, where he heard talk about trials, camps—he bears witness, he says he's changed his mind; and he was called a fascist.

There was a whole debate in the thirties. . . . When Souvarine wrote his book about Stalin, it was Malraux, at the Gallimard publishing house, before the Spanish Civil War, who said to him, ''You're doubtless right, Souvarine, and I will be on your side *when it is the stronger.*'' Look at Aragon and so on. People *knew*. In fact, they talk about ''not causing Billancourt to lose hope,'' but it's not just Billancourt; it's the intellectuals themselves who, in order not to lose hope, refuse to recognize the truth.

It's very hard, in fact, to renounce this idealization of the Eastern European countries. With the current diaspora of Russian and other dissidents, it's easier; but you mustn't forget that, from the thirties onward, people had testified. Undoubtedly, you have to see that in relationship to fascism. It's because fascism seems weaker than before that it is not experienced in Europe as an immediate threat—which permits us to accept what should have been evident for a long time, that socialist countries are the opposite of democracy.

But you know, I was also guilty in that regard. I remember when I was in high school in the United States at the end of the forties; there was a little communist group in my high school, and they gave me the 1936 Soviet Constitution to read. I read it, we talked about it—and I never asked myself any questions; I was sure that it corresponded to reality. I was a fellow traveler; I didn't *want* to believe what they told me about the Soviet Union.

Precisely, for someone like you, for an American intellectual who has participated in all sorts of decisive struggles in the United States—on the women's question, on Civil Rights, against the war in Vietnam, and so on—how do you situate yourself now in relationship to a phenomenon like dissidence in the East? What importance has that had in your life, in your journey?

As far as I'm concerned, the shock came first, before Solzhenitsyn, from the book *Against All Hope* by Nadeshda Mandelstam, this implacable testimony on what happened in the Soviet Union in the thirties and later. You know, at the beginning of the fifties, I had never even heard the *name* of Trotsky. I had undergone a real Stalinist ''brainwashing.'' There was a formidably efficient censorship. And even when *The Gulag Archipelago* was coming out, and Solzhenitsyn was already in the West, he said things that I found completely reactionary—I had a tendency not to believe him at all. But Brodsky said to me one day: "Think what you want of him on the political level, but what he testifies to, what he describes, those are *facts*."

I must also say that for me what was going on in the Soviet Union was always a little "distant." I had detached myself from it since 1956, since the Hungarian Revolution. In the sixties, at the time of the Cuban Revolution, I had started the classic journey for many intellectuals, which consisted of transferring our political hopes to the "Third World." We blamed everything we didn't like in the Soviet Union on anti-democratic Russian "traditions." (There's even a text of Lenin's saying in 1910 that, if the Revolution takes place in Russia and not elsewhere, it will be a catastrophe.) Obviously, I had a shock in 1968 with the invasion of Czechoslovakia, but at the time I was thinking more about Vietnam; that's where I concentrated what I had to say.

Yes, but, if you will, it's one thing not to believe anymore that the Eastern European countries can represent something progressive; it's something else to know in what way they constitute the realization of a kind of totalitarianism that we must fight against, here as well. . . . Everything that you have just mentioned about the blindness, voluntary or involuntary, of Western progressive intellectuals, doesn't that bring up the question of their relationship to power? Aren't the dissidents calling us to resist power?

Yes, but for us it's maybe even dumber than that. In Cuba, in Hanoi, in China, everybody refused the Soviet "model" (in Hanoi, important people told me that the Russians were just as horrible as the Americans)—and we believed in it. It's always a question of a double standard. We believed things, coming from the East, that we wouldn't have believed for a second in our own countries. Imagine, if the American government had killed tens of millions of its own citizens, its own leaders, if all of Roosevelt's cabinet had been sent to concentration camps, shot, or died of hunger, what would people have said about this country!

In fact, I never went to the East, except in 1967 to Czechoslovakia, as if I had unconsciously chosen a time and a place which could only confirm my hopes. . . . As for the question of power, I would say that Russian intellectuals are opposed to power just as we are. We also detest oppression, official state language, and so on. No, the most basic question was suggested by something that Konrad said, in Venice, that a writer who becomes a militant is a masochist, that he sacrifices his language, as a writer, to a conformist, militant language. Does that mean that we have to give up on any political action? I don't think so.

But isn't it a matter of transforming our relationship *to politics? Doesn't speaking one's own language, in opposition to any official "state language," constitute a gesture which has political effects?*

But any militant language is a public language. Take the case of feminism; it's the same thing. If you get involved in that struggle, and not just to carry out actions, you lose your language. I know writers committed to feminism who don't write anything anymore. That's the risk. It's perhaps a tragedy, perhaps also something that's quite justified. . . . But I don't think that you can comfort yourself by saying simply that, if you're independent as far as language goes, that's a political act. The most you can say is that we maintain the possibility of pluralism in our society. But this pluralism is *given* to us by capitalism; you aren't doing anything except affirming what is already given to us. No. What we have to get away from is shame at being a bourgeois intellectual. Everybody has been made to feel guilty about that. We exist within the norms of bourgeois society (while to express an independent language in the Soviet Union is an act of dissidence). Beyond that, there's an even harder question: Aren't we finally happy about our society? Maybe it's not as bad as all that?

Do you think that there are no dissident Western intellectuals? That dissidence is a phenomenon only relevant in Eastern European societies?

Certainly. To live the life of a bourgeois intellectual is a sort of conformism, perhaps a positive conformism, but it's not an act of dissidence. Our "dissidence," if you like, would be to carry on very limited, very concrete, struggles over the real problems of our society, that's to say by accepting the authentic privileges and freedoms that are given to us here in order to fight against the injustices that exist, against things that are harmful in the long run. And in these various specific struggles—on the women's question, the question of environmentalism, on everything that is going on in the school system, the way old people are treated, questions of overproduction, waste,

environmental poisoning, which is tending to destroy the planet—
that's political, and not just a simple fact of claiming a personal language.

*But an action that causes a different language to appear, a lan-
guage that dissolves and overturns a whole culture, is that something
a society can tolerate? I'm thinking of Artaud, on whom you worked
for a long time.*

But even in that case, you know, as soon as you're dead, you
quickly become a classic of intellectual life. Artaud finally became the
determining influence on contemporary theater, for example. It's the
genius of this society to be able to use anything, to assimilate
anything. I used to agree with Marcuse's thesis about "repressive
tolerance," the necessity of fighting against recuperation. But it isn't
possible; there aren't any ideas that are "unacceptable" in themselves, if only because we live in a liberal, pluralistic society.

In fact, intellectuals should rather accept the fact that they're part
of the ruling class and use that as a basis for leading specific campaigns
on real issues, the issue of health, of justice, and so on. Perhaps in
the United States (where we have the advantage of having more or
less preceded the Europeans in accepting this message of disappointment) we more easily accept precise, limited actions. I have been
struck, in France, by the influence of ideas or themes of "the"
revolution: We have a revolution, we change everything, it's all or
nothing. . . . Look for example at this story of the destruction of Les
Halles in Paris, the weakness of the protests. What Foucault has done
about prisons, his analysis, his organization of protests, it's extraordinary—but I don't think that there's any need to talk about a "prison
society," as if we needed "global" ideas, as if it were always necessary to broaden the rhetoric so that it becomes "revolutionary"
rhetoric. . . . No, we're fighting about the issue of prisons, *and
that's all.*

We must come to a conception of political struggle that has as its
target specific events or institutions, without necessarily attaching it
to an overall "revolutionary" project. That's the whole question of
the struggle of minorities.

*Yes, it's important to denounce this illusion about "the" revolution,
insofar as when a revolution tries to be total there is every chance
that it will become totalitarian . . .*

Isn't it just because, when you want to change *everything*, the easiest way to deal with the people who already have power is to deprive them of their rights, to put them in prison and so on. When you want to change everything, you're forced to oppress.

Within this framework of specific, limited conflicts, of daily resistance to different forms of power, wherever power manifests itself in a repressive way, what do we have to learn from dissidents, as far as you're concerned?

I think in fact that they are badly placed to help us. We can learn from them essential things about the prison camps, revolutionary illusions, and so on, but in the last analysis they are distant from us. They may even deny phenomena that are obvious for us, like exploitation in the West. Of course, that's comprehensible, you have to see *where* they're coming from, they have made their own journey; but it is a little bit pointless to ask them to join us in our journey. . . .

The encounter is perhaps difficult on the level of "ideas," but don't we have something to learn from them, I would say, subjectively? This ability to be without illusions, not to take any rhetoric at its own word, to look for the reality behind the words, this strength and resistance: Isn't that, for us, the essential part of their message?

But we have these possibilities in our own right. Nobody takes Giscard "at his own word," for example.

But you were speaking yourself of the blindness of progressive intellectuals in the fifties, of this possibility of taking the Constitution of the Soviet Union at its own word, even though it had never been carried out.

Yes, but the essential thing is what you said about the fact that if you want "total" change, you are asking for totalitarianism. You have to refuse to believe the myth of the "new man." All fascist regimes call for the idea of a total transformation of man.

That goes back to the 18th century. . . .

Exactly, I have just reread Saint-Just; it's quite striking! But we also risk falling into another danger, the danger of cynical intellectuals, which is that of a total renunciation of politics. I want to remain Marxist in a certain sense. Of course, Marx has become the flag of a totalitarian regime. Capitalism has satisfied the great demands of *The*

Communist Manifesto. Marxist thinking is dated. We have different, new problems, about which Marx didn't say anything. But he has given us certain keys, certain methods of analysis, that must not be rejected. I think that you have to be *for* "master thinkers," if we ask of them, not the illusion of an ideal society, but help in analyzing things.

Look at the case of Hannah Arendt, whose book on totalitarianism created a scandal, who wasn't translated for twenty years, etc. Well, the fact that she was part of the tradition of "master thinkers" didn't deprive her of a means of analyzing totalitarianism.

Perhaps the danger is particularly the way in which people have speculated on the limits of Marx's thought (although I don't think you can separate thought from the use that one makes of it); it's the way in which they succeeded in making of it a system of totalizing reason, the very source of totalitarianism.

The essential illusion is the one according to which the state can regulate things better than anyone. Marx doesn't permit one to think about the question of bureaucratization; his thought has to be completed by Max Weber on that subject.

As a writer, more precisely, what do you think of the phenomenon of dissidence?

What strikes me is the way in which literature flourishes in conditions of oppression. It strikes me, and, in a certain sense, dismays me. The situation of a writer is *in itself* a situation of opposition. In a very strongly repressive situation, the strength of opposition, of challenge, can be increased ten times. The danger for a writer is our situation, in which anything is permitted. That can lead to a certain complacency.

Are you in agreement with the provocative statement that Brodsky made in Venice, saying that censorship is finally a good thing for a writer?

Yes, it's the importance of limits. We have to build our own limits. The literature that interests me the most at the moment is the literature that comes from Eastern Europe and from Latin America. You feel there a searching, an imagination, a courage that we don't have. It troubles me very much.

It's not that I believe that a writer has to have a tragic history, but you mustn't fall into this complacency which is always our temptation. Nor can you construct artificial barriers or imaginary limits, but you have to find true limits. For example, obscenity, which has mobilized much energy in the fight against taboos since Sade, Baudelaire, Bataille, etc.; you see now that it's a very fragile limit. The taboo has been broken. You have to find true limits, but you don't do that by creating a literature which "shocks." This society is basically "un-shockable." Our enemy, on the contrary, is this consumer society, this freedom which robs everything of its value. It is by constructing certain criteria, rather than by breaking taboos, that one can make progress. Now, any criteria, any moral thought, is devalued. The danger, as Nietzsche said, is nihilism. Nihilism presented as something liberating.

Doesn't that come back to a very essential thing that Solzhenitsyn taught us, that morals and ethics, far from being something repressive, can be a way of resisting, the only possible subjective position for resisting power?

Exactly. We take up again a term that has been very devalued. We were so much taken by the idea of the terrorist intellectual who breaks taboos, for whom morality was nothing other than bourgeois morality. At the same time, we reserved our idea of morality for the "other side," for socialism, communism, anarchism, for an ideal society. But in our society, we were against ethics. It's a terrible thing. Because if you follow the thread of ethics, you find many things, many limits. The limits are less a matter of expression than of principles. This society is a hypocritical society; we must unmask this hypocrisy, but not under the flag of nihilism. The dissidents always have a very moralizing discourse. Our society has a very amoral discourse: happiness, buying power, consumption. So, we are caught between these two terms: nihilism and consumerism.

Susan Sontag: The *Rolling Stone* Interview

Jonathan Cott / 1978

From *Rolling Stone* (October 4,1979), pp. 46–53. Copyright by
Straight Arrow Publishers, Inc., 1979. All Rights Reserved.
Printed by Permission.

"The only possible metaphor one may conceive of for the life
of the mind," wrote the late political scientist Hannah Arendt,
"is the sensation of being alive. Without the breath of life, the
human body is a corpse; without thinking, the human mind
is dead."

Susan Sontag is an exemplary witness to the fact that living a
thinking life and thinking about the life one is living can be
complementary and energizing activities. Since the 1966 publication of *Against Interpretation*—her first collection of essays,
which included the brilliant "Notes on 'Camp' " and "On
Style" and which ranged joyously and unpatronizingly from
the Supremes to Simone Weil, from films like *The Incredible
Shrinking Man* to *Muriel*—Sontag has continued to be drawn to
both "popular" and "high" cultures and to write about subjects
as diverse as pornography and photography, the aesthetics of
silence and the aesthetics of fascism. In doing so, moreover,
she has been continually examining and testing out her notion
that supposed oppositions like thinking and feeling, consciousness and sensuousness, morality and aesthetics can in fact
simply be looked at as aspects of each other—much like the pile
on the velvet that, upon reversing one's touch, provides two
textures and two ways of feeling, two shades and two ways
of perceiving.

In "On Style," for example, Sontag wrote: "To call Leni
Riefenstahl's *Triumph of the Will* and *Olympiad* masterpieces is
not to gloss over Nazi propaganda with aesthetic lenience. The
Nazi propaganda is there. But something else is there, too . . .
the complex movements of intelligence and grace and sensuousness."

Exactly ten years later, in the *New York Review of Books,* she
reversed the pile, commenting that *Triumph of the Will* was
"the most purely propagandistic film ever made, whose very
conception negates the possibility of the filmmaker's having an
aesthetic or visual conception independent of propaganda."
Where she once focused on the "formal implications of con-

106

tent," Sontag has explained, she later wished to investigate "the content implicit in certain ideas of form."

A "besotted aesthete" and "obsessed moralist" (as she recently described herself), Sontag has—in her essays *(Styles of Radical Will),* novels *(The Benefactor* and *Death Kit)* and films *(Duet for Cannibals, Brother Carl* and *Promised Lands,* a documentary about Israel)—persistently rejected and worked against "comfortable" and "received" positions, attitudes and opinions. As she stated in an interview: "We live in a culture in which intelligence is denied relevance altogether, in a search for radical innocence, or is defended as an instrument of authority and repression. In my view, the only intelligence worth defending is critical, dialectical, skeptical, desimplifying."

And her three most recent publications—*On Photography* (a long, dialectical essay, surprisingly a best seller), *Illness as Metaphor* (a book that elucidates and exorcises tuberculosis, and cancer as metaphors, written as a result of having been operated on for cancer several years ago) and *I, etcetera* (eight adventurous works of fiction that explore and extend her concerns in a variety of voices)—have confirmed Sontag's position as one of our most unpredictable and enlightening writers, whose modes of thinking and feeling have been a model and inspiration for many people.

Born in Arizona and raised in California, Sontag was educated at the University of Chicago, which she entered when she was fifteen, and at Harvard. I met her in 1963 when she was teaching, and I was studying, at Columbia University. I saw her again in 1966 in Berkeley, where she had been invited to lecture; I invited Sontag and filmmaker Kenneth Anger, who had just released his dazzling *Scorpio Rising,* onto an informal, late-night radio program that I was producing for KPFA. A couple of years later I saw her in London during a press screening of her first film, *Duet for Cannibals.*

Having run into each other for fifteen years, we decided, early in 1978, to do a "formal" interview. Since her bout with cancer, she has been in good spirits, good health, and has been busier than ever. The following interview began in June 1978 in Paris, where Susan lives half of the year, and continued in November of last year in New York City, where she lives the other half, surrounded by a library of 8000 books ("my own retrieval system," as she calls it).

When you found out you had cancer a few years ago, you immediately started thinking about your illness. I'm reminded of something Nietzsche once wrote: "For a psychologist there are few questions that are as attractive as that concerning the relation of health and

philosophy, and if he should himself become ill, he will bring all of
his scientific curiosity into his illness." Is this the way you began to
think about Illness as Metaphor?

Well, it's certainly true that the fact that I got sick made me think
about sickness. Everything that happens to me is something I think
about. I'm sure that this experience will turn up in my fiction—very
transposed. But as far as that side of me that writes essays, what
occurred to me to ask was not, What am I experiencing? but rather,
What really goes on in the world of the sick? What are the ideas that
people have? I was examining my own ideas because I had a lot of the
fantasies about illness, and about cancer in particular. I'd never given
the question of illness any serious consideration. So if you don't think
about things, you're likely to be the vehicle of the going clichés, even
of the more enlightened ones.

The fact of being ill, however, and thinking about it in the way
you've done would seem to demand a sense of distance.

On the contrary, it would have been an enormous effort for me to
not think about it. The really enormous effort was to get out of that
period when I was so ill that I couldn't work at all. The greatest effort
is to be really where you are, contemporary with yourself, in your
life, giving full attention to the world. That's what a writer does. I'm
against the solipsistic idea that you find it all in your head. You don't.

For about a year and a half I was going to a hospital three times a
week, I was hearing this language, I was seeing the people who are
victims of these stupid ideas. *Illness as Metaphor* and the essay I
wrote about the Vietnam War are perhaps the only two instances in
my life when I knew that what I was writing was not only true but
actually helpful to people in a very immediate, practical way. I know
people who have sought proper medical treatment because of reading
it—people who weren't getting anything, other than some kind of
psychiatric treatment, and are now getting chemotherapy.

Following Nietzsche's idea that "in some it is their deprivations
that philosophize; in others, their riches and strengths," it seems
interesting that while suffering from your illness you produced some-
thing very rich and strong.

I thought that when this started . . . well, of course, I was told it
was likely that I'd be dead very soon, so I was facing not only an

illness and painful operations, but also what I thought might be death in the next year or two. And besides feeling the physical pain, I was terribly frightened. I was experiencing the most acute kind of animal panic. But I also experienced moments of elation. A tremendous intensity. I felt as if I had embarked on a great adventure. It was the adventure of being ill and probably dying. And, I don't want to say it was a positive experience, because that sounds cheap, but of course it did have a positive side.

So it wasn't out of a sense of deprivation that you thought about these things?

No, because it was two weeks after I was told I had cancer that I cleaned out those ideas. The first thing I thought was: What did I do to deserve this? I've led the wrong life. I've been too repressed. Yes, I suffered a great grief five years ago and this must be the result of that intense depression.

Then I asked one of my doctors: "What do you think about the psychological side of cancer in terms of what causes it?" And he said to me, "Well, people say a lot of funny things about diseases." I mean, he just dismissed it absolutely. So I began to think about TB; the argument of the thing fell into place. I have the same propensities to feel guilty that everybody has, probably more than average. But I don't like it. Nietzsche was right about guilt. It's awful; I'd rather feel *ashamed*. That seems more objective and has to do with one's personal sense of honor, but people do feel guilty about being ill.

I like to feel responsible, you understand. Whenever I find myself in a mess in my personal life, I'd rather say, "Well, I chose to fall in love with this person, who turned out to be a bastard." I don't like blaming other people, because it's so much easier to change oneself than other people.

I don't think it makes much sense to worry about what made you ill. What does make sense is to be as rational as you can in seeking the right kind of treatment.

Job didn't feel guilty; he felt stubborn and angry.

I felt extremely stubborn. But I didn't feel angry, because there was nobody to feel angry at. You can't feel angry at nature. You can't feel angry at biology. We're all going to die—that's a very difficult thing to take in—and we all experience this process.

It feels as if there's this person—in your head, mainly—trapped in this physiological stock that only survives seventy to eighty years, normally, in any decent condition. It starts deteriorating at a certain point, and then for half of your life, if not more, you watch this material begin to fray. And there's nothing you can do about it. You're trapped inside it; and when it goes, you go.

What about all the philosophical and quasi-mystical attempts to overcome that duality? Right now, you've been speaking from an experiential, common-sense point of view.

I think the sense of a self trapped in something is impossible to get over. That's the origin of all dualisms—Platonic, Cartesian or whatever. There's no way that we can be conscious and not feel "I am in my body."

Of course, you can try to come to terms with death, try to shift the axis of your activities to things that are less body-dependent as you get older: your body neither is as attractive to other people nor does it function in the way that is pleasurable to you. But it also should be said that a lot of our ideas about what we can do at different ages and what age means are so arbitrary—as arbitrary as sexual stereotypes. People say all the time: "Oh, I can't do that. I'm sixty. I'm too old." Or "I can't do that. I'm twenty. I'm too young." Why? Who says so?

I think that the old-young polarization and the male-female polarization are perhaps the two leading stereotypes that imprison people. The values associated with youth and with masculinity are considered to be the human norms, and anything else is taken to be at least less worthwhile or *inferior*. Old people have a terrific sense of inferiority. They're embarrassed to be old.

Do you think the health-illness opposition relates at all to that between male and female or youth and old age?

Anytime you have an extreme experience, you feel a certain kind of solidarity with other people who have that experience. There's a world of bravery and gallantry that is so inspiring, but I also know some people who are ill who are extremely exhibitionistic and who can be sadistic, using their illness to dominate and to exploit others.

The Goncourt brothers said: "Sickness sensitizes man for observation, like a photographic plate." When applied to both On Photography *and* Illness as Metaphor, *this becomes extremely ironic and fasci-nating.*

It is fascinating. People in this culture have decided that sickness is laden with all kinds of spiritual values. And that's because they don't have any other means to prod or extract something from themselves. Everything in this society—in the way we live—conspires to eliminate all but the most banal level of feelings; there's no sense of the sacred or of transcendence. Today we don't have much. The two things spiritual values have become attached to, since the collapse of religious faith, are art and illness.

In Illness as Metaphor, *you wrote: "Theories that diseases are caused by mental states and can be cured by willpower are always an index of how much is not understood about the physical terrain of a disease." Don't you think that Christian Scientists might agree with this statement while denying—probably just because they don't ac-cept—the "physical terrain"?*

No, I don't think they'd agree with it, because Christian Science is just another version of the same thing. Starting in the eighteenth century with people like Mesmer in France, you have the birth of a kind of modern spiritualism—all kinds of movements, some of which called themselves religions, some of which called themselves forms of medical practice. These movements denied the existence of illness and said that, essentially, it's all in your head. Or that it was something spiritual (Mesmer talked about fluids). Mesmerism, Christian Science or the psychological theories of disease all convert disease into something mental and immaterial.

What about the notion that one is somehow responsible for one's disease—the kind of argument you hear from some est disciples?

There *are* such things as microbes and viruses and genetic weak-nesses. I think this is a kind of demagogic idea in this society, an idea that is taking people away, or distracting them, from areas in which they really could take responsibility. And I'm very impressed by the fact that all these ways of thinking are so antiintellectual. One of the notions of est is that you must not say *but.* You're supposed to eliminate qualifiers of that kind from your discourse. But the very nature of thinking is *but.* Things *are* complicated. It's *and, but, either*—it's all those things. Those are tricks that are the equivalent of lobotomizing people, and I think essentially they're ways for people to become more selfish and egotistic.

I'm assuming that there is a physical basis for disease. Obviously, this wouldn't convince a Christian Scientist who says, "I just don't believe that disease or death is real." Such notions flourish about a particular disease when medicine or science can't give a convincing account of what causes it and, more important, can't furnish effective means of treatment.

Tuberculosis is particularly interesting because its cause was discovered in 1882, but the cure only in 1944. The myths and fantasies about TB—*The Magic Mountain*'s it's-just-love-deferred, or Kafka's it's-really-my-mental-illness-connecting-itself-into-a-physical-thing—started to vanish when almost no one died of TB anymore. And if people discover what causes cancer but don't find the cure for it, then the myths about cancer will go on.

In your book, the TB metaphor gets away with murder, being extremely rich and suggestive. You point out, for instance, that the metaphor's romanticization exemplified the promotion of the self as an image, that the literary and erotic attitudes known as "romantic agony" are derived from it and that it "refined" and made more creative, and even fashionable, those afflicted with the disease. Whereas the cancer metaphor doesn't get away with murder, it is murder.

Cancer really is only a metaphor for evil, but one that has an enormous allure. So often when people talk about what they really hate or fear or want to combat—as if they don't know how to express a sense of evil—a metaphor is the most available and attractive way of expressing a sense of disaster, of what is to be repudiated.

By the way, there's one metaphor that I left out of the book. In the modern period, the things attributed to TB have been split off—the positive, romantic things being assigned to mental illness and all the negative things to cancer. But there is an intermediate metaphor, one that had a career as interesting as that of TB, and that is syphilis, because syphilis did have a positive side. Syphilis was not only something laden with a sense of guilt because of its association with illicit sexual activity and because it was so feared and so highly moralized. It was also attached to mental illness. It is, in a way, the

missing link between TB and what happened in the split: mental
illness on one side and cancer on the other.

In the late-nineteenth and early-twentieth centuries, somebody who
acted very strangely and seemed to have attacks of euphoria was
thought to have syphilis. You get that in Thomas Mann's *Doctor
Faustus*—the idea that syphilis is the price paid to be a genius. It does
take on some of the same qualities once assigned to TB. Syphilis
brings on madness and suffering and eventual death, but between the
beginning and the end, something terrific happens to you. You kind of
explode in your head and are capable of genius. Nietzsche, De
Maupassant—all those people who had syphilis died of it. But they
had those exalted mental states that were part of, or produced, genius.
But, of course, that was as much a result of the fact that they were
geniuses as the fact that they had syphilis.

What about leukemia?

Leukemia is the only part of the cancer metaphor pulling toward
romantic values. It is the one form of cancer—just the most well-
known one—that isn't associated with the tumor. There's no operation you can perform for it. And there's not this idea of mutilation
and amputation that's connected with the fear of cancer.

*You emphasized the romantic function of madness. Yet I think that
during the past few years, this particular notion of madness seems to
have lost a lot of its glamorous cachet.*

Don't you think Laingian ideas are accepted by a lot of people?
That the mad person knows something we don't?

*I suppose it's just that the Seventies "Zeitgeist" tends to be
embarrassed about, or even derogatory toward, a lot of the notions
that flourished a decade ago.*

Let's talk about this decade-mongering, because I feel that there's
something terrible about making the Fifties and Sixties and Seventies
into major constructs. They're myths. Now we have to invent some
new concept for the Eighties, and I'm very curious to find out what
people are going to invent. It's so ideological, this decade talk.

The idea is that everything that was hoped for and attempted in the
Sixties basically hasn't worked and couldn't work out. But who says
it won't work? Who says there's something wrong with people drop-

ping out? I think the world should be safe for marginal people. One of the nice things that happened was that a lot of people chose to be marginal and other people didn't seem to mind. I don't think of myself as marginal in that I don't particularly want to sit on the sidewalk and take drugs, because I'm too restless and I don't want to calm my restlessness. On the contrary, I'd like to have more energy and be more mobile. But part of my efforts is to keep myself marginal—to destroy what I've done or to try something else. As soon as I see one thing is working, I don't want to do that anymore.

We have to allow not only for marginal people and states of consciousness, but also for the unusual or the deviant. I'm all for deviants. There's no reason for people on this planet to live at a subsistence level. Instead of becoming more and more bureaucratic, standardized, oppressive and authoritarian, why don't we allow more and more people to be free?

We want to be free to make new choices: you can't have everything, so you have to make choices. Americans tend to think that everything is possible, and that's something I like a lot about them [*laughing*]. I know I'm *very* American, in that respect, because I like to think I have as many options as possible.

What is essentially different in the Seventies is that there isn't the illusion that a lot of people think the same as you do. I mean, one is restored to one's position as a freelance person, but I don't feel that I've changed what I think. All throughout the Sixties, I was horrified by the antiintellectualism of the movement and of the hippies and of the bright-thinking people that I stood shoulder to shoulder with in various political situations. I couldn't stand how antiintellectual they were. I think people are *still* very antiintellectual.

Someone once told me that you used to read a book a day.

I read an enormous amount and, in large part, quite mindlessly. I love to read the way people love to watch television; I kind of nod out over it. I don't know how intellectual I am. I have these interests, but I also go to CBGB's and do other things like that.

I really believe in history; that's something people don't believe in anymore. I have very few beliefs, but this is certainly one: that most everything we think of as natural is historical and has roots— specifically in the late-eighteenth and early-nineteenth centuries, the so-called Romantic revolutionary period. We're still essentially deal-ing with expectations and feelings formulated at that time. So when I go to a Patti Smith concert, I enjoy, participate, appreciate and am tuned in better because I've read Nietzsche.

How, specifically, do you see Patti Smith's connection to Nietzsche?

In the way she talks, the way she comes on, what she's trying to do, the kind of person she is. That's part of where we are culturally. But where we are culturally has these roots. As I said, the main reason I read is that I enjoy it. There's no incompatibility between observing the world and being tuned into an electronic, multimedia, multitracked, McLuhanite world and enjoying what can be enjoyed about rock & roll. Rock & roll really changed my life.

What rock & roll?

You'll laugh. It was Bill Haley and the Comets. I really had a revelation, and I can't tell you how utterly cut off I was from popular music because, being a child in the Forties, the only things I ever heard were crooners, and I loathed them. And then I heard Johnnie Ray singing "Cry." I heard it on the jukebox and something happened to my skin. Several years later there was Bill Haley, and then I went to England in 1957 as a student and heard some of those early groups, who were influenced by Chuck Berry. It was the beginnings of what would lead to the Beatles.

You know, I think rock & roll is the reason I got divorced. I think it was Bill Haley and the Comets and Chuck Berry [*laughing*] that made me decide that I had to get a divorce and leave the academic world.

At that time, the late Fifties, I lived in a totally intellectual world. I didn't know one single person I could share this with. I didn't talk about it. People say a lot of stupid things about the Fifties, but it is true that there was this total separation between the people who were tuned into the popular culture and those who were involved in high culture. There was nobody I ever met who was interested in both, and I always was.

In your essay on Leni Riefenstahl and the nature of fascist art, you wrote, "Riefenstahl's films express longings whose romantic ideal is expressed in youth/rock culture, primal therapy, Laing's anti-psychol-

*ogy, Third World camp following, and belief in gurus and the occult.''
That covers a lot of territory, and it seems to me that in other contexts
you've been sympathetic to a number of aspects of the romantic ideal.*

It seems to be quite convincing to argue that Buddhism is the
highest spiritual moment of humanity. It seems clear to me that rock
& roll is the greatest movement of popular music that's ever existed.
But it's something else to talk about the way in which interest in
Buddhism occurs in our society. It's one thing to listen to punk rock
as music, and another to understand the whole S&M-necrophilia-
Grand Guignol-*Night of the Living Dead-Texas Chainsaw Massacre*
sensibility that feeds into that. On the one hand, you're talking about
the cultural situation and the impulses people are getting from it, and
on the other, you're talking about what the thing is.

I'm certainly not going to give up on rock & roll. I'm not going to
say that because kids are walking around in their vampire makeup or
wearing swastikas, this music is no good. That's easy to say. No more
do I want to give up on my admiration for Buddhism because of
what's happened to it in California.

Now, I think there is a fascist cultural impulse. A lot of the activities
of the New Left, for example, were very disturbing. It was a thing
one didn't want to say too loudly in public in the late Sixties and early
Seventies, when the principal effort was to stop the American war in
Vietnam. But some of the activities of the New Left were very far
from democratic socialism and were deeply antiintellectual, which I
think of as part of the fascist impulse. They were also anticultural and
full of resentment and brutality, reflecting a kind of nihilism. Of
course, our society is based on nihilism: television is nihilism. I mean,
nihilism isn't some modernist invention of avant-garde artists; it's at
the very heart of our culture.

But, you see, one has to keep on explaining endlessly that this is
not to say that the New Left is fascist, which all kinds of conservatives
and reactionaries are prone to assert now. We're talking about processes, not just objects: it's really the nature of our situation to be
extremely complicated, and you have to keep directing your attention
to what is contradictory and try to sort these things out, try to
purify them.

*In your essay "On Style," you wrote: "To speak of style is one way
of speaking about the totality of art. Like all discourse about totalit-*

*ies, talk of a style must rely on metaphors. And metaphors mislead.''
What is your attitude toward metaphors generally?*

Ever since I began to think, I realized that I could understand things theoretically by seeing their implications *and* the underlying metaphor or paradigm. When, at fourteen or fifteen, I first began to read philosophy, I remember that I'd be struck by the metaphors. And I'd think that if you used another metaphor, it would come out differently.

Metaphors are central to thinking, but it's like a kind of agnosticism: as you use them, you shouldn't believe them; you should know that they're a necessary fiction, or perhaps not a necessary fiction. You can say something is *like* something else, okay, then that's clean, because it's very clear what the differences are. But when you say, for example, that illness *is* a curse, it's a way of stopping your thinking and freezing you into certain attitudes. The intellectual project is inevitably involved with constructing new metaphors, because you have to use them to think, but at least you should be critical and skeptical of the ones you've inherited: unclogging your thought, letting in air, opening things out.

Nietzsche once wrote that truth is only the solidification of old metaphors.

But that's the truth in a very ironic sense. Take the question of women. The truth about women is that the whole system of patriarchal values, or whatever you want to call it, is false and oppressive. The truth is that that is *false*. The basic view is that women are better than children and less than men. They're grown-up children with the charm and attractiveness of children.

Cries and Whispers *is the world women have been assigned to—to use Ingmar Bergman's film title—not that of dialectical thinking.*

In our culture, they've been assigned the world of feeling, because what men are supposed to take care of is action and strength and executive ability and capacity for detachment and all of that, so women are the repositories of feeling and sensitivity. The arts in our society are conceived of as basically feminine activities; certainly they weren't in the past. That's because men didn't define themselves so much in terms of the repression of women.

One of my oldest crusades is against the distinction between thought and feeling . . . which is really the basis of all antiintellectual views:

the heart and the head, thinking and feeling, fantasy and judgment. We have more or less the same bodies, but very different kinds of thoughts. I believe that we think much more with the instruments provided by our culture than we do with our bodies, and hence the much greater diversity of thought in the world. Thinking is a form of feeling; feeling is a form of thinking.

In one of his poems, Baudelaire wrote: "Agile you move, O my mind, and as a strong swimmer/Swoons on the wavy sea, gaily you cleave/The unfathomable vastness with ineffable, male, voluptuous joy." Here, the poet connected thinking and feeling with a specifically "male" type of consciousness and sexuality.

Recently, however, I came across an interview with a French writer named Hélène Cixous, in which, using another swimming image, she said: "To claim that writing doesn't betray sex differences is to regard it simply as a manufactured object. From the moment you admit that it springs from the entire body you have to admit that it transcribes a whole system of impulses, entirely different approaches to emotional expenditure and pleasure. . . . In writing, femininity produces a much greater impression of continuity than masculinity does. It's as though women had the faculty of remaining below the surface, coming up for air only at very rare intervals. So obviously, the result is a text that leaves the reader very winded. But for me, that's completely in accord with feminine sensuality."

Cixous began as professor of English literature at the University of Paris, wrote a book on James Joyce, and now she's thought of as one of the leading women writers in France. Obviously, she considers herself to be a feminist. But I have to say that her statement doesn't make any sense to me. It's a fascinating contrast between Cixous and Baudelaire, but I think those images will yield anything you want them to. Baudelaire, after all, was the person who said that woman is natural, therefore abominable, and who had a very classic kind of nineteenth-century misogyny—the kind you find in Freud, i.e., women are nature and men are culture, as though women are this kind of slime that drags you down, and the spirit is always trying to escape from the flesh.

It's interesting that both of these French authors conceive of writing in terms of sensual experience—one from a misogynist, the other from a feminist, point of view.

I'm very unhappy at the idea of labeling these things in sexual terms, so that, in fact, you'd have to say that Joyce is a feminine writer or working out of a feminine sexuality. I certainly think that there's *some* difference, not a lot, between masculine and feminine sensuality—obviously, a difference that everything in our culture conspires to make even bigger. But I don't see any reason why a woman can't write anything that a man writes, and vice versa.

And if pushed to it, I'd even say writing *is* making objects. I'm comfortable with the analogies Plato and Aristotle used when they compared the poet to the carpenter.

For a certain group of feminist writers and people who talk about these things, Hannah Arendt would be considered a male-identified intellectual: she happens to be a woman, but she's playing the man's game that starts with Plato and Aristotle and continues with Machiavelli and Thomas Hobbes and John Stuart Mill. She's the first woman political philosopher, but her game—its rules, discourse, references—is that of the tradition established with Plato's *Republic*. She never asked herself: "Since I'm a woman, shouldn't I be approaching these questions differently?" And I don't think she should have. If I'm going to play chess, I don't think I should play it differently because I'm a woman.

I think it's very oppressive to be asked to conform to a stereotype, exactly as a black writer might be asked to express only black consciousness. I don't want to be "ghettoized" any more than some black writers I know want to be ghettoized.

Before, however, you said that ill people have an attunement with one another. Also the old. You did talk about male-female polarity as a kind of prison, so why shouldn't a woman, who felt she has been in that prison, wish to align herself with a certain kind of feminism?

I'm not against her doing it, but I would be sorry to see writing start to be sexually segregated.

A feminist response to this might be that you act as if the revolution had already been won.

I don't believe that the revolution has been won, but I think it's useful for women to participate in traditional structures and enterprises, and to demonstrate that they're competent and that they can be airline pilots and bank executives and generals. It's good that women stake out their claims in these occupations. The attempt to set up a separate culture is a way of not seeking power; and as I've said in the past, I don't think the emancipation of women is just a question of having equal rights. It's a question of having equal power, and how are they going to have that unless they participate in the structures that already exist?

I think that women should be proud of and identify with women who do things at a very high level of excellence, and not criticize women for not expressing a feminine sensibility or a feminine sense of sensuality. It would be nice if men would be more feminine and women more masculine. To me, that would be a more attractive world.

When you write, do you feel like a woman, a man or just disembodied?

I find writing very desexualizing, which is one of its limitations. I don't eat, or I eat very irregularly and badly and skip meals; and I try to sleep as little as possible. My back hurts, my fingers hurt, I get headaches. And it even cuts sexual desire. I find that if I'm very interested in someone sexually and then embark on a writing project, there's pretty much a period of abstinence or chastity, because I want all my energy to go into the writing. But that's the kind of writer I am; I'm totally undisciplined, and I just do it in long, obsessional stretches.

I'd like to learn how to write in a way that's less punishing to my body, and I'm beginning to do that. First of all, although I'm not in the same state of medical emergency that I was until recently— according to my doctors, there's considerable optimism now—I still feel fragile, and I still worry about getting in bad shape physically in a way that I didn't before.

I've also thought that changing the way I write would probably be a very good thing for the writing. I try to imagine, for instance, what it would be like to write and feel really comfortable. I tend to write first drafts lying on a bed, stretched out. Then, as soon as I have something to type out, I go to a desk and a wooden chair and from then on it's all at the typewriter. How do you write?

At a desk with a fairly hard chair and lots of things scattered around.

But don't you think you'd write differently all naked, wrapped in velvet?

One thing I've become aware of is that I tend to repress images in my writing. It seems that what was perishable in a lot of writing was precisely its adornment and that the style for eternity was an un-adorned one.

Somebody says: "The road is straight." Okay, then: "The road is straight as a string." There's such a profound part of me that feels that "the road is straight" is all you need to say and all you *should* say.

Don't you think that the nervous system in some way determines one's writing style and that it's not just a matter of changing one's garments?

I think that there are things stronger than the nervous system. My nervous system is certainly different from the way it was twenty years ago, however. I've taken a very modest amount of psychedelic drugs throughout my adult life. Smoking grass—something I've done in a very modest amount—changed my nervous system. For instance, it helped me relax. That's a dumb thing to say, but it's true. I never really relaxed in the way that I do now before I smoked grass, and I smoked grass for the first time when I was about twenty-two. I don't have to smoke grass to relax in that way, but I got in contact with the part of me that could relax. I didn't know you were *supposed* to relax or that it was any good or anything would come of it [*laughing*].

I was a terribly restless child, and I was so irritated with being a child that I was just busy all the time. I was writing up a storm by the time I was eight or nine years old. And when I started to smoke grass, simply the fact that these drugs stupefied you allowed me to know something about what it was like to hibernate a little bit now and then. And that was a lesson that my nervous system learned. But it didn't change my style. That's why I say that things like writing come from something much stronger.

What I'm trying to say is that one writes out of many things. You write out of what you admire. But you can and do exhaust influences. When I was sixteen years old, my passions were Gerard Manley Hopkins and Djuna Barnes, among others. What I want to do is get *away* from whatever I learned from those two writers.

What was the first book that—vocational interest aside—really thrilled you?

The first book was *Madame Curie* by her daughter. I must have
been seven or eight years old when I read it; I was reading when I
was three. The first novel that affected me was *Les Misérables*. I
sobbed and wailed and thought they were the greatest things.

Then much later, when I was about thirteen, it was Mann and Joyce
and Eliot and Kafka and Gide—mostly Europeans. I didn't discover
American literature until much later. I discovered a lot of writers in
the Modern Library editions, which were sold in a Hallmark-card
store, and I used to save up my allowance and would buy them all. I
even bought real lemons like Adam Smith's *The Wealth of Nations*
[*laughing*]. I thought everything in the Modern Library must be great.

*Most people have a very nearsighted and conventional view of
American fiction and poetry and tend to forget about the writings of
Mina Loy, Link Gillespie, Harry Crosby, Paul Goodman and Laura
Riding, for example.*

Well, you've mentioned two people who have been models for me.
Goodman's *Johnson* stories—one of the major accomplishments of
twentieth-century American literature—and Laura Riding's *Progress
of Stories* really set a standard of writing. Almost nobody knows
about this work and nobody's doing anything as good now.

When I started writing in the early Sixties, I was defending the
"modern," particularly in literature, because the prevailing approach
was very philistine. And for about ten years, the views I espoused
became more and more common. But during the past five years, it's
not as if people have gone back to the position they had before; it's
worse. Before, they didn't like this stuff because they were ignorant.
They didn't even know about it. Now they don't like it because they
think they know something about it and feel superior to it. So you
have to defend Schönberg or Joyce or Merce Cunningham.

There's a meanspiritedness regarding high-modern art now that's
so discouraging that I don't even feel like entering the fray in the
essay form. I thought that by the end of the Sixties, the battle had
been won, but it was a very transient victory. You could say that the
reason for this is that people have had enough, that they need to rest
awhile. But I wonder, I wonder: Why should they be allowed to rest?

*Speaking about influential books, I've often thought that, in their
different ways, Mann's* The Magic Mountain *and Svevo's* The Confes-

sions of Zeno *are both about illness and love—almost as if the latter were an ambiguous, graceful and ironic commentary on and antidote to the weight and portentousness of the former. Now, you've just written about illness, but, unlike Stendhal, you haven't yet written about love.*

It takes courage to write about love, because you seem to be writing about yourself and then one feels embarrassed, as if people will know something about you that you don't want them to know. Even if I'm not writing about myself, people will take it that that's what I'm doing, so I'm shy about it. But I've been taking notes on an essay on love for many years. It's an old, old passion.

It's interesting that you mention shyness, since you seem much more open verbally than you used to be. When I reread your essay "Trip to Hanoi," I came across the lines: "I long for someone to be indiscreet here, to talk about his personal life, his emotions. To be carried away by 'feeling.' " And in the second part of the essay you begin to comprehend North Vietnam as if it were a previously opaque work of art that had now become transparent to you. And you understood it better as a work of art.

The reason why I waited until the second part of the essay to write what I did was that I felt it was important to acknowledge that the Vietnamese are different from us. I don't like this liberal family-of-man idea that we're really all the same. I think there really are cultural differences, and it's very important to be sensitive to those things. It seemed like learning a kind of respect for the world. The world is complicated; it can't all be reduced to the way you think it should be.

You mentioned in the essay that you had just recently visited Cuba, and the Cubans were much more like us—manic, intimate, talkative—and that the Vietnamese were much more formal, measured and controlled. To me, it seemed as if you were describing the difference between a film by, say, Pagnol or Renoir and one by Bresson. If these two societies were movies, you would probably have accepted both immediately.

Absolutely right, you're on to something that's very essential to me. Of *course*, I'm much more provincial in my life than in the way I understand what is represented as art. I really do like intimacy—intimacy of a Jewish kind, to put it in a code way. I like people who talk a lot, who talk about themselves, who are warm and physically demonstrative.

I don't have to live in a Bresson or a Pagnol film, and I do have to live in my life. When I'm thinking about films or anything else, I'm thinking about the world, and then I'm perfectly comfortable with the idea that there should be some people doing it like this and other people doing it like that.

When you think about love as a subject, and also a feeling, do you do so in the open way you appreciate films, or the reticent and slightly more narrow way you say you live your life?

The real change for me was that Vietnam essay, because that's the first time I ever wrote about myself at *all*—even though very timidly— and I did it as a conscious sacrifice. I thought, I don't want to write about myself, I just want to write about *them*. But when I realized that the best way that *I* could write about them *was* to include myself, then it was like a sacrifice. And it changed me. I realized I could have a certain freedom as a writer, which I never thought I even wanted, and I have gingerly begun to explore that freedom in some of my stories that are autobiographical.

Writing about the immolation of Norman Morrison, you suggest that the Vietnamese viewed it, not in terms of practical efficacy, but in terms of the "moral success of his deed, its completeness as an act of self-transcendence." Strangely, that's what you were writing about in your essay on the aesthetics of silence, and I felt that in your Vietnam essay, art and life were somehow coming together a bit.

Well, I think they are. And in my illness book, they come together in a certain way because it's a product of a very passionate experience. The place where I hope they come together most is in my fiction. And when I had to proofread the stories from *I, etcetera*, I was struck by the fact that they seemed to me as a *reader*, not as the writer of them, to have a theme in common—which is the search for self-transcendence, the enterprise of trying to become a different or a better or a nobler or a more moral person.

I'd like to get back to your stories later. But to return to the idea of reticence versus openness. . . .

It's so complicated because I do have—and I don't know whether it's any good as an idea—but I do have in my head an idea about

being a child and being an adult. I turn those notions around and
around, and sometimes I think, there's no difference, this is a completely artificial distinction. We shouldn't try to impose any idea about
what we should do that depends on whether we feel something is
childlike or adultlike. And I have fantasies about childhood—not the
childhood that I personally had but the values represented in the
child's innocence and vulnerability and sensitivity to things, and I
think, how terrible that we don't preserve those qualities as adults.

So I have all these notions, along with completely contradictory
ones that I'm always wrestling with. In fact, just this morning, when I
was at the hospital, a friend came with me and somehow our conversation, while I was waiting to be seen by the doctor, turned precisely on
this theme. I was saying, "Well, I'm an adult. I should behave like
this." And my idea of adult behavior, in *that* context, was that I
should be independent and shouldn't be afraid. So adulthood represented very positive values—nothing like the romantic loss of imagination or the sense of drying up or petrifying.

I'm trying to say that I think our ideas of love are terribly bound up
in our ambivalence about these two conditions—childhood and adulthood. And, I think that, for many people, love signifies a return to
values that are represented by childhood. I mean, love is sensuality
and play and irresponsibility and hedonism and being silly, and it gets
to be thought of in terms of dependence and becoming weaker and
getting into some kind of emotional slavery and treating the loved one
as some kind of parent figure or sibling. You reproduce a part of what
you were as a child when you weren't free and were completely
dependent on your parents.

We ask everything of love. We ask it to be anarchic. We ask it to be
the glue that holds the family together, that allows society to be
orderly and allows all kinds of material processes to be transmitted
from one generation to another.

Why do people want to be in love? That's really interesting. Partly,
they want to be in love the way you want to go on a roller coaster
again—even knowing you're going to have your heart broken. What
fascinates me about love is what it has to do with all the cultural
expectations and the values that have been put into it.

I've always been amazed by the people who say, "I fell in love and
I had this affair." And then a lot of stuff is described and you ask,

"How long did it last?" And the person will then say, "A week."
I've never been in love for less than a couple of years. I've been in
love very few times in my life, but whenever I've been in love, it's
something that's gone on and on and ended up—usually, of course—in
some disaster. But I don't know what it means to be in love for a week.

When I say I've been in love, that means that I've actually had a
whole life with that person: we've lived together, we've been lovers,
we've traveled, we've done things. I've never been in love with
anybody I haven't slept with, but I know lots of people who say
they've been in love with someone they haven't slept with. To me,
what they're saying is: "I was attracted to somebody, I had a fantasy,
and in a week the fantasy was over." But I know I'm wrong, because
it's just a limit on my own imagination.

What about platonic love?
Of course, I have loved people passionately whom I wouldn't have
slept with for anything, but I think that's something else. That's
friendship-love, which can be a tremendously passionate emotion, but
it certainly doesn't mean you want to take off your clothes with
that person.

Certain friendships can be erotic.
Oh, I think friendship is very erotic, but it isn't necessarily sexual.
I think all my relationships are erotic: I can't imagine being fond of
somebody I don't want to touch or hug, so therefore there's always
an erotic aspect to some extent. But, I don't know, maybe I'm again
speaking out of my own sexuality, but I'm not attracted to that
many people.

What about Stendhal's notion of love?
I'm fascinated by *Love,* because it's one of the few books that we
have on the subject, but I think he was so much involved with who
people were . . . you know, this *was* the countess of such and such
and here she was in her clothes and there she was in her drawing
room and there she was with her husband and there with the ambassador, etcetera. Don't you feel you're turned on by people who are
famous?

*Not really, because I'm more attracted to people who are childlike,
and anyone can be like that.*

A famous person is always eager to tell you how he or she is really a vulnerable little child, haven't you noticed [*laughing*]? They're so tired of being treated as formidable that they'll tell you quicker than anybody else.

You don't do that, and you're certainly formidable.

Yes, I do. But we don't know each other in that way. With people I want to get close to, I immediately try to explain that I'm just like a child. One does want to stop talking sometimes, and if you're well known, people expect you to be performing or talking all the time or displaying your personality. I meet a lot of people who know who I am before I know who they are. So if a person interests me as a friend or lover or companion or pal, I want to introduce them to a creatural, silent person whom that other person doesn't feel nervous about. I like the silence that's transparent so that another person can see behind it.

I also don't want to do the thing that I notice some people do— particularly smart people—and this is just to completely split off, so that they say, "Well, don't pay any attention to these books I write . . . it's just little me." I would rather talk about what interests me.

Paul Goodman used to write about boys he was attracted to who weren't interested in his concerns at all.

I wish I could feel that . . . but there's that famous problem of breakfast.

What problem is that?

The problem about what you do the next morning. What do you talk about? I mean, here you have this revelation: you've spent the night with somebody, you're having breakfast together, and you realize that this person is only interesting to you sexually and that neither of you has anything in common. What do you do?

I try to avoid those kinds of nights and mornings.

As a man, you've been told that that's part of male sexuality, that it's okay to have a relationship that is purely sexual. But women aren't told that. If I find myself at breakfast with an idiot, I feel embarrassed. I feel—and that's part of the feminine condition—that I've been exploitative. And then I feel, "Well, men do that with

women and they don't feel embarrassed.'' But I do; I feel as if I'm
slumming. Male sexuality has been *built* on slumming.

I think that women, culturally, exercise an inhibiting force on men
sexually. No heterosexual man can be as promiscuous as a homosexual man, because he still has to deal with women, who demand a little
more than just two and a half minutes someplace.

They might even want breakfast in the morning [laughing].

They might even want breakfast in the morning. . . . I have a
homosexual friend who said to me: ''I feel I've repressed my hetero-
sexuality, but I'm so afraid that if I'd start being with women, I
wouldn't have as much sex.'' Sex is a habit like anything else, and
you can get used to a certain quantity of absolutely impersonal, easily
procurable sex that lasts two and a half minutes.

I think the sexual impulse is infinitely malleable. It seems unlikely
that people don't go through periods of general withdrawal from and
resurgence of sexual feeling. That incessant pursuit isn't about sex,
it's about power.

So sex becomes a kind of metaphor.

It becomes terribly loaded. There seems to be a real connection
between sex and cruelty. Think of all the ways in which sex is fed by
the impulse to be powerful. And it sometimes seems to be a culturally
sanctioned way of combating feelings of insecurity, unworthiness or
unattractiveness.

*One family therapist stated that there are either symmetrical or
complementary relationships—the marriage of true minds or the
marriage of dependency, so to speak.*

By those standards, there must be one percent of one percent of
one percent of symmetrical relationships in the world. All these ideas
that we have about the family and love and relationships are only a
couple hundred years old. You know, people have this terrible metaphor about a relationship *working*—as if a relationship is a machine.
We're filled with this imagery and these sorts of expectations. I mean,
do family therapists talk about the built-in inequalities that are orches-
trated by the culture concerning male and female and older and
younger persons? What does it mean to have an equal relationship
between a man and a woman in this society? Most people would be

satisfied with something that is not equal at all. You talked about "the marriage of true minds," but one mind is staying home while the other mind is going to the office.

What about women who are in between that? What about yourself?
I was lucky enough to have a child and be married when I was very young. I did it and now I don't have to do it anymore. But that's not an example. I chose not to be married anymore, and then I already had a child, so I wasn't going to miss out on this great experience of being a mother, and then I decided to live a freelance life, which has a lot of insecurities and unpleasantness and anxiety and frustration.

Was this a conscious choice?
No, but I did have the idea that I'd like to have several lives, and it's very hard to have several lives and then have a husband—at least the kind of marriage that I had, which was incredibly intense; we were together all the time. And you can't live with someone on a twenty-four-hour-a-day basis, never be separated for years and years and have the same freedom to grow and change and fly off to Hong Kong if you feel like it . . . it's irresponsible. That's why I say that somewhere along the line, one has to choose between the Life and the Project.

You're a well-known writer, but you seem to have avoided becoming a "media" celebrity.
There's a story about Cocteau going to see Proust, who was already working in his cork-lined room. Cocteau brought him some of his early work, and Proust said: "You clearly could be a great writer, but you must be careful about society. You mustn't go out, or go out a little, but don't make it a main part of your life." I'm not saying that one has to be in a cork-lined room, but I think that one has to have enormous discipline. And the vocation of a writer, like that of a painter, is in some deep way antisocial.

Coming back to what you said before, however, I don't think sexuality is a metaphor, but an activity that has been invested with all of these spiritual values. There hardly seems to be anything that is *purely* sexual: it's overloaded with other forms of affirmation and destruction that you are declaring when you engage in a sexual act. We've been instructed that it's the central or only natural activity of our lives. That's nonsense. I mean, it's very hard to imagine what natural sexuality could be. I don't think it's available to any of us.

Sexuality is a much bigger, more anarchic thing than one imagines, and that's why, throughout human history, it's been the subject of so much regulation. I don't think people understand why there's been this problem of repression. I would turn it around and say that the reason most societies have been repressive about sexuality is that people *have understood* that it can get out of control and can be completely destructive.

Four months after we started this interview, I called you in New York to ask when we could complete it, and you said, "We should do it soon because I may change too much." That surprised me.

Why? It seems so natural [*laughing*]. I feel I'm changing all the time, and that's something that's hard to explain to people, because a writer is supposed to be either engaging in self-expression or else doing work to convince or change people along the lines of his or her views. And I don't feel that either of those models makes much sense for me. I mean, I write partly in *order* to change myself; it's an instrument I use.

In your story "Debriefing," you talk about the desire to "change your feelings altogether, like getting your blood pumped out and replaced." And in "Old Complaints Revisited," the protagonist says: "You can't become other than what you are. Only more or less what you are. You can't walk over your own feet." Throughout I, etcetera, characters are trying to become someone else, someone "other."

Yes, but not in the sense of a specific other or of the "opposite," but rather in the sense of changing your life, of waking up. I hate the feeling that I'm just executing what I already know or have already imagined. I like to *not* know where I'm going, and at the same time to be quite a way down the road. I don't like to be at the beginning, but I don't like to see the end, either.

You like to be in the middle.

Yes, I always feel I'm in the middle, more toward the beginning than the end. I always have the impression that the work is apprentice work, and that if I can just finish it, then afterward I'll really do something good.

*Bach said that when he was performing with a group of instrumen-
talists, he preferred playing the alto or tenor parts because he could
listen to the more individualized soprano and bass lines. So by being
in the middle, he could really hear what was going on around him.*

That's so interesting about Bach. I think it's wonderful. There's an
active notion of neutrality that people don't understand. Transcendent
neutrality isn't an attitude of "I won't take sides," it's compassion.
Where you do see more than just what separates people or sides.

*In your story "Project for a Trip to China," you wrote: "Travel as
accumulation. The colonialism of the soul, any soul, however well-
intentioned." And in another story, "Unguided Tour," we read: "I
don't want to know more than I know, don't want to get more
attached to [famous places] than I already am." In your essay "The
Aesthetics of Silence," you said that "efficacious art work leaves
silence in its wake." And in another essay, "Against Interpretation,"
you wrote: "To interpret is to impoverish, to deplete the world—in
order to set up a shadow world of 'meanings.' It is to turn the world
into this world. . . . The world, our world, is depleted, impoverished
enough. Away with all duplicates of it, until we again experience
more immediately what we have."*

I didn't know this, I must tell you. I had no idea that I'd been
saying the same thing since I started writing. It's amazing, but I
almost don't want to think about it too much because something might
happen to the material in my head. Most of what I do is so intuitive
and unpremeditated and not at all that kind of cerebral, calculating
thing that people imagine it to be. See, I've always thought of the
essays and the fiction as dealing with very different themes, and I've
been irritated by carrying what I thought to be a double burden of two
very different kinds of activity. It's only quite recently, because it's
been forced on my attention, that I realized the extent to which the
essays and the fiction share the same themes, make the same kinds of
assertions or nonassertions. It's almost frightening to me to discover
how unified they are.

*Film critic André Bazin believed photography could strip from the
world "that spiritual dust and grime with which our eyes have
covered it."*

Sure, I talk about that in the fourth essay of *On Photography*—the notion that photography gives you new eyes, cleanses your vision.

And this connects with the idea of disburdening oneself.

I think that the idea of various notions of disburdenment is probably central to my work, beginning with my novel *The Benefactor*. I mean, what is it but an ironic, comic story about a kind of Candide who, instead of looking for the best of all possible worlds, searches for some clear state of consciousness, for a way in which he could be properly disburdened. It's there also in those half-comic, half-straight reflections of this eccentric narrator. And I notice now that there are things about photography, too, in *The Benefactor*.

In On Photography, *you use certain verbs over and over in referring to photography, among them: to package, to appropriate, to aggress, to patronize, to imprison, to consume, to collect, to colonialize.*

But a lot of other words too: *fascinate, haunt, entrance, inspire, delight.* The word *aggression,* which a lot of people have picked on . . . for me to say that something is aggressive is, in and of itself, not a bad thing. I thought that was understood, but now I realize this is a word that, quite hypocritically, people have made very pejorative. I say *hypocritically* because this society is involved in colossal aggressions against nature, against all sorts of orders of being. I mean, to live is an aggression. I think there are particular heightenings of a certain kind of characteristically modern form of aggressiveness that are represented in the use of the camera, as when you go up to someone and say "stand still" and you take that person's picture. They see something and they want to take it home; they collect the world. But I don't want to be understood as suggesting that it's photography that *introduced* appropriation, collecting and aggressiveness, or that without it there would be none of these things in the world.

Look, I love photographs. I don't take them but I love them, I collect them. I'm fascinated by them . . . it's an old and very passionate interest. But I got interested in writing about photography because I saw that it was a central activity; it reflected all the complexities and contradictions and equivocations of this society.

In "Old Complaints Revisited," the narrator-protagonist is purposely never defined as being either male or female. In a recent

interview, I. B. Singer says: "If you are going to write, let's say, a
cosmopolitan novel and write just about a human being, you will
never succeed. Because there isn't such a thing as 'just a human
being.' " Your story, however, seems to disprove Singer's statement.

"Old Complaints Revisited" plays with the notion that it isn't so
important to be specific because the real specificity lies in the use of
multiple references. In the same way, my story "Baby" plays with
the notion that you can have a first-person-plural narrator, and it
doesn't matter which is the mother and which is the father talking to
the psychiatrist, because they talk as one. They're Siamese-twin
parents.

What I really would have liked, of course—but grammar locks you
into these stereotypes—would have been to refer to the child as "it"
instead of "he."

I remember that when David was born, my husband and I used to
say, "The baby, how's the baby?" Because it wasn't "David" yet. I
don't know whether it's during the third or fourth or sixth month, or
maybe when the baby begins to use language, that it becomes appropriate to use the name. But since I decided that the child in my story
was supposed to be the child at all ages—babyhood, adolescence,
early adulthood—I couldn't say "it." It would have been too odd,
and I had to choose. So I made it a "he," but I hated doing so.

"Baby" is one of my more autobiographical stories, and it draws
on incidents from my own childhood, from my son's childhood, and
the rest is made up. So I could play both the victimized child and the
monster parent. I think I've been a good parent, but I know that
parents are also monsters and are experienced correctly by their
children that way. They're so much bigger; when you're a small child,
your parents are giants! So I had to face up to all those complicated
feelings in a nonsimplified way: my feeling of victimization as a child,
which every child understands, and my also having been a parent.
And then just let those feelings run.

In "Project for a Trip to China," you talk of your own "desert
childhood."

I had a completely rootless childhood. In fact, I lived in many
different places when I was a child. There was one place, however,
that made the greatest impression on me, and that was southern

Arizona. That's *imaginatively* my childhood. The rest of my so-called
childhood was spent in L.A. I went to North Hollywood High School.

*There are all these geographical oppositions that people set up,
between California and New York, between Northern and Southern
California, between New York and Paris.*
But I like that. I like living in two places at once. New York and
Paris. That's the way I've tried to lead my life during the past ten
years, ever since I've had the freedom to.

But you seem to have an affinity with French life and culture.
Sure I do. I did. That's how I ended up there to begin with. I had
an imaginary France in my head that consisted of Valéry and Flaubert
and Baudelaire and Gide. I knew that that was the past, but I liked
being on the site, in that beautiful architecture where these things had
happened, and hearing that language.
People think that I'm a New Yorker, but I only arrived here when I
was twenty-six . . . and I came very much in the spirit of Masha finally
getting to Moscow. I'd always wanted to live in New York and I found
that finally I was going to get to do it. I'm a New Yorker by choice,
by election. In terms of this moral geography we're talking about, I,
as I said, prefer New York . . . with, let's say, access to the
Mediterranean or to California. I couldn't live twelve months or even
ten months a year in New York. This is a totally artificial life. But so
what? You have to create your own space which has a lot of silence in
it and a lot of books.

*This discussion reminds me of the cliché that culture is a function
of geography.*
People define themselves to an amazing degree by their ideas of
place. I met a woman recently in Indiana—a very interesting, intelli-
gent woman who's lived there for many years—and she decided finally
to move east. And she said: "Well, I think the right city for me would
be Boston. It's *east,* and it's got a lot of *things,* it's close to Europe,
and New York would be too much."
This is totally on the level of myth. She defines herself as a woman
who can make the move from Indiana to Boston, but not from Indiana
to Manhattan because that's a much *bigger* move. In fact, it's not.

But I know what she means.

But it's based on a myth, a myth that's so alive.

But you yourself, feeling drawn to California and New York, still prefer one over the other and are therefore involved with that myth.

Yes, but I'm involved in it perhaps to a second degree. When I say that I like to live in New York, I mean that I like to live in a place where people have chosen to be. It's a world capital and the cultural capital of the country. For better or worse, it is. There are more people here doing things than in any other single place.

When I first came to New York, I must tell you that I did feel that New Yorkers were all short, rude, mean. I was very used to Western friendliness, hospitality, kindness. The way I talk, moreover, the way I smile a lot, is very Californian. The way I'm not defensive or guarded or suspicious of people.

Yet in "Project for a Trip to China," you wrote: "Somewhere, some place inside myself, I am detached."

I don't identify completely with the voices in the story, but it's true I've been hiding out at different times in my life, fearful of the world because people were going to tell me to stop doing what I was doing with my work. And I didn't want to hear that. I didn't even want to be bothered by those cues. Many people ask me, particularly women: "How come you didn't get discouraged?" And I feel that I never did because I never listened to that message. But in order not to hear it, I certainly must have had my hearing apparatus turned off in some way. So if detached, detached only in the sense that I instinctively protected myself against things that could have discouraged me.

In "Unguided Tour," you wrote: "How far from the beginning are we? When did we first start to feel the wound? . . . This staunchless wound, the great longing for another place. To make this place another." This suggests, in microcosm, a lot of what we've been talking about.

That's why that story is the end of *I, etcetera.*

But I want to connect it to the beginning of that book. In the first story you wrote: "To be good one must be simpler. Simpler, as in a return to origins." The Austrian critic Karl Kraus wrote "Origin is our goal." Is it yours?

I don't want to return to my origins. I think my origins are just a starting point. My sense of things is that I've come very far. And it's the distance I have from my origins that pleases me. That's because I have this rootless childhood and an extremely fragmented family. I don't have anything to go back to. I can't imagine what I'd find.

I think of myself as self-created—that's my working illusion. I never was anybody's disciple or protégé; it wasn't because I was some-body's lover or wife or daughter that I "made my career." I don't think it's awful to accept help. If you can get help, fine. But I like the fact that I did it myself. It excited me.

In fact, I have a persistent fantasy of stopping writing, disappearing, and then starting all over again under a pseudonym, who no one would know was Susan Sontag. It would be wonderful to start again and not have the burden of the work that's already done. I think I'd probably do things a little differently . . . and maybe not. Maybe I'm kidding myself. Maybe if I'd publish something under the name of . . . whatever, everyone would roar with laughter and say that's obviously Susan Sontag, because I can't write in any way that would not be easily recognizable. But I just want to say that my notion is very much that of going further and further, of new beginnings and of *not* going back to origins.

As You Desire It

Leonardo Sciascia / 1979

From *L'Espresso* (July 1979), pp. 67–68, 71, 73. Introduction by
Rita Cirio. Translated from the Italian by Kathy S. Leonard.
Copyright *L'Espresso* 1979. Reprinted by permission of *L'Es-
presso* and the Leonardo Sciascia Estate.

The American writer and essayist Susan Sontag will stage *As You
Desire Me* in Italy. We had her meet with an expert, Leonardo
Sciascia. Two rather diverse Pirandellos came out between them. Not
a little Pirandellian. Rome. At the table, accompanied by the sonorous
soundtrack of concrete music, the banging of plates, and a clinking of
glasses, together with us, is the Invisible Presence. It's Pirandello,
whom Susan Sontag will bring to the stage in October in *As You
Desire Me,* presented by the Theater Company of Turin, with Adriana
Asti playing the lead. As if for this reason, Sciascia arrives on the
very morning of the announcement of the Pirandello prize.

They have never before met. Susan Sontag displays her pleasure at
the meeting with sincere and playful American pragmatism. "I'm very
happy to meet you because I'm sure you will become the president of
the Republic in six years. And it's never a bad idea to have met the
future president." Leonardo Sciascia defends himself. "No, no, my
experience as a politician resulted from a sudden decision, and it
won't go beyond that for the two and a half years in which the radical
parliamentary deputies remain in office." The dialogue progresses as
they discuss what a rarity a political career is for a writer: Sontag
remembers South American writers employed as diplomats, Sciascia
thinks about Zola "who potentially could have been a member of
Parliament." He then lists the large and small privileges of the
members of Parliament—the price of coffee, the barbershops, the
theater, free transportation—specifying, however, an attitude just the
opposite of the radicals'. "There's even a women's hairdresser that's
free. The honorable radicals have just now discovered it: It was
Macciocchi who revealed it to them."

What follows is a conversation made up of advice, doubts, digres-

137

sions dealing with Pirandello, but also a conversation about the writer's craft.

Sciascia: This morning I reread the play. I hadn't read it for ten years. Today's reading is very different from that of the past. Ten years ago the central problem was one of identity. Today it seems to me that the problem is about women's identity.

Sontag: It's not the case that a woman is the protagonist. It's not Henry IV in search of his own identity. Ignota is not simply someone who might be insane or who has lost her identity. She's a woman, a woman whom everyone wants to possess.

Sciascia: You've seen the film version of *As You Desire Me*, with Greta Garbo and Erich von Stroheim? I saw it before the war.

Sontag: It's a Hollywoodish film that I saw four years ago. Pirandello had gone to Hollywood and one presumes that he also worked on the script. But the film reproduces an image of Pirandello which is completely outdated. It's almost comical; Garbo recites as if she were Zizi Jeanmarie, the great movie star.

Sciascia: It's curious because, until you read the first lines of the play, you think only about Marlene Dietrich and not about Garbo. Is it presented on the stage frequently in America?

Sontag: Pirandello is the only well-known playwright of the modern Italian theater in the United States. He quickly became a classic. In the 30s his plays were already seen as classics. He's a modern classic; many people would be surprised to discover that some of his plays were already written by the 30s. He is considered a great European playwright, in a kind of sacred dynasty where he joins Ibsen, Chekhov, Shaw.

Sciascia: How do you plan to stage it?

Sontag: I ask myself the same thing. I want to respect the text because I'm not interested in doing a fantasy "of" Pirandello in the style of Carmelo Bene. I want to follow the text because out of it comes a kind of madness of language; all the characters talk continuously, there's a kind of verbal hysteria.

Sciascia: Sometimes it seems as if it wants to arrive directly at poetry, poetry in verse.

Sontag: There are also some political temptations. It's the only

Pirandello play set abroad, not just in any foreign country, but
in Berlin.

Sciascia: In the post-war period it was staged anachronistically, with
many references to Hitler and Mussolini.

Sontag: The first idea that comes to mind is that of a political piece,
but it's so evident that it's necessary to reject that idea. One can well
imagine, for example, the three men who arrive at the beginning
wearing swastikas on their arms. But this would be too Visconti. Tell
me, was there a reaction against Pirandello after the war because of
his connection to fascism?

Sciascia: Of course, and I believe that the idea of Pirandello as a
fascist remains today. He supported fascism, but his work is in no
way fascist. That's important.

Sontag: And is there still a conscious or unconscious resistance to
his work?

Sciascia: In Italy there's an unconscious resistance toward real
writers. Once they die, one tries to bury them for good. No one wants
to talk about Pirandello anymore; they want to put a gravestone on
top of him. His works are presented frequently in Italy because they
are presented frequently abroad. In short, his works are brought to
the stage automatically, because they can't be ignored.

Sontag: Why? Because he's still thought of as a fascist author or
because he's considered out of fashion?

Sciascia: The label of fascism can function as an alibi, because of
the need to forget about it. This touched Pirandello during his lifetime,
also. Even then, without foreigners, he would have remained nailed
down by the sharp criticism of Croce. Renato Serra, who was a very
fine critic, placed him in a category with Renato Zuccoli; that can't
be forgotten. Among Italian critics, he was supported only by Adriano
Tilgher. Gramsci was interested only in a certain Pirandello, the
sociological and regional one, the Pirandello of *Liolà;* that could be a
good formula for understanding him, but it limits him very much.

Sontag: And Croce?

Sciascia: Croce put him down. He used to say: Pirandello is a half-
philosopher, therefore he's not a writer. He thought he was a type of
amateur philosopher, unsuccessful, therefore he couldn't be taken
seriously as a philosopher and even less as a writer, since he made
use of a half philosophy.

Sontag: We Americans never search for a writer's philosophy. That's a very European approach.

Sciascia: Now, is there a political point of view in the production that you are about to present?

Sontag: I am tempted to do something very abstract and "excessive" at the same time. I want to allow myself to be transported by emotion, by melodrama; it's not necessary to restrain these things. But at the same time, it's important to render them as abstract, stylized, and not realistically. I have the impression that Pirandello had a very simple idea of these characters and I ask myself if by chance he wasn't influenced by Wedekind's *Lulu,* written four years before, because the character of Ignota is exactly that of a divorced woman. Everyone is in love with her and no one can possess her; she destroys everyone. It's as if the author had begun to delineate a character who is completely different from his usual ones, and little by little he transforms the character into one of his own.

Sciascia: In fact, rereading *As You Desire Me,* I immediately thought about *The Blue Angel,* about Dietrich, and not about Garbo.

Sontag: I believe that this cliché of the lost woman of the 20s in Berlin should be treated with distance, with irony. If I had done this production ten years ago, I would still have been able to believe in it, but now, after Visconti. . . . Even the character of Mop, the daughter, resembles the Countess Geschwitz, the woman who is in love with Lulu, who is rejected by her and sacrifices herself for her. Mop is a kind of Geschwitz in miniature, aborted. Pirandello departs from these stereotypes but then goes very far and arrives at the second part, a story of money, property, and inheritance, which would be inconceivable in Lulu's world. Here Pirandello becomes practically like Brecht.

Sciascia: It's a very complex work, full of criticism, self criticism. What most attracted you to it?

Sontag: Because everyone is so unhappy. It's a play about desperation, about the desperation of a particular woman. The stereotype of identity that American critics have always applied against Pirandello is, here, no longer true, it's superficial. Here is madness, then, but not in the sense of Artaud. The characters become insane due to some cause, for some reason.

Sciascia: But in Pirandello, madness applies to everyone. Therefore, it's the norm.

Sontag: It seems to me, however, that the idea of madness as the norm is more an idea of our era than of Pirandello's. Yes, for him the madness is everywhere, but it always surfaces for some reason, sex, injustice, cruelty.

Sciascia: There's a different reason for everyone. But everyone ends up there, in this equality of madness.

Sontag: Do you believe that Ignota is truly Piero's wife, or not?

Sciascia: I don't think that even Pirandello knows that. I remember seeing *Right You Are, If You Think You Are* for the first time, when I was a boy in Racalmuto, presented by a traveling company, the D'Origlia-Palmi company. The next day the whole country was betting on who the insane person was. They weren't satisfied with the play; they believed that it should continue and that there was someone besides the author who knew but didn't want to tell.

Sontag: How do you explain that Pirandello became a fascist? I'm familiar with his speech of 1935, which is so in favor of Mussolini, with all the classical themes of fascist ideology. Was it truly his way of thinking or did he let himself go because he was old and there were pressures? In short, was he really converted?

Sciascia: I think the reasons were autobiographical (everything is found in the novel *The Old and the Young*). Pirandello was absolutely anti-parliamentarian and his anti-parliamentarianism had a connection with fascism, which was anti-parliamentarian. I don't believe that he was truly a fascist. In 1935, it's true, he gave that speech, but in 1934 he wrote the short story "There's Someone Who's Laughing," which is very antifascist: That someone is laughing at fascism. He was a very contradictory personality. The telegram expressing solidarity that he sent to Mussolini after the Matteotti incident was due to the influence of Sicilians, I think. Let me explain myself. It seems that at that moment fascism was collapsing and he was inscribed in fascism. He wanted to show that he wasn't afraid to proclaim that he was a fascist in a time of danger. In spite of his personal obstinacy and resentment, he wasn't really fascist. I clearly distinguish between the man and his work. He seems to me to have been the least fascist writer that there could have been in Italy during those years. Nevertheless, he played the fascist. A contradiction.

Sontag: My question was about him as a human being; his 1935 speech was so stereotypical that it seems like it was written by someone else.

Sciascia: I believe he may have adapted what he said about fascism to what everyone was saying.

Sontag: There were times in my life when I felt great resistance to the Vietnam War. Everyone was making speeches. I believed that you could preserve a certain personal style and yet continue to say what needed to be said. But little by little I became aware that clichés about the war were surfacing, and although they were clichés, they were also true, and I also began to believe them.

Sciascia: Fascist rhetoric was so common that we all made use of it. When you wanted to talk, you had at your disposal a ready-made linguistic repertoire.

Sontag: What's funny is that, in his 1935 address, Pirandello speaks in favor of a theater for the people and against a theater for the elite. Yet the theater he created is a bourgeois theater. It's as if he renounced his own work.

Sciascia: The fascist dictatorship was like that. A little bit like what also happens today; there's this duplicity, this double language, you say one thing and do another. Today, for example, if you read books enough, you discover that certain authors who are believed to be left-wing aren't. Returning to fascism, those were not happy times. The only one who enjoyed himself during fascism was D'Annunzio.

Sontag: And he was an awful writer. What's interesting about him is his life, not his work, or better yet, his work through his life. His works are like furniture, like beautiful furniture. But political language is an enormous danger for a writer. There are also those who say, like the Russian writers, that to use political language means to commit suicide.

Sciascia: For D'Annunzio it's somewhat the opposite. D'Annunzio used political language and he didn't commit suicide completely. He continued to enjoy himself.

Sontag: Nevertheless, a writer always plays politics, even when he doesn't need to. He plays politics with what he writes—and above all—with what he does *not* write.

Sciascia: The important thing is to do politics impolitically.

An Emigrant of Thought

Jean-Louis Servan-Schreiber / 1979

As transcribed from the "Questionnaire" television program broadcast on TF1 December 13, 1979. Translated from the French by Clyde Thogmartin. Reprinted by permission of Jean-Louis Servan-Schreiber.

J.-L. Servan-Schreiber: Americans, who are very fond of classifying things, asked their intellectuals a few years ago to designate the best among them. The winner is with us this evening: Her name is Susan Sontag. In fact, her audience goes far beyond the borders of the United States since she writes in Paris as well as in New York, has made films in Sweden, has directed Pirandello on the stage in Italy and speaks five languages, one of which, luckily enough, is ours. Even if she has become, in her own words, an emigrant of thought, the eclecticism of her interests is in the tradition of American curiosity. Of her two books most recently published in France, one is about cancer and the other is about photography. She has been involved in all of the conflicts of intellectuals in her country—Vietnam, feminism—but being more individualistic than is customary in Paris, she does not belong to any movement; that is perhaps why she seems to be more and more modern. Susan Sontag, being modern seems to be at the heart of your search; how is it important?

S. Sontag: I think that one must understand what one is. We are all necessarily modern. That is to say, to be modern is to inherit the problems of our civilization, which are extremely complex problems, and, in part of my work, I try to think about the paradoxes of the modern condition. That is to say, to be modern, for me, is not a choice: The choice is between understanding and not understanding. Personally, I prefer to try to understand.

J.-L. Servan-Schreiber: But, for example, is the aesthetic and, to a certain extent, intellectual fashion for nostalgia something to avoid at any price, because it isn't an effort toward the modern, or is it part of being modern?

S. Sontag: No. I don't think modernity has any value in itself. The taste for nostalgia is a phenomenon of modernity. That is to say, one of the aspects of a modern consciousness is nostalgia; it's the feeling of having lost something of the past and it's a continual recycling of the past as a consumer commodity. There's no contradiction. For me, the nostalgia phenomenon is a phenomenon of modern consciousness.

J.-L. Servan-Schreiber: But isn't a recycling of the past a constant aspect of evolution? In the 19th century the recycling of the past was done not to make consumer products but to make cultural products. Finally, it's a constant process.

S. Sontag: Personally I think that modernity began in the 19th century. In fact, it is people like Rimbaud, like Baudelaire, who were the first to understand this phenomenon that began in the 19th century. Obviously, there is now a magnitude to the activity of recycling that Baudelaire and Rimbaud would never have imagined.

J.-L. Servan-Schreiber: You have the advantage of living in a way that is almost bi-cultural, even multi-cultural. French people are often interested in trying to measure their similarities to and differences from this civilization that has basically been a model or a counter-model for everyone for the last thirty years, and that is the United States. You say yourself, on the one hand, that you've never much liked the United States and, on the other hand, that the impoverishment of French culture disappoints you very much. Do you feel at home anywhere?

S. Sontag: No, I don't feel at home. It's not good for me to feel at home. I like to be uncomfortable. I like to be in opposition.

But to answer in a little bit more detail, I think I have an advantage. I am neither patriotic nor chauvinistic, but I think that as an American I have a certain advantage in that the United States is already a multi- or pluri-cultural phenomenon. I don't say that I'm representative, but the United States is a constructed country, an artificial country, made of many different cultures. I think everyone is a foreigner in the United States; we are a country of foreigners who decided to form a nation, which puts us in a very different situation from older countries like France.

Myself, I love to travel, in every sense of the word, rather more intellectually than literally, but also literally. And I like to be uncomfortable, I like to see from afar. I also like to come back; I'm always coming back to my country. When I say "I don't like this, I don't like that . . . ," it's always a matter of love.

It's the same thing for France, which is the foreign country I have adopted. Nobody asked me to do it, but I did it in my head when I was a child in the farthest reaches of provincial America. I had never set foot in France, and I decided that it was French culture that fascinated me the most. My three sisters wanted to go to Moscow, but I wanted to go to Paris when I grew up and, actually, that's what I've done.

J.-L. Servan-Schreiber: It's a little bit the ambient myth of American intellectuals between the world wars.

S. Sontag: Yes, a little. My childhood was in the 40s. But actually the literature that I read was the literature of the period between the two world wars.

J.-L. Servan-Schreiber: You say that America is already a multi-cultural nation, naturally so, and effectively, by contrast, that France is a sort of monolith that, from time to time, takes in foreigners, but doesn't completely accept them. Finally, I have the impression that you find greater value in this catch-all American pluralism than in the grand, well-organized French tradition which runs the risk of becoming sterile. Don't you?

S. Sontag: I don't very much like to make that kind of judgment because I think nationalism is to be avoided. It seems to me that we're going toward great admixtures at all levels and that France is at the same time a great refuge, an ideal for foreigners—it has been for the last century and a half—but also a country that has a great cultural conceit, which perhaps, in the present situation, is not sufficient for a cultural future. Obviously, France almost dominated European culture for centuries. A great German critic said Paris was the capital of the 19th century. Obviously that's no longer possible. But I don't want to create a rivalry between countries; that's a stupid and basely political game. I will simply say that it is impossible not to be an internationalist of the mind; that's the only possibility, now, I think.

J.-L. Servan-Schreiber: One can measure your love of France by the hard words that you use when you talk about it. As the French say, Whoever loves well punishes well. You say that the French are complacent, narcissistic and xenophobic.

S. Sontag: You're putting words in my mouth that other people have already put in my mouth. I don't come here as a judge; that would be a very stupid position to take.

J.-L. Servan-Schreiber: Your remarks interest us insofar as you have an avowed bias in favor of France, even if you have had some disappointments . . .

S. Sontag: No, no, I can't agree with that. People always ask me to say that and I have the impression that, often, I'm falling into a trap that's not at all of my own making. As a foreigner who spends a lot of time—I've spent practically half my adulthood in France—I am often asked what I think of France and, stupidly, naively, I often answer. Now I've decided not to answer anymore.

J.-L. Servan-Schreiber: You've become suspicious.

S. Sontag: That gives the impression that I come to judge. I don't come to judge. I answer when people ask me questions. Obviously, if you ask me what I think of current French cinema, for example, I can't say that it is now what it was twenty years ago or fifteen years ago or ten years ago. Everybody knows that. But I don't come here to say that French cinema is in decline in comparison to the golden age of Godard or Bresson or Resnais. Everybody knows it. But if I say it, it sounds as if I'm coming here to judge and that's stupid. What I know, all French people know.

J-L. Servan-Schreiber: We believe that.

Let's not talk as judges; instead, I'm going to ask you some questions as an analyst, not a psychoanalyst.

Can you tell us how you see the role of intellectuals in the United States compared to what it is in France? We have the impression that their social position and their influence are exerted in a very different way.

S. Sontag: I think the idea of the intellectual is an idea more or less created in France, like many things which have been invented here. It was invented more or less by the philosophers of the 18th century: Voltaire is perhaps the first intellectual in the modern sense; that is, he wrote plays, poems, novels and essays. He was involved in all kinds of intellectual activities, questions of conscience, the equivalent of demonstrations and petitions. But he went even further in the Calas affair, etc. It was this vocation of being at the same time an artist, a creator, or writer, a person of conscience who gets involved in moral and political questions that was invented here. And that has a certain prestige in France, even now. It's an imported idea in the United States. We have intellectuals but they don't have the same prestige and perhaps not the same importance in the United States as here in France.

We don't have any equivalent of Sartre, for example.

J.-L. Servan-Schreiber: But that's, let's say, almost an accident of birth. You think in general that the position occupied by intellectuals in the whole of American society is less eminent, less central, less important?

S. Sontag: It's less central in regard to the writer. It is perhaps more central in a purely sociological sense. That is, most American intellectuals are professors and our universities, I think, are more important in the whole of American social activity. The university plays a very big role. Now more than fifty percent of young people go to the university; that is, it's really the institution at the center of American life. The universities are our cultural centers. We don't have a ministry of culture, we don't have cultural activities subsidized by the state; the universities subsidize them.

Then there's a connection between intellectual life and university life, which means that university professors are less evolved on the purely university level, in the European sense. Our institutions are perhaps more popular, less purely scholarly or scientific. That's another role. We don't have a great tradition of men or women of letters as you have in Europe and particularly in France, someone who would really be the spokesman of his generation; but we have a class of people who are rather instructors or professors and who are very important.

J.-L. Servan-Schreiber: According to what you seem to be saying, they are far more cut off from contact with the masses since, as you say, for example, it is inconceivable in the United States that an intellectual would work for television. It's a surprising remark. Can you compare it with what is going on here?

S. Sontag: Yes, because some of your institutions are better than those in the United States, if I dare say so. French television is incomparably better than American television. The French publishing industry is better overall than the American publishing industry. You have intellectuals who work for radio, for television, who are journalists working for the weekly magazines: It's inconceivable in the

United States where, generally speaking, radio, journalism, television and even book publishing, for the most part, are vulgarly commercial institutions without the slightest intellectual interest or the slightest intellectual openness. On the contrary, the universities are much more open.

J.-L. Servan-Schreiber: But what role do you think that television could play? Because I believe you don't have a television in your apartment?

S. Sontag: No, I don't have a television set. If I live in France, I have access to television, but not in New York.

J.-L. Servan-Schreiber: Doesn't it communicate anything to you? Wanting to be a modern intellectual, you have tried to work in all the media: You work in movies, in theater, in writing, but, for you, television is not within the range of possible activities?

S. Sontag: In the United States, when you've seen American television once, you've seen everything. Even to watch old movies isn't worth the trouble because every three minutes they cut in with three minutes of advertising. Then, what good is that?

J.-L. Servan-Schreiber: There are what one would call some creative programs on the public television.

S. Sontag: Very few, really, very, very few.

J.-L. Servan-Schreiber: So if you were functioning as a French person you would be a television viewer?

S. Sontag: I watch television when I'm here but I'm not functioning as a French person. I appreciate the effort made by television to maintain a certain level, certain criteria that don't exist in the United States. For instance, it is not possible in the United States to have literary programs on television.

J.-L. Servan-Schreiber: Even so, there are programs where authors are invited to talk about their books since authors in the United States just like here . . .

S. Sontag: You're going to defend the United States and I'm going to defend France!

J.-L. Servan-Schreiber: It's normal that we don't agree.

A propos of this problem of authors on television, I would like to ask you your feeling about the way in which modern ideas are created or spread. That reminds me of a cartoon in which a publisher said to a writer, "Well, we really like your book but we're not going to take it because you aren't as good looking as you need to be to defend it on television.'' As for yourself, I have a feeling that, when we read articles about you, whether they're written in the United States or in France, finally what you say holds people's attention, but the fact that it's accompanied by your personal looks and not someone else's counts in the impression that people get. Isn't that something that seems evident in your experience?

S. Sontag: I never think about that. I can't tell you really.

J.-L. Servan-Schreiber: But people write it.

S. Sontag: Yes, but I don't read what people write about me.

J.-L. Servan-Schreiber: Really? Writers often say that.

S. Sontag: No, it's true; I'm not boasting. It's perhaps a little bit of cowardice on my part because it's very embarrassing.

Here again, I notice an enormous difference. For books, for the big bestsellers, perhaps, if you do a lot of television, that helps. But as for myself, for example, I don't think the success that I have had in the United States has the slightest connection with television. If from time to time I've done a little television, some interviews, some conversations, it's because I had something to say during the war in Vietnam or when I wrote my book on illness. Invitations to appear on television interested me very much because I wanted to reach a wider audience with the ideas in that book. It was a moral duty for me. But I think that you can perfectly well have an important career, can be taken very seriously, and even sell books in the United States, without doing any television. It does not have the same impact, it's not of the same importance there, because it's not expected from television.

J.-L. Servan-Schreiber: That's the way it is. But don't you find it lacking? Doesn't the French system, in this respect, seem more useful to you?

S. Sontag: I don't know. From the point of view of the writer, I find it a little embarrassing; from the point of view of the public, I find it somewhat helpful.

J.-L. Servan-Schreiber: About your book on illness, many people who, like you, have had cancer have felt the same need to write, to offer personal testimony. You took quite a different approach, which was to write an essay on the illness itself. What made you decide to do that?

S. Sontag: Besides my own suffering and my own battle, I was horrified by the myths that surround cancer, I was horrified by the taboo, and I think that these taboos kill. That is, people don't get treatment because when they find out they have cancer they think that they are condemned to die, that there's nothing to be done, they feel guilty, they're treated like pariahs. For me, cancer is an illness like any other. It's a very serious illness, very grave; at the present time, only about fifty percent of cancers are cured, but that's already a lot. If you have cancer, speaking in global, statistical terms, you have one chance out of two of being cured. I thought that I could bring something valuable to the discussion of these myths, these taboos, these phantasms; I wanted to demystify cancer. And that comes from an absolutely personal experience: I spent a lot of time in hospitals, I underwent several operations, I took chemotherapy for two and a half years, and I know hundreds of people who have cancer. I was horrified by their ideological sufferings. It's not just simply a question of an idea, but it's an idea that has real consequences. The fact of cancer is kept hidden, the family thinks that it is too cruel. I think that it is too cruel not to speak of it because you deprive the patient of the possibility of fighting for himself.

J.-L. Servan-Schreiber: But the overall thesis of your book seems to be that psychological theories of sickness—many people say: "Cancer has psychological roots and also, perhaps, is associated with moments of great depression or shock in one's life"—are not valid. You protest against all that and you explain that to a certain extent it's a means of putting the blame for the sickness on the patient.

S. Sontag: Yes, it's also a way of being fatalistic. Perhaps if you're very depressed, you are more susceptible to illness. It's probable, but if it's true, it's true for all kinds of illnesses. Cancer, like ulcers or a heart attack, is a physical illness which should be treated by physical means, which are, at the present time, extremely effective. I was treated by a French doctor and I know that there are some very effective treatments here. I think that the whole psychological discourse is a way of making sickness fate, which is absolutely irrelevant and very dangerous for the patient. It's a way of resigning oneself. That's the starting point for my book. There are also fantasies, absolutely unimaginable myths about tuberculosis, which we laugh about now because tuberculosis is more or less a sickness of the past; but they had these quite ridiculous fantasies about tuberculosis and you can even trace exact parallels between the current myths about cancer and the 19th-century myths about tuberculosis.

J.-L. Servan-Schreiber: But finally the only real way to defeat the myths about cancer will be to reduce the impact of the sickness.

S. Sontag: They are reducing it. There's progress every year on methods of treatment.

J.-L. Servan-Schreiber: But on a personal level, the fact that you had cancer, that you went through this experience, has that permanently changed the way in which you look at everyday life?

S. Sontag: Absolutely, yes, it's absolutely a turning point. I consider myself somewhat posthumous because they told me that I was probably going to die and I think that you're never the same after having undergone this terror of really facing death. Obviously you haven't completely changed; you've become an aspect of yourself. But I think that finally, if I may say so, it was a rather positive experience because you appreciate the fact that you're mortal and that you have to live with the best part of yourself. But I feel myself very, very changed.

J.-L. Servan-Schreiber: Has that had an influence on your work? That is to say are there certain kinds of interests and subjects that seem less important to you or more important or more urgent because of this reflection on yourself? Did that give you the desire to explore other things besides illness?

S. Sontag: No. I always had the idea that I didn't have enough time and I always have the idea that, now that I've done something, I'm just starting out. I think I'll have that all my life; even if I have a very long life, I'll always have the impression that I'm just beginning. That doesn't change my priorities, as they say in English—I don't know if you can say that in French. But it made me a deeper person somehow. I can verify it on the personal level: I have much more sympathy for suffering, for example, for sick people. I had never been sick in my life and I had that confidence that you can have when you have never been sick. Of course, when my friends got sick I was sympathetic. In the sense of being polite, nice, affectionate, but not in the profound sense because it was something I couldn't understand. Now there's something that goes on in me when I see someone who is suffering physically because I know what that means. It's very simple what I am saying.

J.-L. Servan-Schreiber: And you can help them more?

S. Sontag: Yes, obviously. It's also a sort of burden to have this consciousness of suffering because life is in large part suffering. Before, I was more oriented toward moral suffering; now I also know about a physical aspect of moral suffering. But that's what experience brings, it's inevitable.

J.-L. Servan-Schreiber: In your action, in your thinking, politics is never completely absent because you have a meaningful way of interpreting things. Precisely, speaking of France, you have said that you have found that the French were bewitched by the so-called language of the left. But as for yourself, haven't you always considered yourself to be on the left?

S. Sontag: I've never said that the French were bewitched by the so-called language of the left. After all, once again, the left started in France. That started, as you know, by the way they arranged the legislative benches at the time of the French Revolution. It's the same thing in Italy, I must say right away. I think that in Europe there is a prestige to the language of the left that has lasted for a century for the very good reason that many heroic struggles were associated with this language of the left. But we are now in a historical moment where we have to admit that this language is also a language of State, and of Empire, an empire that presents a model which is far from being positive for us. It's one thing to be on the left in the 19th century and it's another thing to use the language of the left more than sixty years after the Bolshevik Revolution. There's also the evolution and the appropriation of this language to account for.

J.-L. Servan-Schreiber: But if the left doesn't have a language any longer, how can it express itself?

S. Sontag: There's always a language of liberty. For the last two centuries, there have been intellectuals who are fascinated by the power of the state: One must disassociate the language of politics from the language which is servile in relationship to the state. One must never love States, any State; I think that's the first duty of an intellectual: not to love a State.

J.-L. Servan-Schreiber: That's what the French defenders of the new philosophy say in effect: that it's an attack on the State. In that respect, you are in agreement with them.

S. Sontag: Yes, they're not the first to say it, of course.

J.-L. Servan-Schreiber: Yes, but they hadn't said it in France for a long time.

S. Sontag: That one mustn't love states? Many people have said that. Simone Weil said that at the beginning of the 30s. If I wanted to find a leftist radical who really understood what Bolshevism is, for example, I would refer to Simone Weil.

J.-L. Servan-Schreiber: A leftist radical [*Radical de gauche*]: You're not talking about a minor French political party.

S. Sontag: No, I'm talking about a "radical" in the sense of someone who takes a position that goes right to the roots, in the etymological sense. I know that we must always be suspicious of those words in French—liberal, radical—because they are the names of parties.

J.-L. Servan-Schreiber: In that respect you have said that to be liberal is perhaps the most radical solution. Well, since these two words are loaded on both sides, can you explain to us what you mean?

S. Sontag: If I can refer again to French thinkers, I can find some reference points, some points with which I can be in agreement, with de Tocqueville and also Simone Weil.

J.-L. Servan-Schreiber: Tocquevillism isn't particularly radical.

S. Sontag: No, but he was a liberal in the Anglo-Saxon sense of the word. He was interested in the idea of liberty; he accepted the French Revolution, which was after all a rather difficult thing for a man of his class, of his upbringing; he understood what modern life could be; he found that deplorable for a minority but better for the majority. Because the liberal position, in the Anglo-Saxon meaning of the word . . .

J.-L. Servan-Schreiber: A little bit libertarian.

S. Sontag: Libertarian, that's also a melancholy position. I don't think that good solutions exist; it's always an effort to avoid the worst.

J.-L. Servan-Schreiber: But today, in this respect, is there a leftist school of thought or a group of intellectuals in the United States?

S. Sontag: No, I don't think so. There are thinkers, intellectuals: We didn't have that very general weakness for the Eastern-block system that French intellectuals have shown for so many decades. American intellectuals understood very well from the 1930s onward what Stalinism was. Our leftist thinking had no common historical reference points; it's not like here, in the 40s and 50s, where many intellectuals—even in 1968 and afterwards—were much too tender regarding the so-called communist governments. We have an anarchist socialist tradition, but it's more moralistic than political. We don't have an important left-wing labor movement at the present time. They are moral movements rather than political movements as such. But I refuse to say, for that reason, that they are not important, because there are certain battles—for instance over ecological questions—that you can't situate in the old terms of right vs. left: They can be claimed by the left as well as by the right.

J.-L. Servan-Schreiber: What disturbs French people when they try to find the intellectual reference points in the United States is that the ideas you have cited as being the only ones that are still on the left, the idea of liberty and the idea of resistance to the state, are often in the United States the ideas of reactionary groups.

S. Sontag: Yes, but we have a little difficulty in accepting this division between the left and the right. I think that is rather outdated. It's going to last for a while, but already people feel it. Which side is the feminist struggle on, or where are the ecological issues? Of course, if you come from a tradition where you think that the best thought always comes from the left, you're going to say that these are left-wing struggles. But why? They are struggles. Feminism isn't a thing that you can situate on the left; feminism is a struggle in itself. The struggle to save nature, to save it from the worst damage of industrial society, of consumer society, isn't necessarily a struggle on the right or on the left.

J.-L. Servan-Schreiber: In France, the difference historically was always between order and movement. It may be that these movements that you talk about, whether they are environmental or otherwise, are movements that challenge the traditional functioning of society. In the end, it's the only criteria they have in common.

S. Sontag: So that means they're on the left?

J.-L. Servan-Schreiber: Very often it means that people of the left are in them.

S. Sontag: Yes, yes, that's true.

J.-L. Servan-Schreiber: It's another way the French have of defining them: Who defends these ideas? In the US, there are people on both sides.

S. Sontag: Yes, actually, you do name the movement by its participants. That means, if you live in France a long time, you can have several ideological careers, you can go from one position to another, etc. I think that you must cut out the idea that it's the person that gives the label and start all over with a new terminology. I think that's what is in the process of being constructed. We're really at an ideological turning point; it's the obvious fall of the moral prestige, of the credibility, of the Leninist revolutionary tradition. And with that, many accepted ideas, Jacobine ideas, if I may say so, ideas that we have inherited ultimately from the French Revolution, will be challenged. But I'm not at all in agreement with the people who say ''We have to give up on politics'' or ''You have to return to the arms of the church,'' where you discover that all the master thinkers are the ancestors of totalitarian regimes, and so on. I don't associate myself at all with what they say and with the thoughts of the new philosophers.

J.-L. Servan-Schreiber: Even so they are carrying out what one would call a radical critique of received ideas.

S. Sontag: Yes, but this critique has been offered many times before!

J.-L. Servan-Schreiber: In your country?

S. Sontag: Yes, but even in yours. Even in yours, during the 30s.

J.-L. Servan-Schreiber: Yes, but of the people who were adults in the 30s, not many are left.

S. Sontag: But the books remain. And it was Simone de Beauvoir who wrote the best feminist book in all of feminist literature.

J.-L. Servan-Schreiber: That was in '47.

S. Sontag: It remains the greatest effort to pull together all the feminist arguments. Even if parts of the book are questionable, it is the great feminist work. It was written in '47, one evolves, but it is always this book to which one must refer.

J.-L. Servan-Schreiber: Precisely to connect politics and feminism you have written that, for socialism to triumph, feminism must first obtain great victories. Can you explain that?

S. Sontag: I'm afraid of falling into a trap of language, because you must use a certain language to make yourself understood.

J.-L. Servan-Schreiber: You have to use code words.

S. Sontag: That is, there's a certain socialism which doesn't exist anywhere. To say socialism means simply to say . . .

J.-L. Servan-Schreiber: A socialism of freedom?

S. Sontag: A better society than what we have now. One of the basic elements of a better society is a change in the situation of women. And we know that so-called socialist societies can very well be societies that oppress women. There is no necessity in the words "socialist ideology" for a change in the situation of women. It's a struggle that can be linked with so called socialist struggle, but that depends on the will of the people.

J.-L. Servan-Schreiber: But after the Russian Revolution a series of extremely liberal measures were taken, from free abortion all the way to liberty in marriage and divorce; the situation had profoundly and suddenly changed. It was after that that conditions went backwards.

S. Sontag: But you always go backwards, which shows that it isn't simply by changing the laws that you get there, that's not enough. Obviously, we know that in many revolutions there's a very libertarian moment, but you can't say that there was no revolution because what happens afterwards is bureaucracy. There are bureaucrats, there's conformism. At the present time the Soviet Union is one of the most conservative countries in the world culturally; as far as feminism goes, for example, you have to construct the argument on the basis of justice, the idea of justice, and not on the idea of socialism, I think.

J- L. Servan-Schreiber: But I'd like to come back to that sentence that I quoted a little bit ago and which is, I think, the opposite of everything that the socialists in the classical sense in France say. It is socialist doctrine to say—whether it is communists or very often socialists themselves who say it—"After the triumph of socialism, the problems of women will be resolved." You're saying exactly the opposite. Can you tell us why?

S. Sontag: Absolutely. I don't think that I'm saying the opposite because more and more I think . . .

J.-L. Servan-Schreiber: You turned the proposition around.

S. Sontag: . . . that socialism is becoming an empty word. You can construct a better society, a more just society, and though you want to call that socialism, I have doubts about whether it is necessary to keep that word. But I think that experience shows us that socialism doesn't bring anything that isn't already given in the culture and in the will of people who create that resolve. Everything is done now in the name of socialism: everything that has happened for the last sixty years. But if I dare pronounce a phrase which often still shocks people, Nazism: What is Nazism? It's national socialism. It also borrowed several elements from the socialist vocabulary. So socialism is a very big flag and I don't ever count on socialism to solve real problems. It may be that this is a structure that works or doesn't work, but concrete struggles, truly important struggles—and the feminist struggle is one of the most important—should be conducted on their own terms.

J.-L. Servan-Schreiber: But the value of the term socialism on the operational level, as they say in modern times, is less the body of ideas than the rallying of the masses. You say that all the elements of socialism have been in the culture for a long time; what serves as a rallying point so that these movements create themselves or become broad enough to aid in the transformation of society?

S. Sontag: Terrible crimes have been committed in the name of socialism. So ultimately you have to take note of these crimes. Why has socialism had so much credit as an ideology? Because it had so many glorious battles and so many martyrs. But now, for nearly the last seventy years, there has also been a series of crimes committed in the name of socialism.

A word is not sacred. The word "socialism" doesn't say anything. It's a word, it's a kind of a flag, a standard that can be changed. Perhaps we should go back to another word or invent another word. All big words like that are empty. But I think that we must use these big words with much lucidity. If "socialism" is the word you want to continue to use, fine, but you must be very lucid about its history, about what people tell us who live in so-called socialists systems. We have lots of testimony; you can't ignore the testimony.

J.-L. Servan-Schreiber: There is a word which doesn't have as long a history but which begins to be given all kinds of bad interpretations; that's the word "feminism."

S. Sontag: Not for me. It doesn't have any bad meanings for me.

J.-L. Servan-Schreiber: Yes, but you know it's interpreted in all sorts of possible ways. There's a remark that you made recently in an interview in *F Magazine* in which you said, "I don't understand women who say they're not feminists." Can you explain your thought?

S. Sontag: For me, feminism is also a stupid word, an empty word like all big words that end in "ism." But it means being aware of the situation of inequality between men and women, of the oppression of women, and wanting to do concrete things to change that situation, in the same way that people realized, in the 18th century, that slavery existed.

J.-L. Servan-Schreiber: Men say right away: "You can't say women are slaves."

S. Sontag: I'm saying it. Certainly it's a much milder form of slavery because slave and master live together.

J.-L. Servan-Schreiber: That was often the case in the southern United States.

S. Sontag: Yes, but it's a form of slavery, it's a form of subordination that's thousands of years old. Changing the situation of women is a radical revolution, completely radical, and I don't mean radical in the Anglo-Saxon sense. It's really changing everything and I never underestimate the importance of the difficulty in this change because all of society is based on a division of roles, a polarization of the two sexes that is to the disadvantage of women and to the advantage of men. To change that will take generations; it will have to take generations, it's impossible to do it in ten years or twenty years.

J.-L. Servan-Schreiber: But finally you have had the luck to belong to the first generation which experienced that in a completely conscious and voluntary way. When you see what has happened in the last fifteen years, from the time when they started to bring up these ideas in the United States until now, how do you measure how far you've come? It has been said that the feminist movement in the United States has run out of steam a little because it lacked issues.

S. Sontag: I think that there is a big change. Something like that, which is really a change in psychic and cultural structures, can't be measured by the destiny of a movement of a little group of people, by demonstrations, magazines, pamphlets, books. It's something which spreads and I think that a change in the situation of women is an idea whose time has come. The time has come, for very profound reasons, which are historical, material, even environmental. It's a change that will take place in the next century. It's a big change. Nothing will stop this change. And it's not a question of a movement: A movement is a little visible tip discussed by journalists, but there's a kind of change that spreads through the whole population, bit by bit, a change in behavior, a change in consciousness compared to ten years ago. It's far from being over: It's perhaps the first five percent that has already happened but I think it's absolutely inevitable.

J.-L. Servan-Schreiber: You're talking as a gradualist, as the Italians say. But, in fact, you declared yourself favorable to the most excessive, most extreme feminist activities. Now, explain this apparent contradiction to us.

S. Sontag: Because I think that helps; it changes the center. Anybody, man or woman, who says "I'm not a feminist" is already a feminist in comparison to what that person was twenty or thirty years ago because the center has changed. It is normal that a woman now has a job; it's a normal, conventional idea in the industrialized nations. Thirty or forty years ago you would have had to have been a feminist to find the idea normal. Now, people say, "I'm not a feminist, but of course I'm for this, this, and this." Those are ideas that were feminist. That is, ideas that were at least reformist ideas if not more than that. I think that the groups, the demonstrators, are a tiny minority that did things that are called excessive, but which do a great service for the majority, because they change the center. That which is normal, conventional, conservative, changes a bit.

J.-L. Servan-Schreiber: Yes, but at the same time, it is often said that the very excess of certain small groups, in feminism as elsewhere—but in this case in feminism—runs the risk of turning women themselves away from feminism. That's something that is being noticed.

S. Sontag: Yes, but I think that the change is too strongly rooted, is too strongly motivated in the historical sense to be sidetracked. It's not important if a particular woman changes her mind and says: "I'm quitting my job, I'm going back home, I'm going to do the dishes, I'm not a feminist." There will always be a range of choices for individuals, certainly, but in general women are leaving their thousand year-old roles as mothers and maids. That's what is important. They are entering into society, they're talking on adult functions beside men. In general, that's what is going on. For an individual to do one thing or another is not important; there are always various cases.

J.-L. Servan-Schreiber: You're talking more with the serenity of an historian than with the urgency of a militant.

S. Sontag: No. I'm a very melancholy person and I always find reasons to be pessimistic, but the future of women is one of the few subjects where I'm optimistic.

J.-L. Servan-Schreiber: Do you have the impression that the machine is running and that nothing will stop it?

S. Sontag: Absolutely. I think often that I'm sorry that I was born in the 20th century because it's such a tragic century, where you see the destruction of so many beautiful things, of a whole civilization. The only thing that reconciles me to the fact of being born in the 20th century is that I was born a woman and I think . . .

J.-L. Servan-Schreiber: This is the time.

S. Sontag: . . . it's a good time for women. If it's not a good time for many values, it's a good time for women. That's perhaps the most positive thing that modernity has brought us. It's a change that after all involves half the human race.

J.-L. Servan-Schreiber: Many women try to explain that feminism is something that will be important, certainly, but that isn't going to change the situation of men. You're saying the opposite. You say deep down that women cannot be freed without the power of men diminishing.

S. Sontag: When the power of man is based on the power of masters, when the classic work situation is the man who bosses, and the woman secretary and assistant who take orders . . . , if this situation is no longer the norm, that will mean that men can't count on being automatically privileged in the work situation. Let me give you a very personal example. My son has finished his studies and he has gone to work for a publishing company; he's already an editor. I am sure that if he were a girl, she would have had to have done an apprenticeship as a secretary and after three, four, or five years, with luck, she would be promoted to editor. My son is very feminist, he didn't turn down the job, but he knows as well as I do that you couldn't ask this young man to be a secretary; he's a boy. He should already have an executive job.

That's going to change. If men aren't automatically privileged, that's a change, it's a loss of power. Power is no longer automatic.

J.-L. Servan-Schreiber: You were talking about your son a moment ago. One of the most difficult problems imaginable is the influence that this deep rooted movement, this evolution of women, will have on the family. I know that you are very sensitive in this regard. How do you see the evolution of the family? The family has been much criticized for the last thirty years. Right now, people are finding once again that it has some virtues. Where do you put yourself in regard to that?

S. Sontag: I've never criticized the family very much. I think the family is a basic institution. And if there's anything that's natural, it is the family.

J.-L. Servan-Schreiber: Yes, but isn't it the very cell of women's oppression?

S. Sontag: No, because a family can be different. A modern family, the bourgeois family, is also a creation. So there will be another form of family, but there will always be a family, certainly.

J.-L. Servan-Schreiber: All right, what form of family can one imagine?

S. Sontag: Everyone talks about that. I don't have any very original ideas. For example, sharing housework: If the husband does as much at home, that changes things; if fatherhood becomes as strong as motherhood on the emotional level, that would depolarize the two sexes. That would be, for me, the ideal. That's going to change relationships. Everyone goes out to work, everyone comes home for love, for affection, for warmth and for food.

J.-L. Servan-Schreiber: Yes, but often the problem of the family is reduced to the problem of who's going to do the housework. What if we get beyond this stage? You have personally studied Freud, who suffered from the feminist movement. What do you think of the problem brought about by the unification of masculine and feminine roles? They say it would be bad if fathers were no longer fathers.

S. Sontag: I don't agree. It's marvelous that fathers would no longer be fathers.

J.-L. Servan-Schreiber: So, the authoritarian function isn't necessary in the family circle?

S. Sontag: Authority can be founded on something other than sexual identity. Personally, I am not against authority; authority is inevitable; parents are authority figures for their children. But I don't deplore at all the decline of paternal authority. I think the decline of patriarchal authority is one of the few advances of our civilization.

J.-L. Servan-Schreiber: Because that means you get rid of values that were not necessary?

S. Sontag: No, that means that authority was founded on the oppression of women. It was founded on the fact that there is a master and his adjunct, his assistant, the mother. Of course, there are all these values within the family, but limited to this family cell, while the father goes out to have a public life and so on.

J.-L. Servan-Schreiber: It is said in France now that women have won, that feminism has become so pervasive that there's not that much left to do. It is a discourse volunteered by men who say: "What is your problem? You've obtained everything you wanted." How do you judge the situation in France when you look at that?

S. Sontag: I think the situation of women is deplorable everywhere.

J.-L. Servan-Schreiber: Not especially in France?

S. Sontag: I think it's better in Germany.

J.-L. Servan-Schreiber: What do you find deplorable in everyday life, for instance, when you live in France?

S. Sontag: Nothing has changed basically. There's just a beginning of a change. Women are educated and raised to be masochists. There has to be a complete psychological change. Of course, we're not an Islamic country but women's freedom is still a formal freedom. Women receive a moral and psychological training which doesn't permit them to use more of the formal liberties that they have won. It's a rare woman who has the psychological confidence to take responsibility for the freedom that is available to her.

J.-L. Servan-Schreiber: That is to say, the important thing is that they are always feeling guiltier than men?

S. Sontag: They also need models. Women have to become pilots for Air France, engineers, they have to enter in to all the jobs, on all levels. It's not a question of supremacy, it's simply that you should see women at all levels. I recently read a study in *Le Monde;* someone wrote a book on the language used in school texts. It's "Mr. So and So and his wife, Claire," "Here's Mr. So and So and his dog Lulu." That is, it's men who exist and, after them, women and children. If a man were treated like all women are treated every day he would realize that feminism, that is to say, a real change, hasn't yet happened. Women accept daily humiliations, even the fact that people always say "man." I remember a headline in a newspaper when Mrs. Gandhi was still Prime Minister of India, portraying her as "Indira Gandhi, the woman who reigns over half a billion men." She did not reign over 500 million men; she reigned, if the number was 500 million, over 250 million men and 250 million women. If you always heard phrases like "women . . ." or "women think . . . ," and if you (a man) were told that "woman" included you every time you heard it, you would find that ridiculous. You'd say right away: "No, I'm not included." But every time they say "men think . . ." or "modern man . . . ," they exclude women. It's not simply a question of grammar; it's a cultural question.

J.-L. Servan-Schreiber: It's true that every language has its problems and that the way in which Americans resolve this problem is different from the way in which the French proceed.

S. Sontag: We don't have grammatical gender, but we have many expressions like that. A long time ago in the United States there was a white man who had himself dyed; he went to the South disguised as a black and he came back with an astonishing book because he understood how much people were suffering. I have a friend, an actor, who pretended to be deaf for twenty-four hours. He told me: "You can't imagine how ill-treated the deaf are, the things people say behind their backs, the looks, all the forms of discrimination." I think it would be good if a man had, for twenty-four hours, the form of a woman—I don't mean physically—but had to take on that kind of language, the kind of treatment that a woman generally undergoes without complaining: He's going to notice that the battle isn't completely won.

J.-L. Servan-Schreiber: Last question, Susan Sontag. It is often said that what is expected of intellectuals is that they project somewhat into the future the urgent or important problems that we must resolve, and that we're living in an alarming era where all intellectuals are resigning one after the other; they don't have anything to say, they don't have reference points, they have spleen. Can you tell us what seem, to you, for the next ten or twenty years, to be our true priorities?

S. Sontag: Is it true that intellectuals are all resigning?

J.-L. Servan-Schreiber: It's said currently. There are no statistics, but people talk of confusion, of despair. That's much more fashionable than to talk about a shining future.

S. Sontag: Yes, yes, of course, because it's always in relationship to this fantasy of the left. No, if the intellectuals have lost some certainties, I think that's positive. Losing false certainties is always a jolt. I think that intellectuals have a lot of things to do; defend liberty, fight for justice; the women's question is a question of justice. There is always a confrontation between dictatorship or censorship and liberty, and I don't know if the domain of freedom is shrinking, but you have the impression that freedom, in several domains, is always endangered, in France as everywhere else, and France is, even so, a relatively free country. So I think that there are always very concrete struggles.

I think that it's a shame that the fight for social justice should be completely identified with an idea of the left; such that, if we decide that the left has betrayed us because the left is no longer what it should be, or because the left no longer exists, you can't have a social consciousness. For me, that's more the havoc resulting from a certain language and, if there is a theme that concerns me, it's the damage caused by phantasms and myths. My book centered on the myths that surround cancer is a study of language, of a demagogic language, I mean a certain way of talking. There are so many myths to demystify. Perhaps this myth of the left, these political myths, should also be demystified, but not in the sense of making people apolitical. I blame for this the many people who are making grand "discoveries" today, in this domain, in France and elsewhere: for leaving people passive and with a very self-centered glorification of private life, leaving them to fall back on this old discovery that we have a private life, that we only have one life, that you have to live, that you have to have fun. I think it's a little pathetic. But it's not the rather old-fashioned language of the left that exhausts all moral and political possibilities: It's that this whole fight for justice is an endless fight.

J-L. Servan-Schreiber: Thank you Susan Sontag.

A Life Style Is Not Yet a Life

Monika Beyer / 1980

From *Polityka,* No. 22 (May 31, 1980), p. 9. Reprinted by permission. A shorter version was published in English as "A Life Style Is Not a Life" in *Polish Perspectives* 23.9 (1980), pp. 42–46. Portions translated from the Polish by Monika Jankowiak.

Susan Sontag was born in New York in 1933. She studied at Berkeley, at the University of Chicago, at Harvard, and at St. Anne's College, Oxford. She was a lecturer in English literature and in philosophy at several prestigious American universities and an editor of the monthly journal *Commentary.* Appreciative evaluations of her literary works brought her many grants, from the Rockefeller and Guggenheim foundations, for example.

She is the author of two novels—*The Benefactor* (1963) and *Death Kit* (1967)—and also many short stories. Her recent collection of short stories is entitled *I, etcetera.* She has also written three scripts for films she directed.

Her essays have aroused the greatest interest. They maintain a very individual style, and are characterized by originality of insight and independence of thought. Among these essays are "Against Interpretation" and "Notes on 'Camp' " (*Literatura na Świecie* 9/79), a set of essays "On Photography," which will be published by WAIF soon, and "Illness as Metaphor" (*Kultura* 33–39/78). She came to Poland, at the invitation of *Literatura na Świecie,* with a group of American writers: John Ashbery, Joyce Carol Oates, William Saroyan, and Raymond Smith.

Monika Beyer: *The United States is a country of overabundance: of material goods, ethnic groups, various minorities, creeds, fads, styles of being, ideas, words and artists. You have a great number of writers, many of whom are very good, but artists of William Faulkner's stature seem to be lacking in present-day America . . .*

Susan Sontag: Yes, indeed, I do not think we have a writer of absolute genius, of the international class.

Can you think of a reason why?

165

No, I cannot really, I think it just happened. America is a country which—as you say—produces and overproduces. I do not know, perhaps there is not a sense of urgency. To tell you the truth, I can imagine Poland more likely to produce a truly great writer than the United States at this moment. Perhaps because Americans are so fortunate, perhaps the great writer of our time has to be produced by some sort of crisis or emergency, and Americans do not feel this sense of historical emergency.

I think we have about ten extremely good writers, of which . . . I am one. But none of us are really great. I am talking of prose writers now. You see, I think American poetry is probably more distinguished than American prose. John Ashbery, for example.

What recent American novels have you read with pleasure?

The Dead Father, by Donald Barthelme, and *Sleepless Nights,* by Elizabeth Hardwick. *Sleepless Nights* is a magnificent novel, beautifully written. Barthelme's book is his only novel; till then he had written many short-story collections. It's written in an experimental style, in the tradition of Joyce, but it doesn't seem especially hard to me.

Americans aren't too fond of experimentation in prose.

This is true, but for the most interesting writers, in America as well as here, one doesn't have to hold with the realist tradition. And the truth is, the 19th-century tradition has a big impact on contemporary writers. Modern narration is still being treated with suspicion.

Why do you think Americans are so very self-critical? It is quite striking, especially when one reads the American press . . .

No, no, it is a form of self-love! We have an extraordinary tradition of freedom. We learned that freedom of speech is not dangerous to society. It does not mean that there is anarchy, despite what it may look like from the outside; America is still a very stable, conservative society. This constant talk is like music that is going on all the time; people pick up ideas from it and things change and then some people are just talking. And it does not matter, but it gives a kind of energy to society; it gives ideas to the people who rule society. It is not just because we are so self-critical that we are masochistic, no, we are exercising a public right.

Is it not a form of self-satisfaction?

Believe me, there is a tremendous amount of self-congratulation of a more direct kind as well. In *Newsweek* or in American literature Americans like to show off how self-critical they are. But all over the country, between New York and California, there are people saying: "America is wonderful," "America is perfect." We have many old-fashioned, patriotic, conservative people, such as you will probably find here too.

Hence the American flags often displayed in front of private homes?

Yes, exactly. You see, our society does not prevent dissidence. Or rather, it does not allow it. If we say everybody can be a dissident, then there are no dissidents. You could say, and people have said it, that it is a more sophisticated form of censorship. So in America you cannot be a dissident because you would get your picture on the cover of *Time* magazine. . . . I do not say that I do not like the system, but I also see that it is in a way also very diabolical. It is a more advanced idea of what a society could be. Your society seems more paternalistic, more old-fashioned. We are more radical in a certain way.

One often hears that, after the stormy 60s, after Vietnam and Watergate, America lost confidence in itself. One could think that chaos and confusion rule.

Indeed, for many political and intellectual reasons, a certain confusion rules. But I am sure that if someone today were to read the statements of literary critics and journalists—for example, of those who wrote in Paris a hundred years ago—one would find the same complaints concerning chaos and confusion. But still we think today that it was much better back then.

In his last interview the late Roland Barthes said: "Gide was one of the last people playing the traditional role of the intellectual who at the same time remains a great writer. Now writers seem to be in retreat . . . They have been massively replaced by intellectuals, by professors."

I absolutely agree with Barthes and I am trying to play this dying role that he talks about. I do not want to be a professor and I do not want to be a journalist, I want to be a writer who is also an intellectual. My ideas are very traditional in this respect. But people are not educated any more to play this role.

Let me return to the American writers. It seems to be a universal complaint (recently voiced by William Saroyan, Saul Bellow and by yourself too) that writers lose their confidence in fiction and many of them reject it. What to write about when everything has already been written about and when la réalité dépasse la fiction?

I would say that writers are always terrible complainers. It is our job to complain; one of the functions of a writer is to complain. That is why it is so terrible where they do not do it. So writers complain about society, and they complain about themselves. They are always saying literature is dead, nobody is doing anything, but I think the real truth is that literature goes on. Of course it is true that *la réalité dépasse la fiction.* We do need writers who can deal with it. I think there are writers in Eastern Europe and Latin America, for instance, who are doing it.

It seems that much of today's world fiction is limited to reflections upon human failure, pathology, maladaptation, incompatibility, anxiety and impotence. Today's world is by no means a happy place to live in, so it is no wonder that this is reflected in contemporary fiction. However, it is a rather one-sided view of the human condition. Is it not one of the reasons why many readers today turn away from fiction?

I think there is a tremendous crisis, or world crisis, not just in the sense that all kinds of dangerous things are happening, like the destruction of nature, the threats of nuclear weapons and overpopulation. I think there is a real moral or spiritual crisis. So if literature mainly deals with various forms of unhappiness, of incompatibility, as you say, I think it is correct in doing so. And I do not think that is why people turn away from literature. I think there is a challenge to literature by other forms of narration.

And entertainment . . .

Yes. In the 19th century, for instance, in England and in America and France, the three countries which had a fairly advanced reading public, the novel was a genuinely popular form. It was the 19th-century television. People used to read novels aloud in the evening to each other and it was really popular entertainment for those who could read, the middle class. Now we have new forms of entertainment through modern technology: wide-screen films, television and recorded music. Therefore literature is "condemned" to being an art. I think it has no other choice. It can either be the most vulgar entertainment competing with television or it must become an art, and consequently have a limited audience.

Still, many well-educated people outside the literary scene often say that no matter how much they appreciate Borges, they cannot face his gloom any more . . .

Some people may not like Borges, but there is Calvino, there is Lem. . . . Take Lem, he is a very interesting phenomenon, a writer who is very serious and at the same time he is writing fiction which many people find very valuable. In America, for instance, Lem is very well known. Engineers read him, and scientific people, those who are not members of the literary community; they like him because of the scientific knowledge. People might feel that life is too sad to read Borges or Beckett. . . . I am thinking now once again of East Europeans and Latin Americans because I think they are about the best writers today, along with some Italian and German writers. You have someone like Lem. You have someone like Garcia Marquez. Well, there is very little happy literature, I will agree with that, but there is more range than this would suggest.

Even those who are very well-read, having gone through various experimental works of fiction, sometimes long for the good, old story, so much spurned by many contemporary writers. Should not the story coexist legitimately with formal experiments and subjectivist exercises of individual vision and imagination?

Yes, absolutely. I am absolutely in favour of pluralism in politics and in literature and in everything else. I myself would not want to see a world in which there is no story-telling. A lot of his later work does not interest me so much but I absolutely approve of the kind of writing of Singer, a writer who was, as you know, born in Poland and who represents the old story-telling tradition. And I think some of his things are wonderful, the earlier ones.

In your essay "Against Interpretation" you call for a sensual perception of art. I am all for it, but how can we learn that in a civilization that is being increasingly cut off from nature?

That is the problem, you are quite right. We are almost pathologi-cally dependent on art to give us all kinds of things a more organic life might provide. By the way, many people say to me: "You are against interpretation—do you mind interpreting your own work?" Of course I am not against interpretation in any ultimate sense, all thinking is interpretation, but I am against a certain kind of reductive interpretation which treats works of art as messages of some kind of social or political or moral content. I think that one of the functions of art is to be autonomous. It is really an entertainment kind of function on a much higher level. People understand this with painting and with music but they have a hard time understanding it with literature or film.

With film as well? In spite of the pictures and colors?

Yes, since they badly want to find out what a given film means. And I think that this does not matter when a film means nothing, when it is simultaneously something abstract and sensory.

Is it not true that the ambiguity of form or content, justified in many great works of art, has nowadays in many cases become a smoke screen to cover up lack of discipline and clear thinking or insufficient mastering of the craft?

This question has always concerned bad literature. There are people who do not write clearly because they are not good writers. But I do believe in the verdict of posterity. I think that time is never wrong in these matters. A writer can be lost for a while because the work is unavailable. Take a writer like Bruno Schulz; he is a classic example of a writer who in his own lifetime was not famous. Only a few people in Warsaw that he was in touch with knew about him; Gombrowicz of course was one of them. But he was certainly a writer who did not have a public in his own lifetime. Now he is a writer known all over the world to everyone who is interested in literature. Why? Because his work is good, and if something is as good as Schulz's work, it will not be lost. So I think that everything that is really good now will be clear in another generation or two, and for the rest—it does not matter.

"Diddy, not really alive, had a life. Hardly the same. Some people are their lives. Others, like Diddy, merely inhabit their lives."

A quotation from my novel *Death Kit* . . .

Yes, I think you hit the nail right on the head in these few lines. Few people are successful in their search for identity nowadays; many of

them simply lose their biographies in the fantasy world of TV and in
the lives of popular idols. At the same time in present-day America
the diversity of individual opportunity and of "life styles" seems to
be overwhelming. Or is it just an illusion?

There are very contradictory things going on in advanced industrial
societies. Obviously we have a tremendous number of possibilities of
living our lives in different ways, but I think some of this diversity is
very superficial. And I think there is also a tremendous conformity.
In other words, I would sacrifice some of the diversity for more depth.
In America for instance a lot of people are talking about their "life
styles." This expression drives me crazy.

A life style instead of a real life?
Exactly. I think there is something deeply wrong if you speak of
your life as your life style. So you change your life style the way you
change your style of clothes. I think there is a deep corruption in the
pluralistic, post-industrial consumer society, as desirable as it may
seem and undoubtedly is in many ways. It does tend to destroy a
certain kind of spiritual possibility.

Sometimes, while in the United States, I had the impression that
people readily talked about democracy and their rights, but in fact
were not always making use of them.
That is because they have no sense of urgency, they are not being
oppressed. But they also run the risk of being empty.

Is Alvin Toffler, in his new book The Third Wave, *painting the*
increasing individualization in the US in a slightly uncritical way?
This individualization does exist. The question, however, is on
what level, because this is not a matter of form. I believe that a part
of this is very superficial and spiritually very empty. Many people
maintain so and I believe that this is true.

Still, when I visited the US last year, after a gap of 20 years, I had
a feeling that the situation in this respect had improved.
Yes, I think we are starting to grow up! You know, we are not a
very young country; most countries in the world are newer than the
US, but it is a very immature country in many ways because for most
of our history we have been so isolated, the rest of the world has been
so far away. Only in this part of the 20th century are Americans

beginning to deal with the world. It may take another couple of generations before we grow up, also politically. American foreign policy is very immature, I am sure you realize that, very incoherent. We do not have the experience but I think we are getting there. I can only hope the rest of the world does not suffer too much from American immaturity, while we are learning.

Let's now turn from the world of politics to the world of women. In your student years most women in America went to college to get some education and to catch a husband. But you have attained international renown as a writer and intellectual. Was it easy for you to make your way in what was predominantly a man's world?
It is always easy if you are willing to make the sacrifices.

What were they in your case?
Well, certain sacrifices of one's personal life. Actually I did get married when I was in college, I was married when I was 17. And I had a child when I was very young. My son is 28 now. He is my best friend. But the life of a writer is a very ascetic life; you spend an enormous amount of time alone. It is always easier for a man, because a man can have a wife. A woman always has to do more. I was divorced when my child was 5 years old and I raised him myself. I had all kinds of responsibilities that a man would not have. I had to take care of the apartment, raise the child, put the shoes on him in the morning, take the laundry and so on. You have to be stronger than a man.

What do you think of the women's movement?
I think it is wonderful. It is fantastic; it is one of the greatest things that has happened in the world. And one of the reasons to be glad one lives in the 20th century. There are not many reasons to be glad, this is one of them.

Will not the changes in sexual roles result in time in obliterating certain differences between the sexes; are we not in for a sort of a chummy world of unisex; will the mutual attraction of the sexes not be endangered?
I do not think we are going to have unisex. And I do not think the attraction of the sexes is really going to be endangered. I think that to some extent it would be better if the sexes were less opposed. I would

like a world in which women were more aggressive and men were kinder; in other words I think it is good if they are not so polarized. I would like women to have more qualities of men and men to have more qualities of women. I think it would reduce violence. Today men have a monopoly of violence; they are brought up to be violent, while women are brought up to repress their energies and aggressiveness. I think that if men were a little more repressed and women would be a little more violent, the total level of violence might be reduced. It would be liberating tremendous energies of half of the population of the world.

You said recently: "I do not feel like an American writer. I am American by nationality and language. But I like the feeling of being an alien, a vagabond; I like loneliness. It is not my fault that I feel an alien in this country."

Perhaps I could explain it by my origins—I am a wandering Jew whose grandparents came to America from Poland. And then I wander all over the world . . .

Miss Joyce Carol Oates also said at Warsaw University that she felt "a citizen of the world in the cultural sense."

Well, you see—she has nothing of my background and yet she feels the same way. I also think that for an American it is perhaps easier to be international. I do not love America, but I am glad America exists. But I also feel it is very limiting to be an American; the culture of my mind is European.

Your background . . .

No, not my background, it was completely American. I grew up in the American provinces, not even in New York, in provinces of no European background where one did not talk of Europe or European literature. I found Europe when I was an adolescent, when in the little local library I began to read the writers that mattered to me, that I really cared about. They were not American writers. The background that I invented, that I discovered, that mattered to me, was Kafka or Mann. These great discoveries that I made when I was about 14 changed my life. So was born my attachment for European culture which I still think of as the source of culture. I still think of America as a colony of Europe. A Polish writer, or—say—Dostoyevsky, matters much more to me than any American writer who has ever lived.

So how can I just be limited to being an American when the writers, the spiritual teachers who matter most, are foreign, European? I want to be a member of the international world and I think that everybody wants that. I am sure Polish writers do too, although they realize their roots are here and they must address the specific problems of their country.

You see, I am very interested in Polish literature. As I said, in some ways you are more likely to have a good writer here because I think people here have a better sense of reality.

Have you read many Polish authors?

Yes, of course. Everything there is to read, the ones who have been translated. I had read Milosz, of course, then Herbert, Andrzejewski and Lem of the living writers. Of the dead writers Gombrowicz, Witkiewicz, Bruno Schulz, and from the 19th century Mickiewicz, Sienkiewicz and so on. As I said, I am very interested in Poland, I have always been. And I like Polish music very much, I like Szymanowski.

I must admit I had not given it much thought before, but once I am here I realize that I could have actually been a Pole, living in Poland. I want to come here again, this time alone, not with a group of writers.

I am looking forward to seeing you again in Warsaw.

Susan Sontag: Me, Etcetera . . .
Charles Ruas / 1980

From *The Soho News* (November 12–18, 1980), pp. 8–9, 16.
Reprinted by permission of Charles Ruas.

Charles Ruas: Many people ask you about your critical work simply because your last novel appeared at the end of the '60s. People assume that your imagination's been taken up with your essays.

Susan Sontag: It's a little bit askew. In '62, when I started writing for publication, there were some first things, and then the novel *The Benefactor* came out in '63. There were two novels, and then all those essays. In '68 I went to Vietnam and the war made it very hard for me to write, as for a lot of people. I couldn't get it out of the forefront of my consciousness. In '69 I decided to make movies. I went to Italy—that was my first love—and tried to find a producer because I had an idea for a script. While I was looking for somebody there, I got an invitation to go to Sweden from this producer and stayed there the better part of two years doing these two movies. I wasn't basically a writer in those years—I was a filmmaker and a political activist. In '72 came a great crisis. I thought: Where am I, what am I doing, what have I done? I seem to be an expatriate, but I didn't mean to become an expatriate. I don't seem to be a writer anymore, but I wanted most of all to be a writer. It doesn't make any sense to make the films because I not only didn't make a penny from the films, I had to go into debt to support myself while I was making them.

This is the situation that I opened the essays with, where I'm in this room the size of a bathroom in Paris saying where am I, who am I, what am I doing? So, it isn't just the '60s and the '70s, there was this whole period of about four years where I was not basically a writer. I feel that I got caught up and responded to various crises. I was really lost without help and I didn't find any help.

There was a second crisis in '75 when I got cancer. I tried to respond to those crises. I feel that this book, *Under the Sign of Saturn,* is the end of that process and now I've discharged my debts to my own obsessions. A tremendous liberation.

175

CR: You speak of purging yourself and yet there's a loving quality in your essays about these writers.

SS: Yes, I would much rather write about things that I like rather than things I don't like. That's why I'm not a critic. I really do think an important job of the critic is to savage this, to say this is garbage, this is terrible, this is pernicious. Although it is a lot of fun to do, the essay that was written most quickly was, of course, the Leni Riefenstahl because it's much easier to write when you feel angry, self-righteous and you know you're right.

CR: Was the Paul Goodman the most difficult to write since it's more personal?

SS: No, the hardest to write was "Syberberg's Hitler." Paul Goodman? Someone brought me the paper in my closet-sized room in Paris, and I saw that Paul Goodman was dead, and I just wrote this thing in an afternoon and sent it to the *New York Review of Books*. It was a breakthrough for me. I have no journalistic talents at all. I will worry about a comma. I am perfectly prepared to spend an hour thinking is the word "fast" or "rapid"? Is that the adjective I want here, and of course they mean the same thing and it's just the most evanescent matter of tone. I'm not bragging about it. It's a question of temperament. I am that obsessional a person.

CR: Was your illness the decisive event that changed so many of your attitudes? In your essay "Approaching Artaud" you write about his Gnostic concept of the body as mind turned into matter, and the physical thoughts of the body.

SS: Becoming ill, facing one's death, being in the company of people who are suffering terribly—and many of them dying—for several years is, of course, a watershed experience. You are not the same afterwards. I was told that very likely I was going to die. I didn't die. I was lucky. I had good medical care—better than most people get, which horrified me because I know that many people would not die of cancer if they had the proper treatment. But the fact is that I have survived, that I am not now ill. I'm in remission and perhaps that means I am cured. It doesn't mean I can cancel that experience. And it has changed a lot of things for me. In some ways it has been a strengthening experience.

It's like any one of the great emergencies that bring out the best and the worst in people, and that's very impressive. I saw it in other people, not just in myself—other people with the most extraordinary amounts of courage, intelligence, beyond anything that they were ever capable of before.

It's also weakening because you realize in a very painful way your own mortality and once again the extent of all this needless human suffering. Which enraged me, which is why I wrote *Illness as Metaphor*. It has also given me a sense of how little time there is, because I have this very American childish attitude that I'm just beginning, that there is always a new frontier. I'm 47 years old. I've done a lot of work which I can hardly renounce; therefore if I believe I can do work much better than I've done up to now, I'd better start doing it. I might live to be 90 years old. There are people who have done their best work when they are older. I hope to be one of those people because I don't feel that I've done the work that I want to do—and I mean fiction, different kinds of fiction. On the other hand it remains for me to do it and not talk about it. People think that I have written a lot, but I haven't actually.

CR: You said that you think of the film as your own creative work.

SS: I think of film more like writing. It's a creation, from beginning to end. The films I have made have been on miniscule budgets. They were just sort of first attempts. If I had a little more money—I don't mean a lot, just a little more money—I think I could do much better films than the ones I did. But what I mean when I make a film is something like what I mean when I write a novel; that is to say, I write the script and I conceive of all the shots, and I determine how it looks, and I work with the composer to make the music, and I direct the actors and I edit the film. And I do all those things myself from beginning to end so that it is the creation of a work in terms of images and sounds—as the writing of fiction is a creation of a work in language.

Directing in the theater or the stage means taking a play or an opera that already exists and trying to make it wonderful for the audience—even better than it is if possible. It's doing something with that preexisting work which I like.

CR: What sort of films are being proposed to you?

SS: They're what I call nonfiction films, but not documentaries. Italian TV is doing a series of portraits of cities and somebody asked me if I wanted to do one. I would be, as usual, the only foreigner. It used to be I was the only woman. Now, thank God, I'm not the only woman, but I'm often the only foreigner. I said I was interested in doing some kind of Venice fantasy. I love doing a lot of different things, but it's important to do them wholeheartedly and not just say I want to make a film so I'll make this small film because I have a chance to do it. I wanted for a long time to direct an opera, and recently a couple of people have suggested this or that situation in which I could do it, but it's not really an opera that I want to do.

CR: Which is the opera you want to do?

SS: I would like to bring something new to people, not just say I have this wonderful idea of how to do *Rosenkavalier*. I have become extremely fond of the operas of the modern composer Janacek, and I think he is just as accessible as Strauss and could be just as popular with audiences. Janacek is a Czech composer, early 20th century, roughly contemporary with Strauss. He wrote eight or nine operas, and most of them are absolutely wonderful, and they are not known here at all.

CR: Do you find that there is a burden of consciousness because of your critical faculties? Does the superego clamp down on the creative and imaginative faculties?

SS: No, I don't think so. I'm perhaps not the best person to answer this question, although I don't know who else could. I'm not aware of it at all, as a matter of fact. Do you mean in the writing of fiction and in the making of films on the one hand, as opposed to the essay writing and the directing on the other?

CR: When you're with yourself, in the range of writing from critical to imaginative to your own fiction, it would be clear whether there would be a conflict.

SS: Not only am I not aware of a conflict. I'm not even aware of any relation between the two. When I write fiction, which is what I am doing now as a writer, it is the only thing that interests me. I feel that I have the usual naive relationship to my own fantasy that everyone has to start with—and then I struggle with verbs and adjectives, commas. I don't have any preconceptions of how it ought to be, and I certainly never did write fiction in order to illustrate any idea that I had as an essayist.

I don't think of myself as a critic, but I did write a lot of essays—more in the '60s than recently. It's not that I think when I write that this is the kind of thing that should be written; I don't have that kind of self-consciousness. I have probably, I was going to say, less than I should; but I don't think about what I am doing except when people ask me questions about it.

CR: When you've done a page of fiction doesn't your critical consciousness start rewriting?

SS: Only in the sense that every writer has to be both the idiot who goes in there and takes out handfuls of raw whatever-it-is, fantasy, and also the shrewd, tough editor who says that's self-indulgent, that doesn't work, that's boring, that part should go here and that part should go there. I am not at all the kind of writer who writes very easily and very rapidly and only needs to correct or change a bit, as many people are, particularly English writers. They have a fluency that American writers don't have. I also think they are much less ambitious than we are. My writing is extremely painstaking and painful, and the first draft is usually awful. It has some elements that are worth keeping; then I have to find what those are and build from them and throw out what doesn't work, whether it's just treading water, or what simply is not alive, so that there is a process of rewriting, of accumulation. In that sense the critical faculty is active, but I don't dignify it by calling it the critical factor; it's me functioning as an editor of my work. It's a very artisanal kind of consciousness. It is not theoretical, it is absolutely practical and intuitive, and what I'm responding to are criteria that are very simple-minded—is this well-written or is this moving or is this alive.

CR: You mentioned contemporary American writers who you think are seriously trying to do something literary.

SS: I think I mentioned Barthelme, William Gass, Elizabeth Hardwick. These are writers who have nourished me and turned me on, given me pleasure and taught me something. They are all writers I feel I have learned something from. I don't know what I've learned, maybe the pleasure was the learning. I love Elizabeth Hardwick's book *Sleepless Nights;* I think it is really a marvelous accomplishment as a book. I love Donald Barthelme's novel *The Dead Father*. I think it's so extraordinary that it hasn't received the acclaim I think it deserves. A writer whom I didn't mention, and it illustrates something a little different, is John Updike. He is certainly one of the best writers in America and yet I don't like his books; I don't like what he writes about. I'm not interested in this main story that he has to tell about suburban adultery and the roué of a divorced father. I am not interested in Philip Roth's account of his particular sexual anxieties and Jewish self-consciousness and his funny, sweet, pathetic, vulgar parents. And yet Roth also is a wonderful writer in terms of sentence-by-sentence quality of writing. In other words I'm getting a very microscopic sort of my-nose-against-the-page view of things as I read. It might be a sentence that influences me—not a story, not a book, not even a writer.

CR: It dawns on me that your interest is in the process rather than the content, because these are all formalist writers.

SS: My interest is in the quality of the prose. I sound like Nabokov, I realize now, and to my astonishment, because this is the last thing in the world I would have predicted that I would feel. I am coming around as a reader—I can't say as a writer—to something like a Nabokov sensibility. I want to be enchanted and delighted, and I can be enchanted or delighted by very odd things. It might be part of something—a sentence, an image. I'm not seeing things anymore as a reader in terms of great blocks. I'm talking about my contemporaries—not Dostoyevsky or Kafka, that's another way of reading, another way of being inspired. I think often that the best work reflects some difficulty about conceiving large-scale works. That certainly is true in the case of both Hardwick and Barthelme.

CR: On the other hand you deplore the fact there is no American novelist who faces up to American society.

SS: Well, I think there are several reasons why that's true. I think there is a vice of American letters, which is the practice of unrestrained egotism. The notion that writing is above all an expression of the unrestrained, expansive self. Mailer has enormous gifts, but at the service of—I'm not saying anything original but I think it's true—at the service of subjects and displays of ego which I think are the ruin of his talent and the ruin of his stature as a potential major literary figure. The temptations of egotism and the temptations of commercialism are so that you have to be very eccentric to be a writer in this century who loves literature and is not mainly concerned with promoting himself, herself. I don't think I am talking about myself. I don't think that's my main job. I'm lending myself to the work when necessary. All sorts of mediocre writers try to portray the society as a whole. I think the writers who are going to last are the writers who care about language, and it may be that the best writers that we have right now are these people who work in these smaller fragmented parts, like Doctorow. Doctorow is a writer who is commercially successful and so rare. But as many people have noted about his new book, *Loon Lake,* it is a form of collage. It certainly isn't a novel in any conventional sense.

CR: Susan, in fiction, is your own material something you've always had and wanted to write down?

SS: Well, I'm taking Doctorow as a good example, because I want to do something really different from what I've done before. One is stuck with one's basic pool of fantasy but I feel that these stories that I am working on must be as different from the ones I have published in the '60s as they are from each other. That's important to me. I can't say why. Maybe because, like everybody else, I am profoundly uncertain about how to write. I know what I love or what I like because it's a direct passionate response. But when I write I'm very uncertain how it should be or whether it's good or, above all, whether it's good enough. That is, of course, the writer's agony.

CR: The public has many ideas about you. Are you bothered by the fact that people often refer to you instead of your work?

SS: Yes. But I live in the second half of the 20th century and I am an American and I have to be visible in a way that people are visible, otherwise I'm not visible at all. I want people to read my books. I have often had a Pynchon and Salinger fantasy and wished that very early on I had made that kind of decision not to be visible because I deeply respect that position. I wish I were crazy enough to do it without being aware of how pretentious it is, but I'm not crazy in that way, and it would be as if I were saying to everybody, "I am superior to all of you." The democrat in me with a small "d" could not bear it. After all, I'm not even a New Yorker. I grew up in southern Arizona and California; and I would just laugh at myself. To answer your question, of course it's true and infinitely discouraging that people say "Oh, I like your work so much. I saw you on Dick Cavett."

CR: With your sensibility and your saturnine definition of the self as a text to be deciphered, is it terrible having these reflections of your image brought to you again in all these distortions?

SS: I don't even read what's written about me and still I feel

scorched by it. I ask my son, David, to read them and tell me what
they said. And he'll tell me, "Oh, the *Village Voice* is really terrible."
Apparently the guy starts by saying he's never read any of my creative
work and has no intention of doing it. That's a nice beginning. I just
learned that today. I'm not going to read it, but just knowing that it's
there is very painful to me. And also a lot of the praise is painful. I
know it sounds ungrateful, but it's not, if one's heroes are Beckett
and Kafka as mine are, among others. How can one take this seriously? It's hard to be dignified. I hate the constant invitation to be
undignified and the constant assault on one's dignity. I hate that and
yet I feel I must stand still for that. You see, it's not bad reviews as
opposed to good reviews; it's a quality of attention that is very trivial.
Certain kinds of triviality are more visible because writers are makers
of consumer products, and so you are rated and treated in this way.

The Habits of Consciousness

Roger Copeland / 1981

From *Commonweal* (February 13, 1981), pp. 83–87. Reprinted by permission.

Roger Copeland: I don't know if it's possible for a brief passage in a short story to sum up an entire body of work, at least not one that includes films, novels, and essays as well as short stories. But let me give it a try. There's a paragraph in your story "Debriefing" which begins, "We know more than we can use. Look at all this stuff I've got in my head; rockets and Venetian churches, David Bowie and Diderot, nuoc nam and Big Macs, sunglasses and orgasms. How many newspapers and magazines do you read? For me, they're what candy or quaaludes or scream therapy are for my neighbors." Now here's what I'm getting at; regardless of whether you're writing about Sartre, Godard, Cioran, Syberberg, or Canetti, you seem to return obsessively to a single theme: the predatory habits of consciousness, the desire to hold the whole world in one's head. Do you agree?

Susan Sontag: Certainly. Consciousness as a form of acquisition; and the counter-projects of disburdenment and silence—the temptations of silence. These are unifying notions in my fiction and the essays. My first novel, *The Benefactor,* is about acquisition and disburdenment; and in *Death Kit,* the very notion of the kit, assembling the elements of a death, is another working out of this idea. "Unguided Tour," the last story in *I, etcetera,* is also about travel and tourism as a form of accumulation followed by a project of disburdenment. These ideas are not only obsessions and fantasies, but formal strategies as well. Ideas of this kind naturally give rise to disjunctive forms of writing, to the techniques of collage, assemblage, and inventory. In that sense, my work is an example of my thesis that form is a kind of content and content an aspect of form.

R.C.: Is it fair to say that the dilemma you describe in "Debriefing" is your own dilemma? One that you've experienced in an immediate, visceral way? I ask that in part because you own one of the most extraordinary personal libraries I've ever seen. It feels as if the entire history of the world is contained here in your apartment, and for all I know, here in your head. I can't help thinking of what you say about Elias Canetti in the last essay of *Under the Sign of Saturn*—that unlike Walter Benjamin, who collected books as objects, Canetti's sole obsession was to put the content of the books inside his head. When you write about Canetti in that way are you also writing about yourself?

S.S.: There's a part of me that identifies with most of the people I write about; it's almost as if I'd invented them, as if they were fantasy projections of part of myself. Please understand that I'm not attempting to put myself on the same level with these people. But particularly with Canetti, I felt I had invented a figure to dramatize my own fantasies. I don't mean that what I say about Canetti isn't true; only that it's a very selective view of him. For example, I talk about the way Canetti must have projected a lot of himself into the figure of Kien, the "bookman" in his novel, *Auto-da-Fé*. And there were moments while working on the essay that I felt I was making Canetti into my Kien. Again, I don't mean to suggest that this isn't also a valid portrait of Canetti, but it *is* an invention, a construction—as is the portrait of Benjamin in the new book. To single out the melancholy element in his temperament is obviously limiting, but that's what I identify with. Certainly my relationship to books is more like Canetti's than Walter Benjamin's. You know, Benjamin once sold his complete edition of Kafka—and there was no writer he loved more than Kafka except perhaps for Proust—because he saw a rare book, an 18th-century children's book which he coveted as a beautiful object, not because it held any intellectual interest for him. But I don't have that sort of relation to books at all. My library is what I have in my head. Of course, like any person who's had a traditional education, I prefer hardcover to paperback because I like the way hardcover books feel in my hands; but basically I don't care at all about the difference. Any book, in any edition, as long as I can read it.

R.C.: Aside from those recurring images of acquisition and disburdenment, are you aware of any other similarities—either formal or thematic—between your fiction and your critical essays?

S.S.: Jean-Luc Godard once said that he wanted to make fiction films that are like documentaries and documentaries that are like fiction films. And I suppose—at least at one time—I would have said

I wanted to write essays that are like fiction and fiction that has the quality of essays. I believe to some extent I have done that. I think of the essays in *Under the Sign of Saturn* as seven stories in essay form, seven portraits of consciousness. I suppose you could also say that the stories in *I, etcetera* contain essay elements.

R.C.: A few moments ago, you said that you identify strongly with the melancholic element in Benjamin's temperament. Something else that you seem to share with him is a fascination with certain surrealist ideas. I think it's in *On Photography* that you credit Benjamin with the most profound surrealist sensibility on record. What interests me about your definition of surrealism here—and in so many of your other essays—is that it has less to do with the actual content of dream life or the subconscious than with techniques of collage and radical juxtaposition, Lautreamont's sewing machine and umbrella meeting by chance on a dissecting table. What strikes you as surreal about Benjamin is his practice of collecting quotations, not any special interest in dreams.

S.S.: All of my essays, without exception, are attempts to ask what it means to be modern, to delineate the modern sensibility from as many different angles as possible. One of the names I've found for this sensibility is surrealism; but I'm aware of the fact that I conceive of surrealism in a very personal way. The reason I've always been so shy about allowing myself to be called a critic is that I know how eccentric these essays are—although I believe them to be true. The people officially called "Surrealists"—Breton and Company—all had a particular view of romantic love and a cult of woman with a capital "W." But this surrealist attitude toward love has absolutely left me cold, so I've simply left it out of my version of the surrealist sensibility.

In a sense, I suppose I stretched the term surrealism in much the same way I stretched the notion of camp so as to examine the phenomenon of dandyism in modern life. In "Notes on 'Camp,' " I was taking a piece of slang that had a certain currency in the homosexual world and trying to generalize it, to go beyond whatever meaning it might have had as a code word. Of course, I pulled back in horror when I learned that I'd hatched this "thing" that people wanted to transform into a commercial enterprise. The essay came at a moment when all this Warhol stuff was starting and people needed a catchphrase to describe it. But that of course wasn't what I was talking about at all; and I really felt my essay had been kidnapped, hijacked. Consequently, I haven't allowed that word to pass my lips since 1964—despite all the offers I've received to elaborate on or update the essay. Perhaps I latched onto the word surrealism fleeing from notions like camp and kitsch. Better to use a word that people won't get so excited about.

R.C.: We've talked about some of the concerns that you've voiced over and over again in many different contexts. But let me suggest one way in which I think your ideas have changed over the last several years. Elizabeth Hardwick wrote a very admiring profile of you in 1978; but she said something in it that struck me as terribly ironic: she thought she was praising you by writing, "Scarcely anyone is more alive to the interesting. . . ." Now that might have been true in the mid-sixties; but in the last few years, it seems to me that you've become increasingly critical of the promiscuous way people use the word "interesting"—you seem to me to be arguing that it's not enough anymore to be merely "interesting." Am I right?

S.S.: Yes, you're quite right. I was astonished by Elizabeth's remark. She was 100 percent wrong. In fact, for a couple of years now, I've been accumulating notes toward a critique of this notion of "the interesting." It started with the sixth essay in *On Photography* where I argued that one of the ways in which photographs are untrue is that they make *everything* "interesting." And then, of course, in *Illness as Metaphor,* I talk about this 19th-century notion that tuberculosis makes one more interesting. Actually, the first person to attack the idea of the interesting is Hegel. Early in the 19th century, it's already being proposed as a criterion for art; and Hegel says it's not enough.

R.C.: But certainly, at one point in time, you thought it was "enough," perhaps even preferable in some ways—or on some occasions—to "the truth."

S.S.: In the sixties, there was a whole period in my life when I was spending a lot of time with Jasper Johns, John Cage, Merce Cunningham, and Marcel Duchamp. "Interesting" was a favorite word of theirs; and in the mouths of people like Cage and Johns, the word sounded very glamorous and aristocratic. It was terrifically liberating for me to be with these people and hear their babble—I don't mean that condescendingly—it's just that they had a very special way of talking.

R.C.: I think I know what you mean. They all seemed to exude a sort of cool, detached, euphoria, a sophisticated cheerfulness. Cage is certainly one hell of an alternative to someone like Cioran—which explains, I suppose, why you contrasted the two of them in your essay on E. M. Cioran in *Styles of Radical Will*. Certainly, Cage is much more optimistic than Cioran; and he doesn't feel the least bit burdened by "history."

S.S.: I now think the juxtaposition of Cioran with Cage was sophistical. If I were to write about Cioran today, I would proceed rather differently. There's a political dimension to Cioran's pessimism that comes from having witnessed the failure of Communism in Eastern Europe. It became clear I situated his work in too abstract a way.

If there's been a real change in my views over the years, it's that I've had to give the historicist approach a more central role in my reaction to things.

R.C.: In your essay on Cioran, you seem to be lamenting the rise of historical consciousness in the 19th century—Kleist's notion that there's no return to innocence, that we have no choice but to go to the very end of consciousness. And that of course is the same conception of history that helped bring the avant-garde into being, with one movement or "ism" displacing its predecessor at a dizzying rate of speed. Do you see any way off the avant-garde escalator? Or is the desire to somehow escape this cul-de-sac simply one more consequence of the avant-garde conception of history, more hunger for change?

S.S.: Today, we are living out the paradoxes of eschatological thinking. Actually, the various avant-garde "isms" were not supposed to replace one another. Each conceived of itself as the terminal "ism." But we've discovered that there is no terminal "ism"; the messiah doesn't come. History doesn't end—although particular histories end.

R.C.: But people today seem terribly eager to declare this phase of modernism dead and done with.

S.S.: Absolutely. And now one is obliged to start defending again the things that one had begun to take for granted. For example, in literature, John Gardner's dreadful book, *On Moral Fiction,* is only the most outrageous of the new manifestos declaring that modernism is over. Of course, these views are also moral and political. They suggest that this modern or experimental or avant-garde literature was elitist and that the only good writers are also commercially successful. And so, John Fowles and a lot of writers whose names I hardly know are the people Gardner proposes as the only serious writers. It seems that people don't want books—or any form of art—to be *hard*. They want art to be decorative. That's why photographs are so popular, because photographs seem easy to encounter and decipher. But the great achievements of 20th-century art have been *hard,* demanding a certain kind of commitment, piety, and investment of attention.

It's not just that people want things to be easy; things that weren't so hard in the past seem more difficult today. I recently met a young woman at a major university who is writing her Ph.D on Proust. This is her sixth year as a graduate student; and she asked me, "Don't you find it hard to read Proust—all those long sentences?" And I asked, "Hard compared to what? Kurt Vonnegut? Yeah, I guess it's harder than Kurt Vonnegut." I submit that twenty years ago, no graduate student in her sixth year at a well known university would even have been able to utter such a sentence. It wouldn't have been sayable. She would rather have gotten undressed in the middle of the street than say, shamelessly and rather wistfully, "Don't you think that Proust is kinda hard?" People don't even know what they can't say anymore. The whole question of decorum tells you a lot about where you are. It's not just what people do or feel; it's also what they think can be said. There are all sorts of changes like this, of people more and more finding things hard, of people not having the necessary energy.

R.C.: What accounts for that loss of energy, do you think?

S.S.: For one thing, the acceptance of television, the mentality and kind of attention that is the given of television. The condition of our attention, the condition of our seriousness has been progressively altered.

R.C.: Do you own a television set?

S.S.: No, never. Not even in 1950. For me, it's an absolutely visceral dislike. The first time I saw television, it just gave me a headache. I thought it was so dreadful to look at this tiny, out-of-focus image and then have everything interrupted all the time by commercials. You can tell me till the cows come home that I've missed this or that interesting program; but that doesn't justify it for me. I know this sounds terribly cranky and eccentric; very few people say this and even fewer of the people who say it actually live it. But I really think it's the death of western civilization. It's the death of literature, the death of literacy, and the death of politics. You can see the way people live now; it's different from the way they lived before.

R.C.: And you don't even feel a sociological curiosity about television? It's not that I imagine you putting down a book of Roland Barthes's because "Laverne and Shirley" is about to come on; but you're so attuned to the tenor of the culture, it surprises me that you never watch.

S.S.: I think that's an alibi. I think you're kidding yourself if you believe you're on top of it because you're looking at it sociologically or because you have an ironic relationship to it. What's actually happening is that it's destroying your ability to concentrate and pay attention. I'll match my detailed sociological knowledge of American popular culture and more against anyone's. But I don't believe for a minute that it's actually necessary for me to *watch* television. To know about America, you only have to travel around and listen to people *talk* about television. I do confess to reading television reviews; but I don't think I'd learn any more from actually watching television than I already know from movies, magazines, spending time with a lot of young people, and going to bars, rock concerts, and discos.

R.C.: I think what you're saying right now is going to surprise some of those children of the McLuhanite sixties who saw you as America's premier intellectual swinger, someone whose consciousness was large enough to take everything in without compromising its seriousness. After all, you were the intellectual who said it's all right to listen to the Supremes.

S.S.: But I haven't changed in that respect. Today, if it's not the Supremes, it's Bruce Springsteen. I'm still the same person, enjoying the same or an even greater range of pleasures. One of the chief ideas of modernism was this new relationship between high culture and popular culture. That goes back at least to Apollinaire. And it was my reiterating of this older, modernist position in the early sixties which seemed so distinctive because there was nobody else around who had my commitment to the traditional literary and philosophical culture who also seemed to know about these other things and to enjoy them. But I still think television is the enemy. The fact is, I don't think you can have *everything*. Whatever I said about high culture and the Supremes, they still have to be in certain proportions.

R.C.: Why is it, do you think, that people insist on putting you in one category or the other? Either they see you as the defender of some new barbarism or as a sort of closet Arnoldian, the "Eminent Victorian" as *The Village Voice* recently labeled you.

S.S.: One of the more discouraging reactions to my new book or to my recent work in general is that people always want to find some great change from the work of the sixties. I think it's part of everyone's over-eagerness to repudiate the sixties. I carry this fortuitous, journalistic label as a spokesperson for the sixties. So then if people continue to like the work I'm doing in the seventies and eighties, it has to be shown that I'm not really the person I was labeled as—the intellectual passionaria of the sixties—that I'm really humane or conservative.

R.C.: I remember Hilton Kramer's article in *The Times* after you published your piece on the aesthetics of fascism. He argued that you had repudiated your earlier commitment to aesthetic autonomy, that the new essay on Riefenstahl was at odds with what you said about *Triumph of the Will* in an older essay, "On Style." But I don't think you ever pitted the aesthetic and the ethical against one another.

S.S.: I don't think I did either and who could? Of course, I *have* indulged myself from time to time in neo-Wildean sallies as one does sometimes when one gets impatient with other people's insensitivity to beauty. But it would be imbecilic simply to *defend* beauty or to contend that there is something called beauty which exists absolutely apart from any kind of historical coloring or ethical mandate. No one believed that, least of all Oscar Wilde, Baudelaire, Valéry, or Barthes.

R.C.: I'd be interested in hearing you talk about some of the less obvious influences on your work, less obvious than say, Ortega, the Bloomsbury Group, or the New Critics.

S.S.: Lionel Trilling, for one, was a great influence on me. "The Fate of Pleasure," particularly, was a major event in my life. The first time I read it, I just couldn't believe what I was reading, something that addressed so many of the problems I was worrying about. Even if I couldn't subscribe to the way he was resolving these questions, I felt that somebody was talking about the things that mattered. In fact, long before that, when I was a fifteen-year-old kid at North Hollywood High School, I discovered a newsstand on the corner of Hollywood and Highland that carried literary magazines. I'd never seen a literary magazine before; certainly I'd never seen anybody read one. I picked up *Partisan Review* and I started to read "Art and Fortune" by Lionel Trilling; and I just began to tremble with excitement, and from then on, my dream was to grow up, move to New York and write for *Partisan Review*. Then within a year, I'd read all the New Critics and had become a great fan of Kenneth Burke's. The following year I went to the University of Chicago where I became a student of Kenneth Burke's. Nobody knows that I was a student of Burke's.

R.C.: That's actually not as surprising as it sounds at first. There are some real similarities between you and Burke. You're both wide-ranging generalists, you're not academically pedigreed.

S.S.: He was the first *living* influence on me. I'd had many influences in my head from the time I was born till the time I was sixteen, from Edgar Allan Poe to Lionel Trilling—but the first person I met who exerted an influence on me was Kenneth Burke.

R.C.: Were you influenced by Burke's ideas about dramaturgy, or his conception of language as symbolic action?

S.S.: I think by temperament I was attracted to dramaturgical kinds of language. I think of the essays in *Under the Sign of Saturn* as *stagings* of a certain kind, dramatizations.

R.C.: Also, you've directed both films and plays. I understand you recently staged a Pirandello play in Italy.

S.S.: Yes, *As You Desire Me* for the National Theatre. And what I did with Pirandello is not so different from what I did with Canetti in the last essay of the book. What fascinates me about this Pirandello play is the theme of psychological cannibalism. So I moved the character played by Greta Garbo in the film version to the center of my production as a sort of queen bee who entraps the other characters; but ultimately she is their victim. Of course to do this, I had to leave a great deal out. But I think in some ways I've made it into a better play than it really is. By finding something in it that is also part of my repository of fantasy, I could make a very strong experience out of it—but at the same time, a very limited, idiosyncratic experience. It's the same sort of thing I've done with Canetti. I've probably left out 90 percent of what Canetti is about. What's there in the essay is filtered through my temperament. It's . . . my Canetti.

Interview with Susan Sontag

Wendy Lesser / 1981

From *The Threepenny Review*, No. 7 (Fall 1981), pp. 6–7. Reprinted by permission.

Susan Sontag published her first novel, *The Benefactor,* in 1963. Since then she has published another novel *(Death Kit)* and a book of short stories *(I, etcetera),* and has also made several films, including a documentary about Israel.

However, Sontag is perhaps best known for her essays, which in their range and seriousness are unlike anything written in this country, at least since Edmund Wilson. And, like Wilson, Sontag has chosen to remain outside the university setting, thus preserving a kind of "unacademic freedom" in her choice of topics. In *Against Interpretation,* published in the mid-1960s, she introduced the general American reader to such European figures as Lukács, Sartre, Simone Weil, Godard, Bresson, and Lévi-Strauss; she also, in essays like the now-famous "Notes on 'Camp,' " explored and defined America's own underground culture. In subsequent essays collected in *Styles of Radical Will* and *Under the Sign of Saturn,* she turned her attention to topics ranging from American politics and German fascism to the works of Elias Canetti, Ingmar Bergman, Antonin Artaud, and Walter Benjamin. In *Illness as Metaphor*—written while she herself was ill with cancer—Sontag used literary, historical, and contemporary medical sources to compare the myths about tuberculosis and cancer. And in *On Photography,* she examined the nature of photographic representation in a series of essays unadorned by a single illustrative photograph.

Throughout her career, Sontag has been attracted to what might broadly be labeled "modernism." Yet she is an odd and therefore engaging spokesman for this cultural trend, for her own essayistic style is in high contrast to what she chooses to write about. Sontag is drawn to what she once called "the artist as exemplary sufferer"—to the fragmentation, exaggeration, morbidity, and lunacy with which art has responded to the modern world. Her own tone, however, is one of eminent rationality. If she is the modern version of the nineteenth-century sage, then she is certainly a toned-down Ruskin, a sane Nietzsche—and in fact a great part of her appeal as a stylist lies in that reasonable tone of certainty, that restrained assertiveness, that assurance of her own well-groundedness. This contradiction between the objective voice of her analysis and the subjective flavor of the art she examines is not, I think, one that

Sontag would wish to evade or deny. On the contrary, as the following interview makes clear, she does not shy away from apparent contradictions—between the personal and the impersonal, between certainty and uncertainty, between acceptance and rejection of what the twentieth century has produced.

This interview was conducted in New York City in March of 1981.

Wendy Lesser: Since Farrar, Straus & Giroux is bringing out a *Susan Sontag Reader,* I assume you've been going over your old work to make selections. How do you think you've changed, in terms of your writing? That is, how do you feel about your earlier work, and what kinds of content or style changes do you notice in yourself?

Susan Sontag: It's difficult to answer that question. I am necessarily my own editor—there's a first draft, and then the re-working of it many times. But I have no inclination to be the critic of my work.

Lesser: Do you wish you could revise when something appears in a new edition?

Sontag: There are some sentences in *The Benefactor* and in *Death Kit* I would like to tamper with, and more than a few passages in *Death Kit* I would cut. But I'm not in fact changing anything for the *Reader*.

Lesser: You're tempted to rework fiction, but not essays?

Sontag: The fact that I may have other ideas now doesn't make me want to alter an old essay. At most, it might make me want to write another essay. But the novels and stories are not part of an ongoing argument but objects, language—whose flaws, when I perceive them, torment me.

In general one is ill-advised to rewrite published work from the past—one is likely simply to make it uniform. I don't think there is much to be said even for re-reading.

Lesser: You don't re-read your work at all?

Sontag: Public readings of fiction excepted, no, I don't re-read what I've published. I'm too prone to draw discouraging conclusions. If I like what I read, I may think I can't now write something as fine. Or, if I don't care for it, I may think that I never was much good. . . . Anyway, it seems futile to try to be the caretaker of one's work. It belongs to me until it is published, when I can still make changes, try to get it as right as I can. What readers do with it, whether I am (as I hope) making work which will last—my part ends with my doing the best I can.

Lesser: Are you ever conscious, when you're writing, of disagreeing with your own earlier opinions?

Sontag: If so, very dimly. Rather, I am relieved to be able to go on, to say something else. Even in the throes of what I deem a salutary exaggeration, I'm burdensomely aware that there's always more to say. Everything I've written—and done—has had to be wrested from the sense of complexity. *This,* yes. But also *that.* It's not really disagreement, it's more like turning a prism—to see something from another point of view.

Lesser: Do you think there are writers whom you know of now but are not yet interested in—just as there may be writers whom you've grown out of? Can you locate yourself between writers, in terms of tastes?

Sontag: I'm always between. Most of my reading is re-reading. Last night I opened *Mrs. Dalloway* to look up something (I thought I remembered a reference to Wagner, whom I've been thinking a lot about lately) and started to read and couldn't stop. I read until two in the morning and woke at eight to read until eleven, when you arrived—something I had no intention of doing. I first read *Mrs. Dalloway* when I was sixteen; and each time—this was the fourth—it has seemed like a different book. This time I thought it more extraordinary, more original, even stronger than I had remembered. Since the books are here, I will be able to come in and out of them many times in my life.

A certain kind of brilliant, rapturous writing appeals to me more now than it used to. When I was very young, my tastes were more ascetic. I was suspicious of prose that was nervous or too succulent. I wanted from writing something more assertive. I look for enchantment from literature more than I did then. I'm also a subtler reader of poetry now. When I was young I liked only the masterful—Milton, Hopkins, Eliot.

Lesser: What do you think accounts for the fact that *On Photography* was a best seller? I mean, why that rather than any of your other works?

Sontag: You're asking me now to be not only my own critic, but my own agent. I have to assume that it's because people are interested in the subject.

Lesser: Do you think about the audience?

Sontag: As someone said, "A writer is a person with readers." I have only a very tautological notion of the audience: that the audience for a book of mine is the audience that would like this kind of book. And here I am only speculating—or rather, refusing to speculate—about a book's initial audience. What I understand by literature implies that a book will have an audience thirty or fifty years after it's published—which means that most books acclaimed as literature when published are *not* part of literature. Whether one's own writing is part of that tiny body of work that is valuable enough still to be read by the end of the century—this haunting ambition makes other calculations seem beside the point.

Lesser: Both *On Photography* and *Illness as Metaphor* seem to have required an enormous quantity of research. But the research is such that it's obviously not the kind where you select a subject, read about it, and then write—it's a much more various kind of research. I was wondering how you got all those pieces of information.

Sontag: But I didn't do any research for either of those books. Absolutely none. I would hardly call curiosity and an addiction to reading, which is part of my daily life, research.

Lesser: But how do you accumulate the very specific pieces?

Sontag: I remember what I read. All the references in *On Photography* and *Illness as Metaphor* are to books which I have on my shelves. If in, say, *Illness as Metaphor* I quote from *She Stoops to Conquer,* it's because I've read Goldsmith's play several times, recall a passage that's relevant to what I'm writing, get the book down and copy it out. . . . If thinking about many things and reading avidly is what, among other things, you do, and you've been doing that for decades, you know a lot. [*Laugh.*] And I've never had a television set.

Lesser: I meant to ask you about that. Why have you not only not written about television, but hardly even alluded to it? It's almost as if television doesn't exist—

Sontag: Well, it doesn't exist for me, in the sense that I have the good fortune to be a natural—I mean, effortless—teetotaller where television is concerned. But I'm very aware of how much it's changed the whole mental and cultural atmosphere. I think television is the death of civilization—the death of politics, the death of literacy. And I do refer to it. Much of *On Photography* is a covert argument about television, and my fiction contains many allusions to the box.

Lesser: This death-of-civilization notion—I wanted to ask you whether you thought of history in terms of progress at all. Do you wish you'd lived at another time?

Sontag: There are several things which reconcile me to the terrible twentieth century. One is that this is the first time in the history of the human species that women have a chance at formal equality. If for no other reason, because I am a woman and not a man—

Lesser: You would have been stuck in an earlier time?

Sontag: No, no. I'm not talking about myself, or about any one person. After all, there have always been exceptional women. If I were to think about myself, I have enough self-esteem to entertain the fantasy that I might have been a writer, and an independent person, even in an earlier era. I am not saying this because of any egotistical concern about what my life would have been like in another time. I say it because, as a woman, I want justice for the half of the human population to which I belong. It matters to me to live during the time in history when this idea has emerged.

Lesser: And the other thing?

Sontag: That notions of distributive justice are alive today as they have never been before. The idea that everyone has a right to a decent wage, comfortable shelter, medical attention; that one should not have to work fifteen hours a day in degrading painful labor; that children shouldn't have to work and that all children should be able to go to school—these are modern ideas, born in the nineteenth century, and generally assented to today.

And there's a third thing. This is the first century that's had any medicine that really works. There was little medical intervention that saved people's lives and cured disease until the nineteenth century, when the theory of germs was discovered. Everything that happened before was just fooling around, and compassion, and art—and self-healing. Most scientific medical knowledge starts no more than fifty years ago.

Lesser: The "women" issue is complicated for you, because I think you've made an effort not to be seen as a "woman artist," a "woman writer"—which is hard to do, given the pressures of the women's movement.

Sontag: But I haven't made an effort. It's natural to me. I'm a militant feminist, but not a feminist militant. My work is both bigger and smaller than I am.

Lesser: Actually, your work has a very complicated relationship to the issue of the personal, or the subjective, I think—because it stems always from the personal and the subjective, but its expression seems finally not that at all.

Sontag: I often feel that the best way to convey the passions I feel is not by speaking about myself. Some people have said to me that they don't understand how I could be so "detached" as to write *Illness as Metaphor.* I find this preposterous. I wasn't in the slightest detached. It was a book written in the heat of rage, fear, anguish, terror, indignation—at a time when I was very ill and my prognosis was poor. It wasn't that I was detached. On the contrary. But I didn't become an idiot just because I had cancer. And I did have an idea, which was liberating for me and I thought would be useful to others trapped by the punitive fantasies that surround cancer. My idea starts from the parallel between the myths about tuberculosis (to which we all feel so superior) and the myths about cancer (still prevalent). Rather than relating how I was terrified when I learned that I had cancer; how I struggled; how I found good treatment and learned that cancer is just a disease . . . rather than writing something about myself, I thought that it would be more enlightening—the book was meant to be a useful instrument—to share this idea.

Lesser: Do you think that having cancer, or writing the book, or both—do you think that it changed your notions about will? Because prior to that—in *Styles of Radical Will,* obviously, and in certain essays, you characterize art as very connected to will. Will is a very strong thing for you in your early work. And then you almost have to turn against will in *Illness as Metaphor.*

Sontag: The criticism of the will is a theme in most of the stories collected in *I, etcetera,* most of which were written before I became ill. But I don't underestimate that being near death was a turning point. Yes. I think that there was something desperate in all that talk about will.

Again, it's something personal—I feel in many ways self-created, self-educated. There's some truth in that, but it's also part of the national cultural equipment. Americans have a tendency to overestimate the will—hence, all these therapy groups, and endlessly renewable projects of self-reclamation, transformation, detoxification, rebirth, that Americans are so fond of. I suppose that will is still central for me, but not in the same raw way.

Lesser: Would you say that you don't like to write about yourself?

Sontag: Well, I take for granted that what happens in art is the transcendence of the personal. There are things in my work which are autobiographical. But the point is not to express oneself. The point is to make something wonderful.

Every time I say "I," I feel it's a fiction. Of course the "I" has some connection with me—I don't want to present a schizophrenic account of what I do. But the I that can say "I" in print is not the same I that speaks to my friends, that leads a life.

Lesser: Is the novel you're working on now in the first person?

Sontag: Some sections are in the first person—there are several speakers. And some parts are narrated in the third person. It's a long, complex book.

Lesser: Any more essays?

Sontag: It's hard to resist, but I'm trying. There are many subjects I'd like to write about. But when I consider that each of the essays takes many months to write, and it isn't that I'm doing it better, I'm just doing another one, I feel reluctant to go on . . .

Someone once asked me who my favorite writer was, and seemed surprised when I said "Shakespeare, of course"—surprised, I suppose, because I'd never written about Shakespeare. But I'm more likely to write about, say, Witkiewicz than about Shakespeare—not because I prefer Witkiewicz to the divine Will but because the world could use a good essay about Witkiewicz. But I'd rather spend the months it would take to write that one essay writing three stories.

A Conversation with Susan Sontag

Amy Lippman / 1983

From *The Harvard Advocate*, Vol. 117 (Fall 1983), pp. 2–4, 26. Reprinted by permission.

Susan Sontag is a novelist, essayist, and filmmaker. Her books include two novels, *The Benefactor* and *Death Kit,* and several critical works, among them *On Photography, Illness as Metaphor,* and *Under the Sign of Saturn.* She is also the author of a collection of short stories, *I, etcetera.*

This interview was conducted in two parts in New York City in April. It followed soon after a lecture Ms. Sontag gave at Boston College, in which she discussed the nature of storytelling in past and contemporary literature and culture.

Ms. Sontag lives in New York and is presently working on a novel.

The Advocate: In your lecture at Boston College last month, you spoke of the atrophying of storytelling. Why do you think this is so?

Sontag: The decline in storytelling is related, I think, to a decline in linguistic skills—the erasing of local differences in speech, of heightened, idiomatic speech; the standardization of speech by television. Even more, to a decline of confidence in language itself. People feel more confidence in the ability of images to convey or sum up situations. Through the aptly-named "media," an unassimilably large number of events swim into view—but these are told in a devalued language, collage-style, with one story succeeding another; it's mostly a gallery of horrors. While storytelling precedes literacy, it does not seem to be surviving in a post-literate society. That 98% of the households in this country possess television sets, with people watching an average of forty hours a week, means not only a decline of time available to reading and gossiping. There has to be a mutation of consciousness.

The Advocate: Do you watch television?

Sontag: No.

The Advocate: But people do talk about themselves.

Sontag: The only institution in modern urban culture that invites storytelling is psychotherapy. But the story told to a therapist or a therapy group is a function of a complaint. To explain why one feels depressed or why one is insomniac, one relates how one was mistreated by one's parents or disappointed in one's marriage. The story's already thematic, illustrative. People treat their experience as alienated from themselves. Experience, thus depreciated in value, is viewed as observing the laws of fashion—such as built-in obsolescence; the self is regarded as a commodity, its decisions as sociologically predictable behavior. When people say, "Well, my lifestyle is . . ." or "I'm planning to change my lifestyle to . . .," what they're talking about are their *lives*. There's a vast and instructive difference between saying "my life" and "my lifestyle." The same self-evisceration can be observed in the current custom of describing oneself as a creature of a certain decade. I've heard "I felt bad because I'm a very 60s person" and "Being a 70s person, I thought . . ."—people treating themselves as if they were products, not subjects.

The Advocate: What about the self in contemporary fiction?

Sontag: There is nothing comparable in literature to the conceptual gridlock in the visual arts, but there does seem to be a certain staleness. The mood is rather dreary and cautious—and there is much expert writing that is little more than cute. Some American writers are going further and further into the miniaturization of the banal. Others reach out for macro-effects—a kind of degenerate picaresque. Releasing the narrative impulse seems easier if the fiction is set in the past, often using historical celebrities. Or in the future—though, of course, most so-called science fiction is just a transposition of present linguistic and psychological customs.

The Advocate: Who are some writers who have influenced you?

Sontag: Hard to say—because I'm not sure I'm influenced by what I most admire. Among the writers in whose work I recognize my own themes are, for example, Poe and Karel Capek, both of whom I read as a child—Poe (I'm thinking of his stories and essays) well before I was ten, Capek at twelve.

The Advocate: Do you think fiction needs to be moral?

Sontag: Fiction needs to be wonderful—Nabokov's idea of aesthetic bliss.

The Advocate: But do you think that fiction has some sort of ethical component?

Sontag: I think the highest duty of a writer is to write well—to leave the language in better rather than worse shape after one's passage. That's an ethical obligation. Language is the body, and also the soul, of consciousness. Our ultimate responsibility is to act chivalrously toward the language we inhabit.

The Advocate: Any other moral component?

Sontag: The fact that plurality is a part of literature—the dialogue among books. Both Austen *and* Beckett. We learn that there are many different ways to be, many temperaments . . . and the fact that to care about literature is to feel at home with the idea that some things are better than other things and a few things are better than everything else.

The Advocate: How do you relate your fiction to your essays?

Sontag: While I'm tempted by Musil's view that there is no longer any essential difference between a writer of fiction and an essayist, I don't believe it. Fiction is what I care most about, but I've written more essays than fiction. Because I read and study and travel a lot, periodically I come to feel I'm silting up. I need to slough off.

But I procrastinate—so that, usually, I write essays only when I am *beyond* the point of view I propose in them. That's probably one reason they take so long to write—the six essays on photography occupied nearly five years. *Illness as Metaphor* and the essay on Riefenstahl ("Fascinating Fascism") are exceptions. They were written with violence and in high spirits, and quickly. . . .

More recently, the essays have a lighter cargo of ideas. Some of the essays in *Under the Sign of Saturn,* in particular the essays on Benjamin and Canetti, are portraits. Behind them is something closer to the project of fiction—the describing of an individual sensibility as distinct from a sensibility in general (an example of which is my "Notes on 'Camp' "). And the individual portraits are less idea-ridden, less expository than they were (an example is the long essay on Artaud). Most of my ambitious essays have been descriptions of a sensibility.

The Advocate: Have you been writing essays lately?

Sontag: Right now I'm finishing a short essay on poets' prose, inspired by reading the prose of Mandelstam and Tsvetayeva. Much of the best prose of this century has been written by poets. And after that, I'll return to a long essay I started last year on politics and intellectuals, called *Before the Revolution*.

The Advocate: And fiction?

Sontag: I've begun a novella, which takes place in the late 1920s— the first time I've set fiction in the past—with a protagonist suggested by a famous woman of the period. I hope to return from this foray into the past with freedoms I can use in setting fiction in the present—as I do in the long novel on which I've been working, on and off. But I've kept leaving it to do other things, such as direct a Pirandello play for the National Theatre in Italy three years ago and—this past winter—make a film in Venice for Italian television. Or write some essays.

The Advocate: Are there thematic concerns that tie your fiction to your essays?

Sontag: Yes, there is a common pool of material and themes. One is duplication or replication—as an image, as a nightmare, as a compulsion, and as a source of poetry, of beauty. This is illustrated countless times in the meditations that circle around the subject of photography in *On Photography* and is also a theme of my fiction, in *The Benefactor,* for example, or in the fable in *I, etcetera* called "The Dummy." Other themes are travel—change—the touristic way of looking at the world—real and derisory projects of transcendence. Similar sentences about the photographic image, about replication, about suicide, about spiritual projects, about admiration occur in my fictions and essays. But the fiction often presents the themes ironically, while the essays stay "responsible." The fiction comes from a deeper place than the essays, a place where I am freer. I'm perfectly free to create a world in which everyone has two heads. The only rules the novel can violate are internal—rules of its own making. I can fly as well as walk. I can change the gait radically from one part to another.

The Advocate: Do you consider the stories in *I, etcetera* experiments in form?

Sontag: I didn't when I was writing them. In the case of each story, I found a form that seemed appropriate to the material, that seemed inevitable. Only when I was selecting the stories for the collection in 1978 did I start to see them as a series of adventures with the first person. (Hence the book's title, which is not the title of any story in it.) Of the eight stories in the collection, six are written in the first person; and one of the six, "Baby," was cast in the first person plural—which, as far as I know, had never been done before. But all those "ideas" occurred to me after the writing. Certainly the stories were not conceived as illustrating formal conceptions.

The Advocate: Is it illustrative of your own experience?

Sontag: My impulse has mostly been anti-autobiographical. Of course, one is always lending oneself—one's fantasies, one's observations—to the work. But the characters are rarely modeled either on myself or on people I've known. I like making things up. And the fantastic or speculative fiction I'm drawn to seemed to preclude the directly autobiographical. At one time I was excluding all that could be self-referring. That's probably the reason that the central characters in both my novels are men. The main character in *The Benefactor* is not only a man but one in his sixties—I was a woman in my late twenties. It was a step forward in my second novel, *Death Kit,* when I made the main character, though again a man, someone my own age. It was later, in writing the stories collected in *I, etcetera,* that I found access to events of my own life in two stories—"Project for a Trip to China" and "Debriefing." Still, even with this new freedom, my life, my consciousness, my concerns are not identical with—in many ways different from—the material in my fiction. There are many subjects I haven't yet found a voice for in fiction. Romantic love is one. But in fact I never start with a subject. What starts me is a voice, or a word. Often it's just a word. Someone says "meretricious" and a whole world is generated by that adjective, and I begin to invent a situation that is meretricious. And then I discover who the characters are—the instruments that are playing this music. Though I do hope that one day one of the instruments will turn out to be, say, a mother, I feel no obligation to write in the voice of a woman (whatever that might be) or to make my protagonist a woman. But of course I want to feel I can do that. In fact, the main character of the novella I'm writing is a woman. . . . One wants to respect and protect one's obsessions. And what makes the work grow is to develop a greater capacity for expressiveness. Greater access to your expressiveness, to your capacity to make something that is expressive in and of itself.

The Advocate: You mean self-expression?

Sontag: I don't think I'm expressing myself. I hope not. But I am the instrument for whatever I can convey expressively. My urge to write is an urge not to self-expression but to self-transcendence.

The Advocate: Do you find that your critical work is greatly affected by the work you do in fiction and film?

Sontag: No, because I try to pen the essay-writing off from the other activities. For instance, I did write some essays on film in the mid-1960s—Godard's work was a great event for me—but when I decided to start making films myself, I no longer had any desire to write about them. Ten years later I made one exception, "Syberberg's Hitler" (in *Under the Sign of Saturn*), because that film supplied me with a pretext for talking about other things, such as the romantic ideas of the work of art, in particular the Wagnerian and Symbolist aesthetics. . . . I've rarely written about fiction, because of my own commitment to writing fiction. Part of the freedom of writing the essays in *On Photography* was that I'm not a photographer. At least two decades of passionate looking at photographic images lies behind those essays—but it's not something I do. Photography has the same status as other passions on which I haven't written, like the history of architecture, or one about which I've started to write a little, dance. I'm more likely to write about things that involve me as a member of the audience, as a student of the subject, rather than as a practitioner.

The Advocate: You once referred to writing as a "desexualizing" process. What did you mean by that?

Sontag: To sit long hours is dephysicalizing. When I'm writing, I'm ears and a mumbling mouth and hands at the typewriter, and I have to forget my body. I eat little—usually I lose weight when I'm working at full tilt—and don't sleep much. All quite ascetic. And thrilling. As Noel Coward observed, "Work is more fun than fun."

The Advocate: Is writing cathartic for you?

Sontag: Writing about something is a form of mastery, and therefore self-altering. But I'm not drawn to thinking about the creation of literature psychologically, or attributing to it any therapeutic benefits. My standards aren't personal standards. Literature comes from emulation.

The Advocate: Have you other projects?

Sontag: Directing another play, and an opera—I'd like to do *The Makropulos Case*. Robert Brustein and I have some as yet unspecified plans about my coming to direct a play at Harvard, at the Loeb.

The Advocate: In conjunction with the American Repertory
Theatre?

Sontag: Yes.

The Advocate: What is the film you just completed in Italy?

Sontag: It's very freely adapted from "Unguided Tour," the last
story in *I, etcetera*. Instead of the unhappy lovers being, as it were,
everywhere—as they are in my story—I set them in Venice, the ideal
location for a meditation on the tourism of melancholy. The woman is
played by the American dancer and choreographer Lucinda Childs
and the man by an Italian actor named Claudio Cassinelli. The film
Unguided Tour was commissioned by the Third Channel of Italian
television. I shot it on a miniscule budget in October of last year, and
then edited it for three months in Rome.

The Advocate: It's your third film?

Sontag: Fourth. And, I think, my best. I've made two fiction films
in Sweden, *Duet for Cannibals* in 1969 and *Brother Carl* in 1971 and a
non-fiction (not a documentary) in Israel in 1973–74 called *Promised
Lands*.

The Advocate: Why haven't you made any films in the United
States?

Sontag: I haven't tried. I'd like to.

The Advocate: Do you look back on the work that you've done with
a sense of satisfaction?

Sontag: Thinking about past work seems a burden. And the process
of moving from one project to another is in large part a sequence of
liberations. It would be impossible for me to write if I didn't think I
could surpass myself. That idea of surpassing oneself is the deepest
theme in my work, and my relation to the work. Therefore, the very
nature of my relation to my work is one of dissatisfaction. It's such
considerations that give me permission to write. It's a most unnatural
activity, and it's not just intelligence or perceptiveness or sensitivity—
even a sense of language—that suffice to make a writer. What I call
permission might be identified as the very capacity for expressiveness.
One is always struggling to enlarge just that, the expressiveness itself.
As I said, I don't think of my writing as self-expression. I don't want
to tell "my story." But I do want to have the freedom to lend to the
work not only my sense of things, but myself. One strives to give
oneself permission to make *everything* available to the writing—amid
all this inertia and intimidation and dread that one can't help but feel.

An Interview with Susan Sontag

Eileen Manion and Sherry Simon / 1984

"An Interview with Susan Sontag" first appeared in the *Canadian Journal of Political and Social Theory,* Vol. 9, Nos. 1–2 (1985), pp. 7–15. Reprinted by permission.

Since the mid-1960s, Susan Sontag has been a highly visible figure on the New York intellectual scene. Her first book was a novel, *The Benefactor* (1963), and since then she has published two other works of fiction, a second novel, *Death Kit* (1967), and a collection of short stories, *I, etcetera* (1978). However, Sontag's reputation is based primarily on her essays, which have done a great deal to propagate her enthusiasms for European writers, thinkers, directors; Lévi-Strauss, Barthes, Resnais, Godard, Benjamin, Canetti, to name a few. Sontag is persuasive not only because she is a good writer, but also because she conveys an impassioned involvement with her subject. To a variety of cultural concerns, Sontag brings the same rigorous scrutiny. Her trenchant analysis often takes the form of regroupings of familiar points of reference. New lists, new contexts for quotations are themselves creators of novel ideas, as Foucault says of Borges, "breaking up all the ordered surfaces and all the planes with which we are accustomed to tame the wild profusion of existing things."

Nonetheless, there are a number of paradoxes in Sontag's position as essayist which quickly became apparent. Sontag is fascinated by "the modern" in art and thought, but deeply suspicious of many aspects of modern life, as is especially clear in her best book of social criticism, *On Photography*. Sontag prefers artists and thinkers who are resistant to easy assimilation by their audiences, but a good part of her writing career has been spent "explaining" difficult, recalcitrant writers, like Artaud. She is known as an interpreter of European, particularly French, writing in North America, but she denounces interpretation in an early essay, the title essay of her first collection, *Against Interpretation* (1966). In "life" as in "art" she repudiates the interpretive stance. *Illness as Metaphor* (1978) is an extended diatribe against those who would "interpret" tuberculosis or, especially, cancer as physical manifestations of psychic conflicts. In her essays Sontag avoids the first person singular, though her writing is very personal; in her fiction, however, she enjoys playing with narrative voice and persona, as is clear from just the title of her story collection.

These paradoxes do not diminish Sontag's work; instead they

contribute to the creative tension between aestheticism and social criticism, sensuality and intellectual rigour. This tension is especially evident in *On Photography* where she diagnoses the "image-ridden" nature of our society and the fundamentally aestheticizing nature of still images (as opposed to narrative, which can explain reality).

In the last two decades, Sontag has published her essays primarily in *Partisan Review* and *The New York Review of Books,* and they have been collected in three volumes: *Against Interpretation* (1966), *Styles of Radical Will* (1969), and *Under the Sign of Saturn* (1980). In 1982 her publisher, Farrar, Straus and Giroux, brought out *A Susan Sontag Reader,* an unusual consecration for a writer in mid career.

We first interviewed Susan Sontag when she was in Montreal for a reading in October. We spoke to her again at her home in New York in early December.

CJPST: In your essay on Barthes you write that he "repeatedly disavows the vulgár roles of system-builder, authority, mentor, expert, in order to reserve for himself the privileges and freedoms of delectation." Would you say that this description applies equally to your own intellectual stance?

Sontag: Well . . . yes. There's a lot of self-vindication in some of the last essays I've written. They are very personal estimates of people whose work has been important to me, though not necessarily important influences. I had not read Barthes when I wrote *The Benefactor* or the first essays in *Against Interpretation.* When I discovered Barthes he was above all for me a model of density and passionateness. There is no waste in Barthes' writing. I don't know another writer who is so exciting to read, always. The essay I wrote on Barthes took me six full months to write and I think it's one of the best essays I've ever written. His work mattered to me a lot and I feel very haunted by him. He is the one French writer to have emerged in the post-war period who I am sure will remain a permanent part of our literature, as a writer—not as a semiotician or literary theorist.

CJPST: In many of your essays you avoid the use of the first person. One has the impression that you speak rather for a community. Is this the result of a conscious decision?

Sontag: Where is that voice coming from? I don't think it's the voice of a community, at least not the sort of community I could take a census of. In fact the essays are extremely personal and yet operate on a strategy by which the first person is renounced. Eventually this formula becomes impossible and I'm finding now that I can't write them anymore. I've been asked to write an essay on Sartre for *The New York Review of Books* and at first I refused because I thought the project was too easy (and I'm a glutton for punishment). In fact six months later I'm still working on the essay. Even a relatively easy topic like Sartre is becoming too difficult, because there's a first person who wants to be born in those essays and can't be. The essays are imploding in a way that makes them extremely difficult to engender. That's what's driving me back to fiction, not reluctantly. I have to come out of the closet of the third person and speak in a more direct way. On the other hand the last essays have become more personal. They are portraits which are in some sense self-portraits: the essays on Canetti, Benjamin, Barthes. And the Sartre essay is a kind of anti-self-portrait.

CJPST: Do you think this problem has something to do with the fragmentation of the left in the States, that there is less of a community for you to represent?

Sontag: I think that there is generally less of a community and that the fragmentation of the left is a symptom. I think that it is less and less possible to take for granted certain cultural references. That's what a community is: taking for granted certain assumptions, not having to start from zero every time. This is no longer true. The decline of education in North America and I suppose in Western Europe makes it harder to have a common body of references. You know that you can't make references to the Classics any longer and less and less to the English classics even.

CJPST: You were one of the first to begin the process of importing contemporary French thought to America. What do you think the balance-sheet looks like now?

Sontag: I didn't think of myself as importing. I thought it was more interesting to write about things people didn't know about than what they did. When I became aware that I was in fact "importing," I stopped doing it. The first French writer I knew well was Gide, whom I read in my early teens. I in fact taught myself French by reading with a dictionary when I was about 14. I went to Paris for the first time when I was 18 and then, starting in my late 20s, I began to go a lot so that by my mid-30s I was mainly living there. So during that period (the 60s and early 70s) it seemed natural to write about things I was excited about. This included Godard, Lévi-Strauss. Now the new things happening in France don't interest me.

CJPST: You're not interested in post-structuralist French writers, then?

Sontag: Their writing is not so interesting to me, but I'm not sure I have the basis to make the proper judgement. I know that I don't feel the need for this kind of theorizing. I feel that I've had enough theoretical speculation to last me a lifetime and I rather prefer the sources of that thought. For instance I'm extremely interested in the Russian formalists and have been for many years. I'm more drawn to their writing, which is expressive and literary, than to writing which is extremely academic or jargon-ridden. What I like about Barthes is that he is first of all a writer. When I read someone like Kristeva I feel that the academic cast of it is a barrier to me. On the other hand it does give you a big machine, a language, with which people can approach texts. I had the experience of teaching a seminar on first-person writing recently at Brown University. The students who had been trained in French critical theory wrote incredibly assertive, self-confident papers, full of ideas about how to use these texts. The students who had not been exposed to this approach simply para-phrased them. They are not even given training in the old-fashioned type of philological scholarship (like that of Auerbach, for instance, who is still a model to me). In other words I think part of the success which structuralist or post-structuralist thought in critical theory has had in literary studies in American universities is due to a theoretical vacuum.

CJPST: At a 1982 Town Hall meeting to support Solidarity in Poland, you distanced yourself from allies on the left by criticizing American intellectuals' tolerance of repression in Communist coun-tries. Have you been led to re-evaluate your own work in light of the ideas you expressed in this speech?

Sontag: In fact the reaction to the speech was a media blow-up. I was not expressing new ideas but rather feelings I'd had since the mid-70s when I started to meet a lot of people, like Joseph Brodsky, who were in exile from Communist countries. I had to believe what they said about how terrible conditions were in these countries. The

60s (when I visited many of these countries) had been a great time of hope even for those in the Eastern bloc. All this ended in 1968 with the invasion of Czechoslovakia.

I had a very discouraging experience with an essay in which I was to discuss the relationship between intellectuals and the idea of revolution or revolutionary power. I abandoned it. It's quicksand! This was the first time in my life that I was bothered by the question of audience. The experience at Town Hall made me realize that you can't limit your audience. When I gave that speech it was directed at a particular audience and I fully expected to be booed. When the speech appeared in the media it took on a different meaning. And so I began to think that if I'm writing about the romance of Communism, about intellectuals, who am I writing for? I'm not interested in giving aid and comfort to the neo-Conservatives. It's a crucifying dilemma. I was finally defeated by it. I spent a year and a half writing hundreds of pages and gave up. Since Town Hall it's been a disaster and I'm still digging my way out of the rubble.

CJPST: How important is feminism now to your work?

Sontag: I certainly identify myself as a feminist. I have been told that I am a "natural" feminist, someone who was born a feminist. In fact I was quite blind to what the problem was: I couldn't understand why anyone would hesitate to do what they wanted to do just because they were told that women didn't do such things. The feminist movement has been important to me because it's made me feel less odd and also because it has made me understand some of the pressures on women which I was lucky enough to have escaped, perhaps because of my eccentricity or the oddness of my upbringing.

CJPST: In the final paragraph of *On Photography* you say: "If there can be a better way for the real world to include the one of images, it will require an ecology not only of real things but of images as well." Do you have any thoughts about how we could develop such an ecology?

Sontag: The last sentence of a book is, of course, where you have to stop. And the answer to this question really involves a new argument which is also a political argument. The question of the social uses of photography opens out into the very largest issues of the self, of the relationship to community, to reality. Jean Baudrillard is a writer who addresses this question of the ultimate implications of the consumer society.

CJPST: What do you think of Jean Baudrillard's work?

Sontag: I'm very interested in his themes and particularly like his essay on the Centre Pompidou and the function of the museum in modern society. I'm very interested in Baudrillard's perspective, extremely rhetorical descriptions. I like his eye. I can't say that I come away with any sense of alternatives, because the way he describes always carries with it an imputation of inexorability. That tendency of social thought to generalize, to describe a leading tendency in a society in such a way that it seems that everything falls within its iron laws, is very common. Of course our own experience tells us that life is not as monochrome as these thinkers depict it. On the other hand they are very valuable because they alert us to transformations we are likely to take for granted. I belong rather to a more classical tradition of social analysis. Max Weber was a very important influence for me. I can't say I know how to change the society, but I share the feeling that this society is full of technology which depersonalizes people, which seems to drain a sense of reality from our lives. It's full of a lot of other things too. What interests me is to understand the nature of the modern. Ultimately that's what the essays in *On Photography* are about: another way of talking about the modern.

CJPST: In *I, etcetera* one character says "My skull is crammed with quotations" and another says "We are ruled by quotations." Do you have a particular strategy for using quotations in your work?

Sontag: What seems distinctively modern as a unit of thought, of art, of discourse is the fragment; and the quotation is one kind of fragment. I became aware, after the fact, that I was fascinated by quotations and lists. And then I noticed that other people were fascinated by quotations and lists: people as different as Borges and Walter Benjamin, Novalis and Godard. Using quotations was at first quite spontaneous for me, but then this use became strengthened through reflection. But originally this practice came out of a temperament. I agree with Nietzsche and Oscar Wilde that ultimately ideas come out of a temperament or a sensibility, that they are a crystallization or a precipitation of temperament. It's not that you make up your ideas to justify your temperament but that it's the temperament first.

In the late essays collected in *Under the Sign of Saturn* I ended up writing portraits which seemed like assessments of the body of a work but are in fact portraits of temperaments that express themselves in art. I'm interested in the possibility of fiction which straddles narrative and essay. A novel is a "baggy monster," as Henry James said. You can include essay elements in fiction; this is a very nineteenth-century practice. Balzac will stop to describe the sociology of a place or profession; Tolstoy will talk about ideas of history. That notion of including essay elements is very familiar, but there are more seductive modern examples: Central European novelists, like Broch.

CJPST: Are you working on that kind of fiction now?

Sontag: In fact after finishing the Sartre essay I'll be going to Cambridge, Mass. to direct a play by Kundera at the American Repertory Theatre.

CJPST: In Kundera's last novel, *The Unbearable Lightness of Being,* he suggests that Western intellectuals are in some way "condemned" to a kind of necessary but futile theatrical activity when they question political power. What do you perceive as the role of intellectuals to influence political events?

Sontag: What Kundera has to say is so shaped by his own historical situation that he comes as a messenger of bad news. His own posture was frozen 10 years ago and things have changed very rapidly since then. Kundera is addressing a situation which is already obsolete. There is an understandable vindictiveness in people who come from Communist countries. They want to keep telling us that we were fools to think that we could make radical changes in our society. Though I understand their dismay, respect their suffering and don't understand the gullibility of some people who don't take in how repressive these societies are, I still think it's important to keep people of all kinds as active in civic matters as possible. Currently intellectuals in Western Europe and North America are extremely demoralized and shaken by the rise of a virulent conservative tendency (which some have even joined). The way in which a certain kind of political idealism has been discredited and scorned makes the danger not that intellectuals keep on making fools of themselves, formulating political opinions when they might not be as informed as they might be, but that they retreat and leave politics to the professionals.

CJPST: Your writing is impassioned and risk-taking . . .

Sontag: It doesn't feel like risk-taking but I know that it is. I've been at it long enough to know the trouble you get into. I write essays first because I have a passionate relationship to the subject and second because the subject is one that people are not talking about. The writers or artists I write about are not necessarily those I care most about (Shakespeare is still my favourite writer) but those whose work I feel has been neglected.

CJPST: Has the reception of your work influenced the way you write?

Sontag: I'm more cautious about what I write. When I wrote *Against Interpretation* I was very innocent about the way work is used. I wrote those essays for the most part very quickly and they reflected some current interests and discoveries. In my own mind I had a model of the transmission of literary work which, at the time when I was starting to publish, was becoming obsolete. I thought there were such things as "little magazines" with a small, passionate, educated readership. When I was in my mid-teens, going to high school in Los Angeles, my dream was to come to New York and write for *Partisan Review* and be read by 10,000 people. Well I did come to New York and write for *Partisan Review*. But it turns out that already in the 60s among the 10,000 people who read the *Review* were a lot of editors for perhaps *Time* magazine, or *Newsweek* or *Playboy* who would want to take the work, recycle and amplify it. When you see your 40-page essay turned into a "hot tip" in one paragraph in *Newsweek,* you get anxious about the way your writing has been used. I have not liked many of the transformations and adaptations of my work. The work is not allowed to remain itself: it is duplicated. It's almost as if this is the fundamental procedure in modern society: duplication and recycling. Therefore when you are writing, you are— from society's point of view—only producing the first version which will then be processed and recycled. . . . We live in a world of copies and we're fascinated when we encounter the originals (in a museum, for instance). In a lot of writing or intellectual discourse we're starting to use that model: "Oh, this is where it comes from!" I would like to concentrate on work which is more resistant to that procedure, as I think fiction is.

One of the things I've been thinking about a lot this year is the word processor. Most writers I know have switched to word processors. I haven't but I'm very curious about why people like it so much. I think it has something to do with the fact that at last writing, which has been such an old-fashioned, artisanal activity, even on a typewriter, has now entered the central domain of modern experience, which is that of making copies, being involved in the world of duplicates and machine-mediated activities.

CJPST: In your Artaud essay, you seem to be attracted to his writing precisely because he resisted easy assimilation.

Sontag: There I was treating a more old-fashioned version of the question of reception by talking about the domestication of something which was basically wild. Some of the exuberance of my essay-writing has gone because I'm worried about the uses they could serve. Shortly after I wrote the essay on Canetti he won the Nobel Prize and a number of people said; "Oh, you predicted he'd get the Prize." That sort of reception—where everything is assimilated to the world of celebrity—makes me dream of becoming a more recalcitrant, harder to assimilate writer.

CJPST: Would that be a writer who couldn't be quoted?

Sontag: No, you can always be quoted. Quotation is a method of appropriation which is invincible, I think. It's not a procedure which displeases me, contrary to recycling. The quote is always fascinating because it changes out of context, becomes different and sometimes more mysterious. It has a directness and assertiveness it may not have had in the original. I think the quality of inaccessibility, the mystery, is important—that whatever matters can't be taken in on just one reading or one seeing. This is certainly a quality of the little of art that lasts.

Nadine Gordimer and Susan Sontag: In Conversation

Nadine Gordimer and Susan Sontag / 1985

From *The Listener* (May 23, 1985), pp. 16–17. Reprinted by permission of BBC Enterprises Limited.

What are the responsibilities of the writer? Nadine Gordimer and Susan Sontag discuss the often fraught relationship between writing and politics.

Gordimer: When I first began to write as a child—I began when I was about nine years old—I would never have dreamt that this would become work for which I would be taken to account by anybody. I never dreamt that to write was an act of responsibility.

Sontag: But you saw yourself as having an audience, as writing for other people—or simply for yourself?

Gordimer: I think I saw it as writing for myself; I didn't ever think of being published, and I didn't think of anybody else reading what I wrote.

Sontag: I had a different experience. I also began when I was seven or eight, but I *did* think of being published. In fact, I really thought that that's what being a writer was. I also had no idea of what the responsibility of being a writer was.

Gordimer: In my case, being born in a country like South Africa, white, automatically privileged, brought up in the colonial life as I was, if I was going to be a writer, there would have to be a time when I would see what was in that society, when I would see how it had shaped me and my thinking. I would bear automatically a certain responsibility for it as a human being and, since a writer is an articulate human being, there would be a special responsibility to respond to it in a certain way. But, you know, I was reading Rilke and Virginia Woolf and Henry James and Proust—not when I was nine years old, but when I was 15 or 16. There was a kind of blindness in me. I simply thought: "Well, I'm writing; it's the one thing in the world that I want to do." I buried myself in it.

Sontag: But I don't think you were hiding when you were reading Proust and Henry James and Tolstoy and Dostoyevsky. You were seeking your essential identity as a writer. You were seeking what would make you a writer and, at the same time, you were coming to an awareness of what it means to be a citizen of your country. Why is that different from what you do now?

Gordimer: Well, the political aspect is something that came into my work implicitly, because the life around me was imbued with it, even the most private aspects of life were penetrated by the effect of politics. Politics in South Africa wasn't and isn't something that you choose to be involved in. The whole political climate—the social order, the way you live—is determined by politics, without any question of choice coming into it. But what I didn't understand, what I felt this kind of innocence about, was that when I grew up and I became aware of where I was living and of my responsibilities as a human being, as a citizen, I saw it as something completely separate from what I was doing as a writer. Even when political situations determined the lives of the characters in my books, because that was happening all around me, I still saw it as part of what I was making, in terms of literature, and the challenge was to make it well. It had nothing to do with whether I was satisfying people who shared my political opinions.

Sontag: Chekhov said that the writer's main relation to politics should be one of flight, and that you should never allow yourself to become captured by other people's demands that you express a progressive point of view.

Gordimer: I would certainly agree with Chekhov rather than with Albert Camus, who said: "The day when I cease to be no more than a writer, or only a writer, I shall not be a writer any more." I disagree with that entirely. I would turn it round the other way: the day when it's more important for me to be more than a writer in the public sense, in the sense of being answerable to some political or social problem, in which I may be very involved as a citizen, the day that that becomes more important than being a writer, I think I'm discounted in the world. I've got no use and no place, because I believe that you must do the thing you do best, and if you're a writer it's a mistake to become a politician, even though you believe passionately in a particular cause.

Sontag: But I don't see why you think writing is private in that sense. I mean, writing is solitary—you do it alone, it is perhaps the most solitary occupation there is. But it's not private; it is simply work done in private. I never think of the activity of the writer as a private activity. You see, I think that the good writer, choosing to write, is always making something social in standing for excellence, standing for a certain hierarchy of values, protecting the language— that's our medium, and ultimately, we want to prevent it from decaying or deteriorating. We want to leave the language in a perhaps slightly better shape because of our passage through it in all our books, rather than in worse shape. The writer stands for singularity, the writer stands for an individual voice. The existence of good writing stands for an independent or autonomous life, for self-reliance. These are all public, civic, moral values that don't necessarily involve the kind of communal or civic engagement that you're talking about. Which I understand perfectly. I don't live in a country where I am very often called on to take a public position. I've taken a lot of public positions in my life, but I've always felt that I volunteered to do it, I stuck my neck out—often the consequences were rather unpleasant.

Gordimer: I want to ask you then why you did that. You had a choice. Why did you get so involved, for instance, in the Vietnam War, and put a lot of creative energy into writing about it and perhaps speaking on public platforms?

Sontag: I think I felt compelled, first of all, as a human being, and not as a writer. That is to say, I felt that it was a privilege to be a writer, that I had a privileged situation in the society and that I had a public voice, and that there was an emergency in which I felt I could use my voice to influence people for something that I cared passionately about. I think it's part of what it is in modern life to be a writer that we think we have—or many of us think we have—an ethical responsibility. But I don't think it's what determines our value as writers.

Gordimer: No. But in my situation it is much stronger because I am living in the midst of suffering, I'm seeing the oppression of black people around me. I've lived in the middle of it ever since I opened my eyes, in my privileged white hospital where I was born, and if I die there I will be buried in a white graveyard where no black is allowed to be buried. So it is literally a cradle-to-the-grave situation of having the unnatural and oppressive social order around you every minute of your life. So the responsibility is staring you in the face, as a human being. Right from the beginning.

Sontag: Having a subject and the relation to that subject is, I think, for serious writers a much less innocent relation than it used to be. To portray one's society and the panorama of human folly and frailty, I think, was much easier to define in the time of Thackeray or Balzac or any of the great Russian novelists than it is for us. On the whole, the writers who clearly have subjects in the traditional sense are kitsch writers—they're entertainment writers, they're not part of literature—whereas most of the major writers, I think, of the last few generations—and you can take this all the way back to Flaubert, who was our original ancestor—most of the great achievements of 20th-century literature have made—seem to make—a claim to be beyond a subject, to be self-referential, to be ultimately about language and about sensibility.

Gordimer: I think what has happened now, though, with writers, for instance, like Milan Kundera, to a certain extent myself, the two coincide. It's shown that it's possible for the inner landscape and the outer landscape to become one, to be melded together in the same work. In other words, the inner landscape, which is really the subjective novel, the techniques, the sensibilities, the perceptions—even the technical side of it, the method—can be used with the outer landscape, the subject. I find it very strange that, to my mind as a stranger to Europe, British writers seem to avoid that outer landscape, almost completely. In 1984 there was this long miners' strike which must have affected the lives of so many people living in the areas where the mines are; it must have changed their whole lives for a very long time. I just wonder whether any novels, any stories, are going to come out of this, any fiction's going to come out of it. Or is it only going to be recorded in the press and on television.

Sontag: I don't think that I want novels to bring me news. I think I look to the higher journalism and to essays, and to film, to a certain kind of film essay, which I think is very important, to give me a sense of how sensibility is altering under the pressure of immediate events. I think the fiction writer is a conjurer and I think I want a certain kind of magic, a certain kind of delight.

Gordimer: But why is it that so many writers seem not to be able to apply modernist sensibilities to a subject, or not to be interested?

Sontag: But could it be something about the way most writers live? They are academics. Very often in the United States they are academics—most serious writers make a living as teachers, they live in a university world. Good writers, on the whole, don't write about where the real sources of social power are. They write about private situations because I think in fact they have a narrower social experience.

An American writer whom I know and admire enormously, William Gass, once asked me: "What emotion do you write out of, Susan?" I said: "Grief." Of course it's a preposterous question to narrow down the source of your writing to one emotion. He then said: "Oh, for me it's rage." I was very struck by my own answer, although his was equally odd. I didn't know that that's what I felt, but I realised that my writing comes out of a deep pessimism. And I think that we do live in a time that we all experience in some way as a time of crisis, as a time in which much has been destroyed and much has been lost, and much more is going to be lost, and we experience the demand on us as writers, and I think also—and why not—as human beings, to be both a radical demand and a conservative demand. It's radical because we want to help change what is evil in our society and bring to birth something that will help assist in the correction of certain fundamental wrongs and injustices. And we are also conservative because we know that in this process so much is being destroyed that we cherish and that we value. It's very difficult to call ourselves either conservatives or radicals, because we understand both impulses. And that informs one's situation as a writer. One is part of a process of civilisation and one is part of a process of increasing barbarism.

Gordimer: I think that we are living in what I have called a state of interregnum, not only in the country I come from, South Africa, where it is most marked, because there there's a perfect illustration of Gramsci's statement "the old is dying, and the new cannot be born; in this interregnum there arises a great diversity of morbid symptoms." So I could almost write a novel now, or a story, and call it *Morbid Symptoms*.

Sontag: I've heard you say on many occasions that you don't believe that capitalism or Western-style democracy can solve the problems of your own country, that there is no evidence that they can solve the problems of your own country. And obviously I could not presume to speak about what the viable future is for your country. But I know that the historical hope in what has called itself socialism has been systematically disappointed by regimes which have started out so promisingly and turned into bureaucratic dictatorships under the domination of an important form of imperialism—Soviet imperialism, or whatever. It seems to me that one has to change the horizon of one's hopes, if history does not support them.

Gordimer: But has history been given a chance? I would agree with everything that you've said about the experiments—one might call them so far—in various countries. But they have occupied really only a moment in history; it's not very long, it's a few generations. Can one then on that evidence accept that the whole idea of socialism, the whole social order, is something that can never be achieved?

Sontag: Well, I certainly think that a more humane society could be achieved, and in that sense, in that very limited almost tautological sense, I, too, remain an optimist, or I, too, have a horizon of hope. But I do not believe that the traditional formulae operate, because we know more about what makes an economy, about what makes a society; the whole situation of modern bureaucracy and the new technologies have altered the way societies are run. I live in a society, and I think it's true largely for people in Western Europe, Britain, at least Canada and the United States, where people no longer have a sense of inexorable and desirable change. They do not believe that certain changes, except possibly changes for the worse, are inevitable. They do not see that they are on the edge of something that they can only assent to or subscribe to. One has a rather defensive feeling toward change. Change is mainly something that destroys the continuity of the generations. The one thing that we are taught as citizens of a rich consumer society is that the future will not be like the past. New technologies are promised to transform our lives, and we are trained to be consumers of these new technologies, to be consumers in the destruction of our past, and our continuity with the past. That has had, I think, an enormous and largely negative impact on what personality is, what individuality is, and what all sorts of cultural and intellectual enterprises might be.

If I write, it's because I make an assumption which is thoroughly anachronistic, that the future will somehow be like the past. But most of the information that my society gives me is that it will not be like the past. And I can only view this with dismay. You do not view the change that is coming in your society with dismay?

Gordimer: Well, with apprehension, because I don't know what kind of change it's going to be. But there is an obstinate belief and a fervent hope—in other words, there's still enthusiasm in me, there's still belief that it would be possible to create an alternative Left. I believe that for people like us, who have seen the Left betray itself in many countries, who've seen regimes turn into dictatorships, new forms of imperialism, I still believe that it's possible to create a new Left to move on from there. And I believe—indeed, it's an almost apocalyptic feeling—that this has to be done, that we've got to do it. Vis-à-vis my own country, the difference is, you see, that we're in this political and ideological interregnum. But *you* believe and you know that there are things worth preserving in the society that you're in and you'd like to see them carried on; you'd like to see that continuity there. Truly, I have to rack my brains to think of something that I would like to see preserved in South Africa.

Susan Sontag: The Passion for Words

Marithelma Costa and Adelaida López / 1987

From *Revista de Occidente*, No. 79 (December 1987), pp. 109–
126. © Susan Sontag. Reprinted by permission of *Revista de
Occidente* and Susan Sontag. Though most of the interview
published below derives from an edited English-language transcript of the original conversation, significant portions derive
from the *Revista* version as translated from the Spanish by
Kathy S. Leonard. A slightly revised version was published as
"Susan Sontag" in Marithelma Costa and Adelaida López,
eds., *Las dos caras de la escritura* (Puerto Rico: Sin Nombre/
University of Puerto Rico, 1988), pp. 179–195.

Q: In the very first pages of *The Benefactor*, you write: "Ambition, if
it feeds at all, feeds on the ambition of others." Could you tell us
something about the development of your own ambition as a writer?

Sontag: One might divide writers into those who start at a very
early age and those who don't. I was reading when I was about three
years old, and writing by the age of six or seven.

Q: What were you writing?

Sontag: Plays, poems, stories. One play, I remember, was about
robots. I wrote a great deal in my childhood, and I also published a
four-page newspaper with stories and articles, all of which I wrote. I
went around the neighborhood on my bicycle and sold it for five
cents. I used a very primitive duplication system called a hectograph.
You type on a stencil that you put face down on a tray filled with
gelatin. I could get about thirty copies of each page.

Q: Did you want to be a writer when you were writing these stories?

Sontag: I wanted to be a scientist, first a chemist, later a doctor,
and a writer as well. I wanted to be a doctor well into my adolescence,
and then I abandoned that idea because it meant an entirely different
program of studies. When I was in my early twenties I had a flare-up
of longing to go to medical school. It would have involved going back
to the university and taking some science and mathematics courses,
and again, I decided against it. I still regret not becoming a doctor.

Q: Some studies reveal that it is necessary to have a mentor or a guide in all processes of learning. Was there any figure in your family who influenced your interest in medicine?

Sontag: No, nobody in my family was influential in any of these decisions. I was lucky enough not to have any influences until I was in college.

Q: Were there any literary figures who guided you in your development as a writer?

Sontag: I don't think anybody has guided me. There have been people I admired, who were models to me, but they're mostly dead. Kafka, for instance, and Nietzsche.

Q: Why Nietzsche?

Sontag: I think he sets a certain standard, let's say a standard of seriousness.

Q: Doesn't he seem intolerant to you, even merciless?

Sontag: He's very vehement, yes. Kafka too was very vehement, and he excluded a great deal, in his life and in his work. These are people whose lives I find exemplary in some respect—their thoughts, their ideas, their work, their seriousness. Van Gogh is another important presence for me. He matters more to me than any living American writer.

Q: It is interesting that these three artists never were accepted by the establishment. Could they be called martyrs, martyrs of their own seriousness?

Sontag: It's true that Nietzsche died insane, Van Gogh committed suicide, and Kafka had only a small readership, but my interest in them is not about that.

Q: What figures in the American intellectual tradition do you feel most comfortable with?

Sontag: I love Emerson, the first great American writer. The stories of Poe and Hawthorne. Whitman. Henry James. Among the contemporary writers I like William Gass, Donald Barthelme, and Elizabeth Hardwick. The first critical essays that I loved were Eliot's, and then Kenneth Burke's, and Lionel Trilling's, which I read when I was in my early teens. I didn't know any of the European critics when I started to write. In the end, I think that Benjamin and Barthes have mattered more deeply to me, but I was already quite formed when I encountered them. It was a question of recognition, in a way, more than a model.

Q: In your essay on Godard, you write that the culture heroes of our time have often been both ascetics and destroyers. You have been attracted to such ascetic figures as Simone Weil, Walter Benjamin, and Kierkegaard. Later, however, you were drawn to the ideas of a different kind of writer, a gourmet of culture, namely Barthes. As a cultural critic, are you more of an ascetic that a gourmet, or do you think that there is a middle road between asceticism and hedonism in cultural criticism?

Sontag: I have lots of appetites, and I enjoy a lot of things, but I don't think I'm a gourmet. As far as the essays go, I like writing about what I admire. The things that I admire are numerous, and if they haven't been much written about, I enjoy supporting them. I don't think I have to choose between being ascetic and being avid. In some ways I'm rather puritanical, I suppose, but there is a puritan tradition of pleasure, which is not incompatible with enjoyment. Some people may think it's ascetic to be turned on by a six-hour movie by Hans-Jürgen Syberberg, but I think it's pleasure. I'm probably somewhat ascetic in my life, that's a question of temperament, but I have a great capacity for enthusiasm and pleasure.

Q: If you like writing about what you admire, is it your reading that has most abetted your career as a writer?

Sontag: I love reading. It's a passion, and that's why I do it, to excess. I doubt if it abets anything. And I'm not so happy with the notion of a "career." I've been writing, and that produces a career, but I don't think of it as one. The struggle is not experienced in that way.

Q: You don't like the word . . .

Sontag: I suppose that I am somewhat resistant to language that sounds opportunistic. Of course there is a career in the simple sense that I have already done all this work, and I'm associated with it. It's also different to be in the middle than to be at the beginning. It's not so easy to have a lot of work behind you and, one hopes, quite a bit of work in front of you.

Q: Do you think it's harder than to be at the beginning?

Sontag: *I* feel it is. My writing exists in the world, and I have some awareness of a variety of responses to it. By and large, these responses are not helpful to me. It's different when you start off. Then it's marvelous to be able to do anything at all, but when what you write goes out into the world, that changes its status. And then you go on, and you have this thing called a career, which is very distracting.

Q: Is it harder because you ask yourself for more, because the standards are higher?

Sontag: I think I *am* setting the bar higher, as athletes do. I'm more self-conscious, more conscious of my standard. I'm in a sort of competition with myself, which is not an innocent relation to one's own work.

Q: Does that self-consciousness become stronger after you finish a piece?

Sontag: No. Immediately after I finish it, I feel relieved that I *could* finish it. The self-consciousness is worse at the beginning of a new work, when I fear that it's not going to be as good as the last piece, or that I'm repeating myself. There are people who say that they enjoy writing very much, but I can't say that I enjoy it. I find it a great struggle. The more I exist as a published body of work, supposedly representing or advocating certain positions or a certain kind of writing, the more I worry. As soon as I write something that I believe to be true, it doesn't seem true anymore. I start seeing some other way of doing it, or another point of view.

Q: Does that happen with fiction, or more with essays?

Sontag: More with essays. They are getting harder to finish, so I'm trying to concentrate on fiction. In the last few years, I have had the discouraging experience of having worked for many months each on several essays, and being unable to complete them. I still may eventually, but in each case, as I worked and rewrote, I just saw more problems and more alternatives. In fiction if you find the right voice, it has its own energies. You're not responsible to the truth in the same direct way that you are when you write an essay. It's much freer.

I recently abandoned a story, although perhaps not for good, because I tired of it. I felt it was pointlessly depressing. I hadn't found the center. I was relating the story of two lives, two friends who meet periodically. They're very different. One is a man, one is a woman; one is middle-aged, one is young; but they have a problem, a burden in common, and they meet and talk. They're both, in different ways, very unhappy, very unfulfilled. I got impatient with them, which is to say, with myself. I felt that what I was doing wasn't rich enough. It was rich in details because the world they live in is a world I know well. I had a lot of what I thought were very elegant descriptions, but in the end I didn't feel that "lift-off" that I want to feel in a story. And I thought, well, maybe these characters are still in my head, though they're very real to me, these two people, their friendship and their dinners, and their suffering, but it's not big enough, it's not deep enough. In fiction that, for me, is a criterion of truth.

Q: Could you talk a little bit about creating a character? About how the characters in your stories come into being?

Sontag: It starts with language. Sometimes it comes with a first sentence. I hear a sentence in my head, and then wonder, "Who's saying this?" Once I wrote a story because I heard the *last* sentence in my head. I knew it was the last sentence when I heard it, and the sentence was "Nothing, but nothing, could tear me away from this rock." And then I thought, "Well, who's saying this?" And when you ask yourself that, you open yourself to the elements, to your own landscape. It was someone being stoical, and this was that person's way of speaking of grief. So I had the stoicism and the grief, and I knew it was in the first person. I began to think about that, and I decided that the person speaking was a woman, and then I decided that her best friend had committed suicide. I worked backward, and I had a story. I don't know how a character appears. It's magical, I would say. Most writers develop characters based on people they know—they may take notes after a dinner on their friends' behavior—but I feel reluctant to use my friends in that way.

Q: Has any character started not as a voice but as a vision? As a body?

Sontag: It's always a voice. It's always language. The other day I heard a sentence, which I wrote down, and I know it's the beginning of a story. The sentence was "It was like having a third leg," and I knew exactly why this was being said. Somebody has suddenly understood something very important, that changes everything. But there's too much information, and the person is crippled by understanding too many things. That's why the character says, "It's like having a third leg." You don't need a third leg to run; two legs are enough. It's an image, a mood, an insight, of someone reflecting ruefully. My fiction usually starts with a dilemma of consciousness.

Q: Do you remember how the main character in *The Benefactor* came to you?

Sontag: I was talking with a friend, in a coffeehouse in Greenwich Village on the corner of MacDougal and Bleecker, called the Figaro. She knew that I was very discouraged, that I wanted to stop writing stories, which I had been doing for a long time, and to write a novel. But every time I sat down to begin a novel, it turned into a story. I brought it up again, my longing to write something long, something that would have a larger energy. My friend said, "Well, why don't you start your novel right now?" We had just sat down and had ordered two espressos. I replied, "Yes, I'm going to." And she said, "No, I mean *right now*." Then suddenly something happened inside me, and I said, "O. K. You pay for the coffees." Our order hadn't even arrived. I'll bless her forever, because that's exactly what she wanted me to do. I took a taxi home, sat down, and wrote the first sentence. Then I looked at it and wrote the next sentence. I stayed up for a couple of hours, wrote around three pages, and these were the first pages of the novel. Of course, the first sentence is a bluff: "If only I could tell you how changed I am since those days!" That kind of sentence is like a blank check, as were the next couple of sentences. But then I began to see a person.

Q: After you started to write.

Sontag: Yes, after. I didn't have any idea for the novel. I just put in a token sentence, a dummy sentence, so to speak, but it generated another sentence. Writing is about sentences.

Q: Was the character created then through the writing?

Sontag: Yes, by the second or third page. I was in my twenties and, given my reluctance to do anything autobiographical, I wanted to make this person as different from myself as possible. So this was a man in his sixties.

Q: And you experienced the character as a voice, not as an image?

Sontag: Yes. One of my struggles as a writer of fiction is to try to get something more visual into my work. I feel that I'm learning to use language in a more sensual way, and that may be taking me towards the visual.

Q: Silvia Molloy's first novel makes extensive use of dreams, and so does your novel *The Benefactor*. Molloy told us that although she paid a good deal of attention to her dreams at one point in her life, they have become much less important to her. At the time you wrote *The Benefactor*, were you very aware of your dreams?

Sontag: I've never paid that much attention to my dreams. When I was writing *The Benefactor*, I thought of dreams as another kind of narration, an enigmatic nugget of narration that I would insert every so often in the longer, more spaced-out narrative, and that would become a point of reflection. But there's nothing psychological or autobiographical about them, although I suppose they could be treated psychologically. They're invented. Only one of the dreams was mine, and I used it only because I thought it was a dream that my character *could* have, not because it was mine.

Q: There is a strong moral sensibility in your essays that sometimes approaches religiosity. Could you tell us anything about your religious upbringing?

Sontag: I had no formal religious upbringing. Throughout my childhood I had a Catholic nurse, and I often went to Mass with her on Sunday. But there was no religious observance in my family, which was Jewish; and the first time I entered in a synagogue I was in my mid-twenties. Visiting Florence for the first time, I passed a synagogue with a plaque listing the names of the Jews of Florence who had been deported to Auschwitz, and I went inside.

Q: Did your interest in ethics begin at the University of Chicago?

Sontag: I think it began when I was three years old. In some ways, I'm not so different from when I was a small child, which is a source of strength as well as a problem. I can remember thinking many of the things I think about now in the years before I was ten. If I could do it all over again, I would give myself the ability to enjoy my childhood. Unfortunately, childhood was just a kind of prison sentence for me and when I was finished with it, when I was fifteen and able to leave home, I was delighted.

Q: Umberto Eco claims that he believes that narrative fiction ultimately invokes an ethical response from the reader. Do you agree?

Sontag: Some fiction does, of course. If I read *The Brothers Karamazov*, naturally my response is an ethical and a spiritual one.

Q: If we get into the problem of the creative process, how would you describe the act of writing?

Sontag: Kafka had a fantasy of setting up shop in the sub-basement of some building, where twice a day somebody would put something to eat outside the door. He said: One cannot be alone enough to write. I think of writing like being in a balloon, a spaceship, a submarine, a closet. It's going someplace else, where people aren't, to really concentrate and hear one's own voice. Then, too, if your work has reached a certain audience, and you become famous, it's harder and harder to find the kind of solitude that you have quite naturally at the beginning when nobody pays attention to you. It's less a question of worldly obligations than of an inner focus. It's up to me not to answer the phone, or not to go out to dinner. I need a lot of turning inwards. It's an effort to find that solitude, because I'm not actually a very reclusive person. I like being with people, and I don't particularly like being alone.

Q: We spoke with other writers about the different motivations that lead them to write fiction and criticism. In the preface to *Against Interpretation*, you state that writing criticism "has proved to be an act of intellectual disburdenment as well as intellectual self-expression." You write, too, that if certain issues no longer preoccupied you, it was probably because you had written about them. Does writing fiction also relieve you of burdens and obsessions?

Sontag: Writing fiction is more intimate. One touches certain kinds of obsessions and fantasies in a more unveiled way. But my essays are also, in fact, very personal. All my writing is involved with personal passions and obsessions, although the fiction is more direct.

Q: What prompted you to write *Illness as Metaphor*?

Sontag: I was prompted to write it because I had cancer. I had never been seriously ill. Then suddenly, I entered the world of the sick. They told me that I had a 10 percent chance of living a maximum of two years. Of course, I felt fear and pain. But I didn't go crazy. I remained aware and I listened to everyone else saying frightening things about being ill. I discovered that many patients in the hospital are embarrassed about being sick. The doctors also treated the cancer as if it were something more than an illness: It wasn't like having a heart attack or another illness; there was a taboo about it. The idea for my book came from my observations. I also wanted to write something useful.

Q: Did you write it in the hospital?

Sontag: I couldn't write the first six months. I was taking tranquiliz-
ers. When they discovered my cancer I was involved in writing my
essays about photography. Four of the six essays had been published
and I had drafts of the other two. When the idea to write *Illness as
Metaphor* came to me, I wanted to begin writing immediately, but I
knew that if I did, I would never return to the essays on photography.
When I began to write again, I forced myself to finish those essays
first, in the spring and summer of that year. Later I wrote *Illness as
Metaphor* in approximately a month and a half. It's one of the things
that I wrote quickly and I enjoyed doing it. I knew it was going to be
important for many people. I knew it would matter to a lot of people.
Hundreds of people have written to me and have said that it saved
their lives, that because of the book they went to a doctor or changed
their doctors.

Q: Professor Ruth Hernandez Torres, a Puerto Rican educator,
launched into frenetic activity after her bout with cancer. Have you
found that your need to write has intensified since your illness?

Sontag: No. But the experience of thinking that you're going to die
and then not dying is a very strong one. You're never the same
afterwards. You are obliged to come to terms with the idea of dying
and, even if you are reprieved, there is some part of you that never
comes back completely. You can never regain that old relationship to
life, and contact with people becomes very important. I do feel a
conflict between the intense solitude that's required for writing and
my need for people, which was strengthened when I was ill. Besides
the excellent chemotherapy, what saved my life was all the kindness
and affection that I received not only from those to whom I was
closest but also from acquaintances and strangers who suddenly
appeared and came through for me in a marvelous way.

Q: Do you do as much rewriting now as before you were ill?

Sontag: I rewrite more than ever.

Q: Rupert de Ventos compared the work of rewriting to forced
labor.

Sontag: That analogy implies that one is being forced to do it. I'd
be very upset if I *couldn't* do it, because I'd feel I wouldn't get it
right. I've got to have the time to rewrite.

Q: He was referring to rewriting as forced labor, as opposed to writing which was labor. To rewrite was even worse than to write the first draft.

Sontag: For me, it's the other way around. The hardest thing is to write the first draft. Once I've got a first draft, unless I'm headed towards disaster, I feel a kind of relief, because I've got something to work with. The hardest thing is to generate it out of nothing, particularly with the essays. And then successive rewritings generally come easier. But I am an obsessive rewriter. I've awakened in the middle of the night and thought, the comma's in the wrong place in that sentence on page 32, and I've gotten up, gone into the study, and changed it. I would love to be able to write straight out, as some very good writers do. First they think, and then they have a sentence, and then they think a while more, and then they have another sentence. When they're finished they're finished, except for a few little changes. There may be more writers who work in that fashion than the way I do. But I don't know how to do it any other way, and, with some notable exceptions, I don't consider my first drafts anywhere near the form where I would want them to be. For me writing is a bootstrap operation: If I end up at the top, it's because I started at the bottom. With each draft I go up another notch. I have to go step by step. And sometimes what I get at the end is very different from what I started with. It may be because my attitude has evolved, because I see the theme differently. Sometimes I use it up, sometimes it doesn't work.

Q: Are those rewriting techniques the same with fiction as with essays?

Sontag: I do go through fewer drafts in the fiction, usually three or four. With the essays, I've done as many as ten or fifteen drafts. I find writing essays harder, and I'm not sure why I've written so many of them. Perhaps it's because I had a lot of views and I was trying to get rid of them. But then there were *more* views behind them.

Q: But that ties up with what you said before, that the responsibility to truth is a bit less in fiction.

Sontag: It's another kind of truth. There's always a reference in the essays, whether I'm talking about Nicaragua or Gertrude Stein. I can look up from the page and think about how it actually is in Nicaragua, or what is going on in the work of Gertrude Stein, and then I can go back to the page and ask whether I've said something interesting or original, have I generated something more.

Q: There's more matching to do.

Sontag: It isn't matching, but I can turn away and try to think about what is not on the page. My text isn't primarily about me, it's about it, and I try to give the most interesting or richest account of what's going on. But also I want to say something that's original, that's useful, that's true.

Q: Finishing sometimes gives a sense of relief. Is that your case?

Sontag: Yes, I feel a tremendous sense of relief that I can go on to something else. Invariably, whatever I'm writing takes longer than I think it's going to take. I feel terribly restless towards the end of that process, because I'm overdue, in terms of my own time, and I've already started to think of other things, before I finish, so I feel trapped. I want to go on to the next thing. I wish writing could be like singing, where one is contemporary with what one is doing. Of course, there's a long period of preparation and rehearsal, but then it's done, and one goes on to something else. In writing, one's whole life is the preparation, and the doing of the writing drags on much longer than is pleasurable. I've found that the more preparation I make for an essay, and the more notes I have before I start writing, the longer it is going to take to write. It's the same with fiction. I've been working on a novel on and off for a couple of years, which I've had to break off for a number of reasons. I have a lot of notes on the unwritten part, as well as single different paragraphs, phrases, and observations. When I get back to the novel, I'm sure these notes are going to cost me a vast amount of additional work. It would probably be wise to dispense with this note-taking, this semi-writing.

Q: One of the genres that you seem drawn to is the biographical essay. What do you understand to be the art of biography?

Sontag: I don't believe that I write biographical essays. I write essays on bodies of work. Edmund Wilson's essay on Turgenev, or any of his major literary essays, are biographical essays. It's a nineteenth-century form in which the focus is the story of somebody's life, and the work figures as an event of the life. I'm not drawn to that. I detest psychological speculation. The only biographical strategy in the essays about someone's work is that sometimes I try to find an idea that permits me to discuss the work in chronological order, the order in which it was done. I think my essays are as unbiographical as it's possible to be, given the fact that they are, as I say, about a body of work, and that I don't write about a "text" in the new critical sense, according to which there is no author at all. I'm very interested in the project of a life work, and in how one piece connects with another, but not in terms of the actual life, nor in terms of any private information. To me the biography of the author is just what is in the work. Although sometimes I am privy to information about the private life of the artist or writer, I chose never to write about these things.

Q: Your essays on Weil, Benjamin, and Bresson seem to want to grasp the essence of those twentieth-century women and men as people.

Sontag: I don't feel it's their essence as people. It's their essence as creating consciousnesses. I don't say a thing about Bresson or Godard as real people. That's exactly what I *don't* want to do. I do like to see work in connection with other work. I can't imagine somebody not being curious about what else someone has written. Once I had a conversation with Mary McCarthy about the work of William Burroughs. When *Naked Lunch* came out, she had praised it extravagantly. That had seemed odd to me, because the book seemed to incarnate everything that's not in McCarthy's work. Burroughs' way of writing or sensibility was something I would have thought would be extremely offensive, perhaps even incomprehensible, to her. Anyway, talking with her a few years ago, I mentioned that when *Naked Lunch* came out, I had liked it too, and that later I realized that I was only seduced by some particularly salient formal aspects of the book, and that now I didn't like it at all. Reading Burroughs' subsequent fictions made me decide that I was mistaken about *Naked Lunch*. I suppose I was really asking McCarthy whether she had ever reconsidered her judgment, and was astonished when she said that she had never read anything else by Burroughs. If I am at all engaged by somebody's work, whether it's a film, a dance, or a poem, then I always want to see or experience more of it. If I'm interested in a painter, I would see every painting I could, if not in museums, then in reproduction. Each part changes for me as I know more and more of the whole work, which means to know the work in a deeper way.

Q: Generally in fiction there is a strong link between marginal characters and their condition as travelers. It is revealing that both your fiction and your criticism reveal an interest in travel . . .

Sontag: Yes, I suppose travel is one of my recurring themes. The book of stories, *I, etcetera,* begins with "Project for a Trip to China," and ends with "Unguided Tour." *On Photography,* too, is really about travel, about taking photographs as the ultimate touristic experience.

Q: Does travel affect or stimulate your writing?

Sontag: It's part of my life, an addiction that I try to keep under control. I love to travel, but travel takes me away from writing. I have to be cautious and not overdo it. I don't need travel for the writing; for writing purposes I've probably done enough travel to last me for the rest of my life. I would say rather that the travel is in competition with the writing.

Q: You wrote that you decided to write about "camp" because it both repelled and attracted you. Do you feel similarly ambivalent about travel?

Sontag: No, no. As I said, it's an addiction, a hunger. It's something I have to discipline. I think less about the voyage or the trip as a metaphor, and more about travel as a reality, as a kind of "fast" reality in which you go from one thing to another. I'm very interested in what it means to go fast and to go slow. Images of velocity are constantly in my mind. They sound abstract and have to be put in a context, but I think they're among the central images in my work.

Q: Could you try to give us that necessary context?

Sontag: There's a story on which I have been working intermittently, called "Speed," which is about different ways, both real and metaphorical, in which people go faster and slower. We live in a time when people prize the idea of going fast very much. I have mixed feelings about going faster, and I like the slowness of travel rather than the speed. Almost all the writers I know, including some very good ones, use word-processors now, and many of my friends and acquaintances have told me that I would be well served by one, especially with my propensity to rewrite. But I've resisted it. And when people say that I would write faster, I think, what's so good about writing faster? I like the artisanal aspect of writing, and I don't mind doing all that retyping. Sometimes I wish I had the patience to write everything in longhand. I like going slow, and doing things over and over. I find it interesting to repeat things, each time in a deeper way.

Q: You state in your essay on Lévi-Strauss that "most serious thought struggles with a feeling of homelessness." Could you distinguish between the homelessness of a North American intellectual and that of a European?

Sontag: I think a true intellectual is never at home. To me, being an intellectual means seeing things in a complicated way. One lives on the boundary, one is aware of many claims, many alternatives, and that precludes being at home, in the simple sense. I'm not so interested in being at home. I accept being uncomfortable, I also don't know how else to be. I don't feel it's so different, for a North American or a European.

Q: In the prefatory note in *Against Interpretation* you state that when you write cultural criticism, you want to expose and clarify the assumptions that underlie certain judgments and tastes. What formal qualities do you strive for when you write an essay?

Sontag: I want the essays to be as well-written and as dense as possible. Ideally there should be a new idea in every sentence. I also try to get the prose to be as eloquent as possible from the point of view of diction and style. To keep jargon out of my prose has been a long struggle for me, because I have an intense academic background. I enjoy reading academic books, but I don't want to write like that.

Q: Although Sartre is not extensively discussed in your essay on Barthes, you observe that Barthes' work is a response and a challenge to the older French writer's system of thought. Are there any "hidden presences" in your critical essays?

Sontag: When I started out, in the insolent way typical of the young writer, I was taking on everybody. Now I don't think about other writers when I'm writing. My "hidden presence," if there is one, is myself—the writer I have been and am trying to surpass.

Q: Although you rarely mention contemporary political events explicitly in your essays, the undercurrent of your criticism carries a condemnation of the tenor of American culture. Could you tell us something about the shaping of your political views?

Sontag: I've had periods of limited political activity, when I have felt very strongly about a particular situation, like the Vietnam war in the 1960s and early 1970s. I did some speaking on behalf of the Equal Rights Amendment. I've been active in campaigns for political prisoners in many countries since 1970. I'm not doing much of this *in* my writing. I'm doing it *as* a writer, using the fact that I'm a public figure.

Though I have a strong civic sense, I don't want to use my writing as
the principal vehicle for my political views. I choose not to devote
much writing time to politics, although I devote other kinds of time.

Q: Your writing also conveys an acceptance of the responsibility of
being a North American intellectual. What is your sense of this
responsibility?

Sontag: It's an enormous responsibility. It seems to me essential to
have some intellectuals in the dominant empire on the planet playing
a critical or adversarial role—one of the things that intellectuals, at
least since Voltaire, are thought to do. It's true that most intellectuals
are conformists, like most people. But I hope there will continue to
be some North American intellectuals who will keep alive a more
complex and more critical attitude toward this society, which has not
only its strengths and good points, but a great many defects, and has
behaved rather badly toward the rest of the Americas.

One Must Defend Seriousness:
A Talk with Susan Sontag

Stefan Jonsson / 1988

From *Bonniers Litterära Magasin,* Vol. 58, No. 2 (April 1989), pp. 84–93. Reprinted by permission of Stefan Jonsson. Though most of the interview printed below derives from an English-language transcript of the original interview, some portions of the *BLM* version are included as translated from the Swedish by Ingrid Anderson.

When we are about to finish, she adds: "A lot of what I'm saying is not very theoretical." It's not an excuse or reservation; more a confession about a critical ideal. "I can construct my ideas, ad hoc, when I need them. But I'm not interested in literary theory as such."

How is it that Lukács, a great theorist, is critically blind to the literature of his time, when the theoretically idiosyncratic Benjamin has a critical eye that can see well into the future? Probably because theories are in some sense like prejudices. They can lead to predictable positions. When the critic derives his or her loyalties from theory, then theory will be the critic's enemy.

With Susan Sontag, theoretical ambivalence seems a condition for the development of critical depth. She exists within the concrete course of events that provide the conditions for thinking and cultural production. She positions herself by using theory as a temporary construct in order, as she says, to "justify necessary positions that have to do with one's deepest loyalties." Her critical sensibility moves dialectically, powered by a radical and human engagement. The result is a kind of thinking that is so fast that it can hardly be methodical, and so rich in concepts and modes of reasoning that it can approach its objects from several different angles at once, restlessly searching for a position from which it is possible to pull the *Zeitgeist* by its tail.

Since you have visited this country many times before, and even lived here for a couple of years in the early 1970s, Susan Sontag has become a name with a special position in the cultural public sphere of Sweden. As a member of that public, I am of course curious about your most recent impressions of this country. Have you been received in Sweden this time by a press and a cultural establishment that are quite familiar to you from previous visits? The writer and politician Jörn Donner, for example, remarked that Susan Sontag nowadays ought to be in charge of "the cultural museum." And one of the large Swedish newspapers wrote yesterday that "Susan Sontag, this radical from the 1960s, has turned out to be this elitist cultural conservative."

That is a caricature. I am not primarily a political writer. I am a writer who has political and ethical principles, just like many writers for the last 200 years. But my writing is not at the service of my opinions. I do believe, however, that I am absolutely committed to the idea of cultural criticism. I think that is what being an intellec- tual—as opposed to being a writer—is. Since Diderot and Voltaire this has become the vocation of the modern writer: to advance critical or adversarial ideas about culture.

If I had to explain my opinions I would certainly start by saying: There are many ideas of the modern, and there are many versions of the modern. People think the modern is just linear economic develop- ment, increasing consumer society affluence, or sophisticated technol- ogy. But we know that all of these things have a tremendous price. They have a tremendous price for culture, for politics, and for the environment. If you point that out—and it is obvious—then people think you are some kind of reactionary.

Another point is that people in Europe always identify the modern with America and Americanization; yet America is only one model of the modern. The prosperity in Asian countries which have become rich gives other interesting examples. These nations can be incredibly modern, very rich and consumerist; but their kind of modernity has nothing to do with democracy, pluralism, tolerance, or similar values. Whereas for Europe a capitalist or mixed economy always does bring democracy, to a certain extent. In the Soviet Union now there may be all glasnost but no perestroika yet. But Gorbachev is right that, in principle, the two things go together. You can't have a greater eco- nomic development in the Soviet Union without some democracy and some degree of freedom.

But in Asia you can have lots of perestroika but no glasnost. You could move China into a capitalist economy and still it would not become anything like a liberal society. So my point is that these cultural alternatives are more varied than people think. And I have a gut feeling that it's hard to criticize the modern in Sweden. The belief in progress is very hard to shake in this country.

From a certain point of view your famous essay about Camp was an inquiry into some specific cultural alternatives offered in the West during the 60s. Even though many have seemed to believe so, your own understanding of the cultural alternatives summed up by the notion of Camp was not one of complete affirmation. Rather, you saw it as the dialectical counterpart of the established canon. The Camp taste, you stated, was a taste that turned its back on "the good-bad axis of ordinary aesthetic judgment." What has happened since then, however, is that this judgment has lost much of its omnipotence. Today there is hardly any theoretically or socially founded consensus on a set system of aesthetic norms. The Camp-mentality, together with the commercialization and commodification of culture, seems to have suppressed the aesthetic standards formerly upheld by the culturally hegemonic bourgeoisie and by the modernist avant-garde.

Camp is not my attitude. It is something I observed and something I thought was very instructive. But in so far as it is something I could appreciate I always assumed that it is a marginal attitude which presupposes certain majority standards. If those standards are no longer there, if instead you have something which is not camp, but the kind of thing that Nietzsche was predicting, which is really the levelling of all taste so that everything is made equivalent to everything else, a kind of relativism which you have to call cultural nihilism and which I think *is* the situation today, as it is administered by television values, then of course the function of this kind of irony, which is rather aristocratic and rather special, is really lost. All cultural attitudes are dialectical, relational, and oppositional. If the mainstream changes, the criticism of it has to change too; which is to say that the oppositional or ironic attitude, the counter-attitude, must change. I am very interested in counter-attitudes. They are absolutely necessary ingredients in culture. If those attitudes are not present, any culture becomes a form of lobotomization. So I am an exponent, in a very unsystematic way (because I am very "anti" and unsystematic), of counter-attitudes. Everything I have done presupposes a mainstream attitude. But it is true that the cultural situation has changed even more radically for the worse than I would have predicted 25 years ago. And so I find myself moved to support things which I did not think would be necessary to support at all in the past. Like seriousness, for instance. I really did not think one would have to defend seriousness, and I do now.

For a critic this is of course a precarious situation. Nevertheless, you seem to be able to keep your good-bad axis quite intact. One of the most amazing things about your essays is your ability to make accurate aesthetic judgments. But how do you defend judgments of aesthetic quality in a situation where there is no generally recognized aesthetic doctrine to fall back upon, no public opinion in cultural matters to which one may appeal?

For one thing I have a very strong sense of the canon. I find it impossible to think without the notion of a canon. I never even was aware of it until it began to be challenged, of course, but then I realized that the notion of the canon is essential to me.

The Nobel Prize is an interesting effort to establish a canon. But although it puts you in the canon it cannot keep you there. Saul Bellow, for instance, is not going to stay in the canon, and Golding certainly did not even belong there. In part, the Nobel Prize is a kind of guessing game about what is good. Because I think you cannot really tell about the worth of the work of a writer until it is over and a certain amount of time has passed. But within a fairly short time, I would say 25–30 years, it is really quite clear who is good and who is not. One of the few consolatory ideas which I have about writing is that the judgment of posterity is correct.

But how does this process of canon formation really work? As I see it, the canon must be a result of many conflicting forces, institutions, and readings at work in society. I suppose you agree with this. At the same time you say that 30 years after the death of a writer we can decide—as if it was objectively true—whether the work is of any value, if it belongs in the canon, or if it should be forgotten. How is it possible to make decisions like these?

If I say that Chekhov is better than Françoise Sagan, there is always someone who can say: "Well, that is just your opinion, how do you know? There is no way of proving it." Yet I am *sure* that this is *true*. I mean I would stake my life on it.

Now, if just one example of this kind is true, then that means there is a possibility of making judgments. It does not mean that we are not wrong sometimes but it means that it is correct or admissible to make this kind of aesthetic judgment.

The other way of arguing to support the idea that you can make judgments of value is to think about the question historically, and to say that there are certain classes of judgments or views which are not validated by sense-impressions, nor are they tautological, self-evident, like mathematical propositions. In other words, these are judgments which cannot be defined, but they have an historical character. Therefore they can only be described.

The project of consciousness is basically a historical project. It is based on an accumulation of understanding and on consensus, which stipulates what it is to be human. It also has to do with an idea that there are better ways of being human as opposed to less good ways of being human, and the idea that there is a range of choices in the very form of being human. It has to do with the idea that there is memory, that there are records, and that there are efforts and versions of this project of consciousness. So you begin to construct a genealogy, and in the arts this means that judgment is a product of experience and that experience is formed out of a body of works which has stood the test of this judgment and which has both reflected and created certain standards. When you are talking about the canon you are not talking about something that is closed. You are talking about something which at any given time has a shape. As with almost every cultural question, you want to do two things at the same time. As I was saying earlier, there is always a position and a counter-position, and in fact every position has to be understood in terms of what it is opposing. So you would have both the creation of a canon and therefore the maintenance of it, the conserving of it; and then you would have constant challenges to it. I am not against these challenges. But these too have to stand the test of a certain kind of experience and spiritual utility. The canon should generate simultaneously its conservers and its critics.

What I don't think works is simply to cut the gordian knot and say that because individual elements in the canon, or the shape of the canon, can be questioned, let's say according to certain standards of justice, this proves that the canon is simply arbitrary or always ideological—in the narrow sense of ideology.

I want, for many reasons, to defend the idea of a canon. The relativist position in its pure form is finally completely incoherent, because if it were true then it would not even be possible to establish relativism as a position; and it would have no greater claim than the absolutist position. To go back to the original example—if a book by Françoise Sagan were in fact the only book ever written, it would indeed be a masterpiece. I mean, I am not a relativist, but I am, as it were, a relationist: The standards come because there is something else that is better; it is not a question of intrinsic value, it is a question of relational value.

This seems to imply that you have to confront the postmodernist challenges to the idea of artistic authenticity, to the notion of a canon, and to the possibilities of making theoretically grounded statements about literary quality. It seems to me that all these notions are of decisive importance to your own critical authorship. Do you regard what usually is called postmodernism as an intellectual atti-tude which goes in hand with this situation of cultural nihilism, as you described it above?

Yes. The answer to your question is—I do. But it is so complicated. Many different things have been embraced in the postmodern attitude. Some of it is just plain old cultural nihilism and cultural relativism. Some of it is an ethical criticism of the authoritarianism of culture and its exclusionist qualities, particularly with regard to non-European cultures, and with respect to women, with which I would associate myself. You have to separate these things.

The most characteristic aspect of what is called postmodernism is the levelling of everything. Postmodernist art is characterized by parody and collage. You see this most clearly in architecture. What did the term mean when it first came up there? It said: "We don't want to be forever limited by this neo-Bauhaus idea of geometrical purity, anti-ornamentation, and total functionalism. We want to play, we want to quote the architecture of the past, we want to have things which are functionally irrelevant, we want decoration, we want eclec-ticism, we want playfulness, we want to accept the modern in its vulgarity, we don't want to confine the modern to any kind of idealism (which it meant for Bauhaus).'' The result is an architecture of facades, a culture of facades, of recombinant styles. I think that the making of everything equivalent to everything is the basic postmodernist impulse; it has a kind of ideological pretext of being more democratic. But I think democracy is just a pretext.

When I visited this new museum in Paris, le musée d'Orsay, I burst into tears. Because we thought it was established what the 19th-century canon was. We thought it was clear that Degas was better than Bouguereau. Now comes a new museum which says it is all the same, or that, in fact, the bad art is better than the good art because it is more entertaining. That's why the great late 19th-century impressionist and post-impressionist stuff is up there on the fifth floor next to the kitchen. And on the great ground floor of this incredible building, reconstructed on the inside as if by Albert Speer, there is all this terrible kitsch, salon kitsch of the 19th century which you thought had been defeated forever.

This is a culture of entertainment, and the easy thing is now revalued in a certain way. People are saying all the time: Well, why be so serious? You only have to be serious if you live in a tragic country, like Poland, or Hungary, or the Soviet Union, or South Africa.

In a world where standards of seriousness and of real accomplishment, real search, real quality—whatever you want to call it—are being institutionally and ideologically challenged by this contradictory set of ideas that goes under the umbrella term of postmodernism, in a world where there is not even place for the older class-braced defenses of quality, which I am not interested in perpetuating—in such a world there has to be another way of defending these standards. Perhaps you have to say that a certain level of cultural accomplishment is just necessary to human ecology.

It seems to me inconceivable that some values would not be acknowledged as superior to mere values of entertainment or distraction. I don't see how in the world anyone could say it is not better to be a more profound person, or a more feeling person, or a more compassionate person, or a more sensitive person. And if the common answer is, ''Well, if you are all these things you are going to suffer more in life because you will experience more,'' then I feel I almost have to give a religious answer which would go: "Well, maybe that is why it is a duty to suffer." One of the beautiful ideas in Buddhism is that if you are in fact at a point in your life where there is no suffering, then it is your duty to go and find some, to put yourself in contact with it. There are, as it were, duties about being human. You don't have a duty to be as unconscious as you possibly can be. But modern society makes some states of unconsciousness seem very desirable. Television is a perfect institutional form of the mandate to be not very conscious.

Writing about the novel in the 60s you stated that it had not kept up with the changes in society and the new sensibility which followed these changes. At the same time, in essays like "Against Interpretation" and "On Style," you expressed certain theoretical views on the morality of art. You write that art is not a criticism of life, as Matthew Arnold would have it. Art is rather the extension of life. It helps us to experience the world by cultivating our senses, and the morality of art is thus to educate our consciousness. You have also referred to Walter Benjamin who, talking about Proust, remarked that every great work in literature either creates or destroys a genre. In line with these ideas, your own novels and short stories were trying to replace the traditional mimetic ways of representing character and setting, much in the same way as the French writers associated with le nouveau roman. *Yet, neither your novels, nor the ones written by Robbe-Grillet, Butor or Sarraute, have managed to set new standards for this genre. The novel—is it then still arrière-garde?*

No, I don't think so. To tell you the truth, I was not being entirely honest with myself in the 1960's about the accomplishment of *le nouveau roman*. What I really liked much more was the idea of it. When I wrote about Sarraute and Robbe-Grillet, I liked their essays and the ideas they had about fiction much better than the fiction that they themselves were writing. Those essays, particularly the ones in *Against Interpretation*, were responding to a cultural situation existing in the English–speaking world at that time. Almost all the fiction written in England and America at that time was very sociological and psychological in its intentions, and always discussed in terms of its ideas. So these ideas of mine, which I guess you could call formalist, were a way of criticizing that literature. But I think that, in fact, the prejudices which are the target or the adversary in "Against Interpretation" are much weaker now. Of course in England most fiction still does follow that style. A writer like Iris Murdoch, for example, is not in any way interested in formal innovation in fiction. In fact, almost all the British writers are very unambitious.

Talking to Nadine Gordimer on British television you remarked that quite a few writers in your country are looking with awe at the situations experienced by writers in countries where various forms of state oppression hamper the development towards freedom and equality, countries like Hungary or South Africa. In such a situation the artistic and intellectual activities have an immediate function in the struggle between oppressors and oppressed. In a country like your own, or like Sweden, this function is not generally associated with literature. But would you say, today, that a writer in the capitalist states of the West has no responsibility whatsoever when it comes to choosing his or her material—the content?

I don't think of the writer, ultimately, as having any responsibility except to literature. If I criticize the writers in my own country it is because I think most of them have a very provincial view of the human situation, and because their writing is very unambitious.

One of the writers I admire most is Chekhov. Chekhov is always talking about how writers must flee any kind of political engagement. A writer practicing literature at the highest level is implicitly making a political statement in the sense that it is a statement in favor of quality, or in favor of the integrity of the language. Sometimes I feel that, in the end, all I am really defending—but then I say all is everything—is the idea of seriousness, of true seriousness. What strikes me is how unambitious and superficial most American literature is. I can't speak for Sweden, of course, but I suppose it is not too different here. That is why the literature which seems serious so often comes either from the smaller countries, or from marginal people or even foreigners in the larger ones. In Hungary, for instance—and Hungarian really is a closed language, from an English-speaking point of view—there is an absolutely extraordinary literary vitality, four or five wonderful writers of fiction and very good poets. Perhaps this is because of the exigencies of their political situation. Things are so difficult, and they have to be serious. They have no excuse.

V. S. Naipaul wrote a novel recently called *The Enigma of Arrival*. It is actually a completely autobiographical book about his experience of leaving London, and of renting a small house on a big estate in the middle of the country. It is about living in this house, and about his experience of the neighbors and the small English village, of the countryside, and of the changing of the seasons.

It is the kind of book which, if the average American or English writer wrote it, would be superficial and very quick. But Naipaul's book is a work into which the writer has poured so much feeling for the language and for the possibilities of description. When reading that book I was thinking that this could be something so simple for another writer, but Naipaul brings this kind of seriousness to the project, this intensity. It is that which is lacking in other works. The politics and the social engagement are almost by-products of this intensity.

What I want to see is a strong literature, and I want to see a literature which is also very conscientious about language. That is another reason to be against the so-called media, because television debases language. Literature has to be against television and similar forms of communication.

Is this kind of literature at all possible in countries like our own, which are not—as you said—tragic? Maybe we have to get used to a situation where the most important contemporary literature, within the tradition of our European cultures, is created in countries situated in the margin of, or outside, our materialistic, commercialized, and comfortable Western world?

If you think of a career of someone like Van Gogh or Joyce, it is just unimaginable today that someone would accept that degree of marginality in order to do his work. They felt that they had to lead strange lives, to a certain degree, in order to do their work.

And they were right. I don't think people understand that it really is the same today. In bourgeois society people perhaps have an idea of novelty, but they don't have a serious idea of originality. It is as if the notion of novelty has cannibalized the notion of originality, or any kind of real search.

Another example, a little bit closer to our own time, is Elias Canetti. He would sit there in London for decades, working on his books, some of them, like *Crowds and Power*, taking him 25 years to write. I suppose people who knew him just said "Oh, he is just some brilliant café-talker from Vienna, with this masterpiece he is working on." In the meantime all these Brits are turning out a book every year, the way they do here in Sweden, and it does not amount to anything. But Canetti is willing to remain marginal in this way because he has this incredible self-confidence. In all these cases, Van Gogh, Joyce, Canetti, it is really a question of an enormous self-confidence, of really feeling something like a mission and of seeing it partly as a religious vocation. Whereas now, writing for most people, including some very talented writers, is a career, it is not a vocation.

This reminds me of the title of your essay on Cesare Pavese, "The Artist as Exemplary Sufferer"; and writing on Camus you make the distinction between the artist as husband, keeping within the borders of convention, and the artist as a lover, always challenging and crossing these borders. It seems as if in your view the artist should be the inverted image of the bourgeois society, should embody its dark side, its counter-attitude.

I think so, I do think so. But those are very early and somewhat immature formulations. I like better the way I discuss it in *Under the Sign of Saturn*, where I don't make it so explicit. But the portraits of Canetti and Walter Benjamin really take up that theme again. With Benjamin it was something else, it was almost as if he had a talent for failure in a worldly sense. He actually tried to be integrated into the system. He did try to get a university job, and he did try to work as a journalist. There was something clumsy about him, and he could not make it work. It was not just that Hitler came and Benjamin had to leave Germany. He was not talented for success. He rather had a kind of talent for failure.

In the end I think that the status of marginality of the writer is very precious. It does not mean that you have to be as marginal as, for instance, Van Gogh or Benjamin. The career of Roland Barthes is interesting. He had what seemed to be a rather normal career, in the sense that he did take a university position, and was a teacher, and lived a rather worldly and mundane life in Paris, and he was very clever at making alliances with people to get support among the Paris intelligentsia.

And yet I still think he was a kind of outsider. He was in some ways like Diderot, who also was worldly, lived in Paris, and knew a lot of rich people and aristocrats, and was involved in public institutional-ized projects like the *Encyclopédie*. But at the same time Diderot was doing some things which were original and extraordinary, like *Le Neveu de Rameau* or *Jacques le fataliste*. With Diderot, as with Barthes, it is almost as if the success was a kind of disguise.

Talking about the literary canon before, you stated that the canon is necessary as an arena where literary issues and cultural problems are discussed. Without such an arena, there would be no possibilities for discussion at all. Now, a consequence of the postmodern situation we talked about before is that the vocation of serious writers and intellectuals is pushed toward the margins of society. This means, in turn, that serious cultural matters disappear beyond the horizon within which the majority of the people do their thinking and lead their lives, that those who are aware of and care about this arena, this canon, constantly decrease in number. This development seems to lead to a situation where the public at large becomes completely unconscious about the mere existence of this arena. They don't even know that there is such a thing as a literary canon. Is it relevant to talk about a canon when 99 percent of the people are not aware of its existence? And what, in such a situation, would be the role of the intellectual?

I am aware that much of what I am saying sounds like a secular version of ideas which are quite familiar in religious discourse. The distinction between esoteric and exoteric knowledge is quite accept-able in all the great traditional religions. There is a body of teaching and practice that is designed for most people, and then there will be a few people who will, through study and spiritual discipline, have access to other ways of thinking and feeling and other teachings, which may even contradict the teachings which are prescribed for the majority of the people. One of the fundamental ideas of a secular, modern world is that this distinction, except for those disciplines or bodies of knowledge which have the prestige of science, is obsolete, oppressive, authoritarian, elitist. Even if we acknowledge that the most important, serious, and profound work of culture is the occupa-tion of a minority, the modern dogma is that we must be committed to extending it to the greatest possible number of people.

It feels uncomfortable to make this argument outside a religious context, but I think we should make it. I think we have to say: It does not matter if there are only five thousand people in the world who care about these things. Then that is all there is, and we could be like Irish monks in the Dark Ages, who were just copying the classics and keeping them alive, perhaps with a hope there will come a completely different time when these texts will be meaningful to a much larger number of people, and when they could be an inspiration for some kind of cultural renewal. But of course we cannot count on that. It seems pretty likely that—barring some extraordinary catastrophe of a political or ecological kind—the condition that you talk about will last, not only my lifetime but yours.

The whole question of democracy and culture is really a very hard one. But I think one has to be prepared to give tough answers, that culture in a serious sense, or art in a serious sense, or the project of consciousness in a serious sense, is not one to be judged by democratic standards, though the access should not be restricted by class, or birth, or race, or gender or any of those things. We are required to continue to make an effort to invite people in who are willing to do the work and to accept the difference in their own lives and their own consciousness that these loyalties will imply. It is a question of recruitment just as you recruit people into a religious order.

But I also think this is a gift. A very good friend of mine is the American painter Jasper Johns, who probably is the most famous living painter now. He grew up in a very, very poor southern family in a village in South Carolina, like really something out of the 1930s and the Depression. His father was the town drunk and his mother ran away with somebody. He had no education, there were no books, there was nothing. Zero. He told me that when he was six years old he knew he was going to be a painter. And I asked: "Did you ever see any paintings?" He said "No." I said: "Did you ever see any pictures?" He said: "Well, maybe I saw a picture in a magazine or something." I mean nothing. Zero. The most absolute zero-cultural level you can imagine. But he said "I knew I was going to be a painter, a great painter." At the age of six! How? I don't mean that it is true for everybody, but you can have these ideas that have nothing to do with your class, with your influences, or with anything that can be described sociologically. And you go to the big city, you meet people, you start to do it, and there it is.

What you have said now seems to contradict two very influential and quite similar ideas of the role of the intellectual. The first is the idea from the early and middle 19th century of the liberal humanist or bourgeois democratic intellectual. This intellectual was a writer and journalist firmly tied to the middle-class, for which he could serve as speaker, as ideological and political strategist, and at the same time as the ethical conscience of his class. The second notion is the more recent idea of the politically committed intellectual, often indistinguishable from the intellectual of the Left. This type of intellectual does not have any organic links tying him or her to a certain social class. Nevertheless, it is a position which usually implies the ideal of being rooted in the working class, or simply in "the people." In other words, these two notions of the intellectual rely on two different ideas of what you earlier called the modern, the liberal bourgeois version and the socialist version of the project of the modern. Are both these ideas of the modern passé?

No, they are not. I absolutely believe in those projects. They may be passé in the sense that they are being defeated historically. But I myself not only believe in those projects, I am willing to devote a considerable amount of time, which really is my activity as an intellectual, to continuing that struggle, the struggle for public education, public enlightenment, social justice, humanization, trying to keep alive humanist values in mass culture. If there is any chance in this society to keep open some alternatives which will permit a few people to make different kinds of choices, and if there is any chance to keep the general level of public and cultural life from sinking to an even lower standard than today, then there must be a considerable number of people prepared to do that work.

The only thing I am saying—and it is a lot and it is a source of great personal anguish to me—is that I know that in so far as I do pursue this project, I am in a certain way betraying or leaving the project of being a writer at the very highest level. To a certain extent the project of the intellectual and the project of the writer overlap, but they also face in different directions. As a writer I have a loyalty to this project for which I think intellectuals are so important. But I know and I feel more and more that it is carrying me away from a kind of freedom and spiritual absolutism which would be better for me as a writer, and in which I would really turn my back on those questions. Maybe a single person can do both to some extent. I have done both, as have Hans Magnus Enzensberger and John Berger. Barthes is another example, of an older generation, who was in a way divided. Toward the end of his life he was tormented by the thought that, instead of writing articles and essays, he should have written a novel with Proust as a prototype. And I earlier gave you the example of Diderot. *L'Encyclopédie* was this public, humanist, intellectual, liberalizing project—of course Diderot would have been a democratic socialist if he had lived in the 20th century—and then he was also writing *Le Neveu de Rameau*, which cannot be included or enveloped in the kind of mentality which produced all his public activity.

There is the mandate of the intellectual and there is the mandate of the writer. Since the vocation of the intellectual is in fact much more socially acceptable—however much it is made fun of—than the radical vision of the writer, which will leave you marginal and much more isolated, it is usually the intellectual vocation that wins over the writer's vocation. I am absolutely not saying I do not believe in the intellectual vocation, but I am saying that I know it is not identical with the creation of literature.

But I think the project of enlightenment, of humanism, of democratic socialism is a project that addresses needs that everyone shares, including writers of course, because writers are human beings and citizens. So finally it is as a citizen that one experiences this mandate. If you acknowledge it you have responsibility to other human beings.

In a way, I almost feel this is an exaggeration, but it is a kind of pedagogic exaggeration: I think you really have to have something of this commitment to the social, and to justice, and to maintaining some kind of idea of rationality, of justice, of quality and of light for everyone, or else, in fact, your position really does lead to suicide. It is humanism or suicide.

Celan did not have any admixture of the intellectual in this sense. He was one of the purest examples of a writer in this part of the century. All of his work comes out of a total absence of hope. And since he also was someone who, like Benjamin, did not have any talent for success, he was just tormented by everything, always haunted by the past. When Celan received the Büchner-prize, which was then the most prestigious literary prize in Germany, he was invited to give a speech. The speech is about two pages long, and it is completely unintelligible. You cannot understand a word of it. It is just a kind of intellectual music, a kind of agony. He makes statements about literature and poetry, which come from so deep inside him that they don't communicate. It is so condensed you would have to add six buckets of water to turn it into something that would be intelligible to people. But he had no instinct for doing that. He was too much inside himself. And if you are too much inside yourself, and if things get very difficult or you have some great personal difficulty, which Celan probably did, you finally don't understand even how to go on living. So I mean it is partly because you want to save your life in a more literal sense—if you have an instinct for life—that you want to connect with other people and assume a certain civic notion of well-being, which then would go back to these enlightenment ideas of the 18th and 19th centuries that you talked about.

I would like to throw another couple of concepts into this distinction between the writer and the intellectual. It is Italo Calvino, who, in his last book, Six Memos for the Next Millennium, *makes the distinction between crystal and flame in a metaphorical way which I find very imaginative. Calvino writes: "Crystal and flame; two forms of perfect beauty that we cannot tear our eyes away from, two modes of growth in time, of expenditure of the matters surrounding them, two moral symbols, two absolutes, two categories for classifying facts and ideas, styles and feeling."*

It seems to me that your own work is constituted in the mode Calvino sums up under the image of the crystal. At the same time I would say that the writers and artists you seem most attracted by create works resembling the image of the flame. They are visionaries, often with a thirst for the absolute, revolutionaries who refuse to compromise, artists whose lives are consumed by the flame of genius—a genius which, permeating their work, will continue burning forever. I am thinking of writers like Artaud, Sade, Cioran, Weil, Nietzsche, Canetti.

I think there is something in what you say, but in my case I think there is a flame in the crystal. And if I am making progress as a fiction writer it means I am able to move the flame to fiction. I have discovered a way to put a more direct kind of urgency and eloquence in the voices of the fiction. That is why I am more excited now once again about writing fiction.

That is an extraordinary image. What I like about it very much, besides that it is so beautiful and convincing, is that it gives another example of the irreducible plurality of models, of highly desirable models of consciousness. If you have enough complexity and experience and breadth of consciousness, you can, of course, understand both these possibilities and appreciate them, as Calvino says—they are equally beautiful. Finally it is a question of temperament, or sensibility. It is something as simple as that.

Calvino was surely a man of feeling. But his characteristic relation to everything was very ironical and rather sad, rather skeptical. He experienced himself very much as an observer, or somebody outside experience. He was very quiet, sort of melancholy, just a little bit child-like. One of his last books of fiction, *Palomar*, is really a self-portrait. It is about a man who is always watching, a man who has the name of a great telescope; and a telescope is an instrument with which you see from afar.

Borges is in one sense the opposite of Calvino. He was no watcher because he was blind. But this blindness gave him an extraordinary opportunity to be in a way very child-like in the later part of his life, also a kind of Mr. Palomar. He enjoyed things enormously. He loved being invited to places and he would go anywhere where he was invited. That is how I happened to meet him first in New York. Then I saw him many times and I visited him in Argentina, not long before he died. He was always travelling. And I said: "What do you get out of travelling?" And he answered: "Everywhere I go people are so nice to me." He was very sweet and rather child-like and completely helpless. And he never really had a full adult life. I don't think he really had any sexual life ever. He had this enormous love of literature. He loved to be read to, he loved to talk about literature. Even though he was so brilliant there was something extremely naive, and in a way very pure about him. He just did not live very many of the ordinary human options. He did marry but he never really looked at his wife. He lived his whole life with his mother, and then toward the end of his life he had a young companion, a young woman who was partly Japanese. She was like his daughter; it was like the old Oedipus and the young Antigone, and they went everywhere together holding hands.

He was also a crystal, such an example of a crystal, but not in a melancholy register—he was capable of great joy. He loved the contact with people, while Calvino would think that contact with people always was strange, desire was strange, intimacy was strange, everything was strange.

Nietzsche says that every philosophy is the rationalization of a temperament. And it is true. The choices these writers are making as literary performers—I don't mean that they are expressing themselves; I mean that this is how temperament takes some kind of linguistic form in the making of these structures—these choices reflect certain kinds of energies or certain kinds of distance or intimacy with experience, a certain degree of yearning and longing or a certain degree of resignation or irony. That arch or reach of temperament is the ultimate limit and the shape of your writing.

AIDS and Its Metaphors: A Conversation with Susan Sontag

Kenny Fries / 1989

From *Coming Up!* (March 1989), pp. 49–50. Reprinted by permission of *The San Francisco Bay Times*.

"Now comes the scary part." Susan Sontag had just delivered a lecture in the Green Room of the Herbst Theatre (February 1). *Now* it was time to take audience questions. "I am aware I am in San Francisco. A lot of thinking about AIDS has gone on here—a kind of model has developed here."

Only days before, a review of her new book, *AIDS and Its Metaphors*, had appeared in *The San Francisco Chronicle Book Review*. Even though in the review written by journalist Randy Shilts the book was called "required reading for those whose lives or careers are intimately joined to the experience of this epidemic," the latter part of his review is negative. Shilts questions the accuracy of some of Sontag's assertions and ends his review by calling *AIDS and Its Metaphors* "only half a good book." He states: "Both the subject and the reader deserve more."

Later, after the question and answer period, when we were setting up a time to meet the following day, Sontag admitted she was stung by Shilts' review. "I'm hurt," she said.

During the lecture she had hinted at her "disappointment" at the early reviews. The book had been given to "science writers or to specialists on AIDS, to social commentators." Sontag would have preferred to have the book reviewed by writers who could see the book as "a literary performance. It is an essay, a literary form with a tradition and a speculative purpose."

I suggested to Sontag that she need not feel defensive. "We'll talk more about that tomorrow," she promised.

I spoke with Sontag the next day at her comfortable two-room suite at the downtown Clift Hotel. Relaxing on a billowy sofa, she said, "Last night I was surprised by the warm welcome." She was obvi-

ously relieved that the lecture was behind her—but just what was she
nervous about?

"Randy Shilts is probably the most visible gay-identified journalist
in the country," she told me. "He has written an important book on
AIDS. He has lots of agendas, lots of purposes. But the review is
more about Randy Shilts than about my book. The early reviewers
just don't seem to get it."

Sontag describes her book as one less about AIDS than as "a book
about how we think about AIDS—a book with AIDS as its primary
example, not another book about AIDS. My ideas of AIDS alone,
stripped of the associations, are the same as any civilized, compassionate, liberal's. What should people do? Weep? Demonstrate?
That's obvious. I agree with them." She calls her book "weird" and
a reflection of the way she thinks. "I have the kind of mind that,
whenever I think of something, it makes me think of something else.
With this book I do what I do best. This book has more to do with
Emerson than with Randy Shilts."

"I mean, what is Debussy doing in a book about AIDS?" she asks.
The answer lies in the fact that while writing the book, Sontag
attended a performance of Debussy's opera, *Pélleas et Mélisande*, at
the Met. ("A very good performance with Frederica von Stade as
Mélisande," she notes.) During the performance, Sontag realized that
the opera, which was based on a Maeterlinck play, was actually about
miasma, a turn-of-the-century medical problem often attributed to
living in dark, dank, cities. Miasma is now medically discredited,
even though the word still lives on in our language.

Sontag wants this book to be seen in relation to what she has
written in the past. She says that "the book reflects my dope, my
exaggerated concerns." But she admits that *AIDS and Its Metaphors*
is not a book she expected to write.

A few years ago, Sontag relates, friends of friends, acquaintances,
and, soon, very close friends began to become ill, and some die, from
AIDS. Her first written exploration on the subject, the story "The
Way We Live Now," which appeared in *The New Yorker* and as the
lead story in *The Best American Short Stories 1987*, was started one
night after she received a phone call telling her a close friend had
AIDS. When she hung up the phone, she burst into tears, and later,
she could not sleep. So she took a bath. In the bathtub, the first words

of her story came to her. "It was given to me, ready to be born. I got out of the bathtub and started writing standing up," she says. "I wrote the story very quickly, in two days, drawing on experiences of my own cancer and a friend's stroke. Radical experiences are similar."

Sontag is "very proud" of her story. She would like to be known as much for her fiction as for her essays. "Fiction is closer to my private life, more immediate, direct, less constrained—more reckless. Essays involve more effort in layering and condensation, more revisions." She describes the process of writing *AIDS and Its Metaphors* as "making soup into a boullion cube."

Sontag has received many letters from people with AIDS telling her how helpful her earlier book, *Illness as Metaphor*, published in 1978, has been to them. This strengthened her determination to write about AIDS, but she still felt that she did not want to return to writing about illness. "I like to move on. I had done that already," she says. But privately she was "talking about little else."

At the time, her publisher, Farrar, Straus, and Giroux, was preparing, one by one, new paperback editions of her books. ("New editions with pretty covers," she muses.) When it came time to prepare the new edition of *Illness as Metaphor*, she decided to write a three-page epilogue about AIDS, and include it in the earlier book with no fanfare, no announcement on the cover, "like a party favor."

Eventually, this epilogue became forty pages, "much too long for an afterword," and when she called her editor to let him know, he said to make it sixty pages and it can be a book of its own. "Oh, it'll never get that long," she recalls telling him.

A year from when she began the would-be epilogue, the manuscript had grown into its current, published, ninety-five page form.

While writing, Sontag kept in mind that the book was a sequel to *Illness as Metaphor*. "It had to follow the earlier book, without repeating it, or contradicting it. And it had to be as good," she says. Eventually, the two books will appear together, as one book—Part One and Part Two. For now, however, the book has a separate life of its own.

I asked Sontag if writing this book felt more second-hand than her experience writing *Illness as Metaphor*, which came out of her successful experience in curing her own cancer. "It doesn't feel second-hand," she replied without hesitation. "AIDS has devastated my world. The most important person in my life died of AIDS and I sat with him every day. I've lost so many friends."

Some of Sontag's friends with AIDS are doing very well. Many are being treated by New York doctor Joseph Sonnebend, a friend of Sontag's and founder of New York's Community Research Initiative. Sontag, herself, is on the organization's Board of Directors. According to Sontag, Sonnebend is "not keen on AZT." He treats each patient as an individual, and thinks that those that do best have less of a track record of immune system depression. Many of her friends have travelled to Sweden for treatment.

Anyone who reads either *Illness as Metaphor* or *AIDS and Its Metaphors* will know that Sontag does not believe in "non-disease specific treatment" for cancer or AIDS. "You can't cure this disease by going on a macrobiotic diet," she says. When I mentioned acupuncture, she said, "These are ways of helping the body, and I'm not against that. But they are not treatment." "I'm not telling anybody not to do what they do," she adds, but she does mention a friend who "died fast" because he "received no treatment."

Knowing that Sontag herself was cured of cancer by traditional Western medicine allows us to understand where her belief comes from. She believes there is good treatment to be found and that the patient must take an active role in finding it amidst the awful treatment that abounds. She believes the metaphors surrounding the illness often prevent people from seeking good treatment. "How would you feel when the doctor says you will be *bombarded* by radiation?"

When I asked Sontag how she felt about the gay community's responses to AIDS, she said our responses were "great." "Look at you," she says, "a few years ago would you have known all this medical terminology—t-cells, suppressor ratios, antigens? This is what I mean by people taking an active role." Referring to that morning's ACT-UP demonstration, she said, "I think things like what happened on the Golden Gate Bridge are terrific."

But she does comment that she is sad to see the gay community become "so medicalized. I don't want to see gay men become largely a medical culture—a culture of succor and death. The fight for gay rights should continue." She mentions, as an example, a gay group at the University of Texas in Austin changing its name from Gay Action to AIDS Action. "I know I'm treading on dangerous ground," she says.

Of course, her concerns are not limited to the gay community. "Something that bothers me is prostitution," she asserts. "Are we thinking about protecting those young boys?" "And in New York," she continues, "a city where it is inconceivable to have a woman mayor or a black mayor, AIDS is becoming a poor person's disease. In these Reagan-Bush-Quayle years AIDS will become a class issue."

Sontag was surprised when I told her that I disagreed with her statement in the book that a difference between the way cancer and AIDS is viewed is that with AIDS "no one is tempted, not yet at least, to psychologize it." She was eager to hear more when I told her that many people have told me that they knew I would test negative for the virus because I don't feel guilty about being gay. And that I have heard others say that people who feel guilty about being gay die faster when they get AIDS. "I never knew that," she admits.

Continuing our conversation along this line of inquiry, we talked about the possibility that people might be embarrassed to say they had AIDS since receptive anal sex has been the primary suspected mode of HIV-transmission. Saying you have AIDS is, therefore, tantamount to saying you like getting fucked. "That's fascinating," Sontag said. "A stigma within a stigma. Such an American way, not having a positive attitude about sex. How could you deny this certain thing you do?"

She reports that in Europe the prejudices concerning AIDS are somewhat different. Whereas here we see AIDS as an African disease, in Europe, they view AIDS as being American. Of course, the common metaphor of AIDS being foreign, invasive, remains intact. "We have a climate of health paranoia," she says, and she believes that if not for AIDS, the new computer lingo would not have called the new computer bug a virus.

As we approach the millennium, Sontag thinks apocalyptic thinking will get worse. "Imagine the kitsch of the evening of December 31, 1999," she offers.

But Sontag refuses to write about her subjects using the "t.v. approach to reality. This is too complex, how people use language and ideas to manipulate. Too much hype can backfire." She views AIDS as a turning point in the way we view sexuality. "The very thing associated with life is now associated with death," she says. "This is a deep psychic wound."

Sontag realizes she has been called the "last of the 18th-century rationalists," and has been criticized for being "too in love with words." Although she enjoys being a "professional foreigner," she feels very strongly that it is of the utmost importance for us to remain "lucid as a form of empowerment, not detachment."

She says it took until the sixth draft of her book to realize that she, too, had succumbed to the belief that AIDS was a plague. Then she realized that calling AIDS a plague was only a metaphor. She writes:

Plague is the principal metaphor by which the AIDS epidemic is understood. . . . Plague, from the Latin plaga (stroke, wound), has long been used metaphorically as the highest standard of collective calamity, evil, scourge. . . . It is usually epidemics that are thought of as plagues. And these mass incidences of illness are understood as inflicted, not just endured. Considering illness as a punishment is the oldest idea of what causes illness, and an idea opposed by all attention to the ill that deserves the noble name of medicine.

Sontag hopes her book will be seen as "a plea against hysteria and facile pessimism" (she reminds us that "no disease yet has proven to be 100% fatal"). Her book, she says, "assumes previous discourse," and in it she refuses "to talk down to people. The words we use are evidence of attitudes," she asserts, and although she knows we cannot live without metaphors, we have to be careful about the ones we choose and buy into.

After a short time with this remarkable, spirited, and beautiful woman, you soon realize that her attitudes and the words she uses are shaped by her probing mind, and that the mind that belongs to Susan Sontag, the so-called dark lady of American letters, is informed by a generous, open heart, as well.

Susan Sontag, Hot at Last

Paula Span / 1992

From *The Washington Post* (September 17, 1992), pp. C1–C2.
© 1992 *The Washington Post*. Reprinted by permission.

NEW YORK—Add this to the list of phenomena you thought you'd never see in your lifetime.

Nixon resurrected.

Germany reunified.

A Susan Sontag novel on the bestseller list.

You can picture, all over the country, reviewers and book buyers alike scratching their heads. Susan Sontag, reigning queen of the New York Intellectuals? The scholar-critic who writes all those dauntingly brilliant essays about European writers and filmmakers whose names you are uncertain how to pronounce? Who can reel off references to Kleist, Artaud, Duchamp, John Cage and Harpo Marx in the space of half a dozen paragraphs of "The Aesthetics of Silence"?

Yes, that Susan Sontag. *The Volcano Lover* is her first novel in 25 years and the first of her books to reach so far beyond the circles that devour the *New York Review of Books*. What's more—further head-scratching—it's a zesty historical novel, a re-imagining of a famous love triangle that's subtitled "A Romance."

The author is startled by this turn of events, but she's having a swell time. "Most of what I've done in the past, I didn't like it so much," she confesses, propping her feet on the living room coffee table in her Chelsea apartment. "I didn't think it was so good; it was just the best I could do. I always felt some dissatisfaction."

Not that she didn't take pride in some of it, she goes on, ticking off a few favorites, such as the essays on photography and *Illness as Metaphor*, which analyzed social perceptions of cancer. "But there was always something," she muses, "like being hungry after a big meal."

After finishing *The Volcano Lover*, though, there was only sweet satiation. "It's a feast," she says.

This is a different Sontag, or perhaps an evolving one. She looks much the same as you've come to expect, after nearly 30 years as a public icon, with penetrating dark eyes and that trademark swath of silver coursing through her black hair. Age has only slightly softened her fierce features. Her erudition still makes an interviewer nervous about asking dumb questions (such as, how does one manage to be 59 and still confine all graying hair to one dramatic battle ribbon?).

But an earlier Sontag would regularly proclaim that she didn't read her reviews, scarcely cared about matters like money or audience. She had grown up dreaming of writing for the *Partisan Review* and being read by 5,000 people, she once said, and was apparently still content to be. "I write to be part of literature, not for other people," she informed a hapless interviewer who'd raised the question of public response to a later essay, *AIDS and Its Metaphors*.

An earlier Sontag, too, kept vowing year after year to devote herself to fiction but somehow never managed to. Through the '70s and '80s she started and abandoned several novels. "Somewhere along the line, there was a failure of nerve," she says. "A *justified* failure of nerve."

Now, Sontag herself talks of having reached a turning point, of feeling "liberated." People come up to her in the street to tell her they cried over her novel and she's delighted. "The response does mean something to me," she says. "It's wonderful to write something that matters to people." She's undertaken a 15-city publicity tour, a high-toned one to be sure, consisting largely of readings (including one at Washington's Chapters, a benefit for the homeless, Tuesday evening) and interviews with NPR affiliates. It's a first nonetheless and, she says, "an adventure."

She's even acquired the first literary agent she's ever employed, leading to a more lucrative arrangement with her longtime publisher, leading in turn to this sunny, book-crammed co-op with a few tomato plants growing in pots on the terrace. "It's not as simple as you're commercial or you're not commercial, or you're idealistic or you've sold out," she thinks now. "It's complicated."

What's fueling much of this change is *The Volcano Lover* itself. It germinated a dozen years ago in the musty antiquarian book-and-print shops of London. Sontag was in search of the 18th-century architectural prints she collects, like those propped atop her living room bookshelves, when she came upon a series of hand-colored engravings of Mount Vesuvius. A clerk eventually ascertained that they had been commissioned by Sir William Hamilton, British ambassador to the court of Naples, for a privately printed book in 1776.

They're hanging now in her foyer. "The altar, as I laughingly call it," she says, leading the way. Erupting Vesuvius, somnolent Vesuvius, close-ups and cross sections of volcanic rock—she bought five prints, five more the next day, and then another seven. She's still berating herself for the prints she left behind. And she's still uncertain why these pictures so attracted her. Perhaps, Sontag muses, recalling a hot summer in the early '60s when she spent air-conditioned hours at a festival of Japanese sci-fi films ("early *Godzilla*, that kind of stuff"), she is "fascinated by images of disaster."

Hanging on her apartment walls year after year, though, the artworks generated thoughts of disaster less often than thoughts of Hamilton: diplomat, collector, amateur scientist and gentleman connoisseur. "It really began with him, ideas about his passions and his avidity," Sontag says, resettled on the couch. She writes here, on yellow legal pads, because the books climb halfway up just two walls instead of overwhelming the room as they do her study.

"I began with some feelings about his character, how he must have been a repressed melancholic, how all these enthusiasms and passions were a compensation. And I knew the story, of course, the famous triangle."

History remembers Hamilton, whose much younger wife, Emma, had a notorious affair with the British naval hero Lord Nelson, as a cuckold. Hollywood remembers him (falsely) as an overweight lecher with a cane in the 1941 weeper *That Hamilton Woman* (Vivien Leigh and Laurence Olivier did the swooning), which Sontag saw and thrilled to as a child. As the rudiments of her novel began to coalesce, "I thought, well, Emma and Nelson, they'll be in the story in a minor way," she says. "Didn't work out that way. Emma kidnapped the book."

Arguably, though, the kidnapper was Sontag herself, supplying a cooly modern narrative voice that recounts the action while commenting on love and grief, cracking jokes, digressing to discuss artistic philosophies, referring to developments (Hiroshima, premenstrual syndrome) that her 18th-century characters could know nothing about. Critics who dislike that approach tend to dislike the book.

They've been substantially outnumbered, though, by those who declare that Sontag has pulled it off, created a satisfying saga of high
literary quality, a brainy page-turner.

Writing it was unlike any other writing in Sontag's long career, she
says—"a great emotional experience." The essays that established
her reputation were always a struggle, revised so endlessly that
sometimes nothing of the first draft survived. Each of the half-dozen
essays that make up *On Photography* took her nine months to produce. Whereas *The Volcano Lover* simply seemed to flow, prologue
to epilogue in three years. "The people were really alive in my head
all the time," she says. "As I went about in my life, I thought about
what they'd think and say."

Afterward, she saw she'd gotten some of the historical details
wrong and hit the reference books. "By the end of it, I was a very
good student of British naval history." She also began to see that
what she had told a friend early on—"I'm writing a book 50 people in
the world will read"—might not be so, as friends and editors began to
respond. A fifth printing has brought the total copies in print to
105,000.

The desire to write a novel she initially saw as "folly"—along with
a disaster that was not merely an image—also brought about an
alteration in business arrangements. Sontag's dated to the early '60s,
when she simply walked into the offices of Farrar, Straus & Giroux
(she liked the books it published) and left the manuscript of her
unsolicited first novel with a secretary. Farrar, Straus has published
all her work, and one reason she never used a literary agent was her
assumption ("quite naive of me") that an agent's shopping her book
around would result in a rupture of that relationship. But she wanted
enough money, this time, to forgo the lecturing, grant-wrangling and
essay-writing by which she had supported herself and to devote
several years to *The Volcano Lover.*

As for the disaster, it occurred in her previous apartment. "I woke
up one night and my bedroom was aflame," she recalls. "Thank God
I woke up. Another five minutes. . . ." Firefighters chopped through
the roof to extinguish the blaze, which caused at least as much
psychic as physical damage. What horrified her, Sontag says, was the
realization that she didn't have enough money in her checking account

to take refuge in a decent hotel. The landlord put a tarp over the hacked-open hole, and she spent the night in her roofless apartment.

"I realized how unprotected I was," she says. Naturally, she could have called a friend; she could have borrowed a few hundred dollars. But, she thought, "'maybe I shouldn't be so carefree about these things.' You don't discover you're undefended until a brick falls on your head."

It's a remarkable statement for a woman who struggled valiantly with cancer in the '70s, without health insurance or enough money to pay for her treatment; an editor friend raised a reported $150,000 from friends and fellow writers to help cover her medical bills. This time, though, Sontag contacted an agent, and not just any agent but one known (feared too) for his aggressiveness, Andrew Wylie.

"I was then 56 years old," she explains. "I'd had more than 30 years of work. It's not so much to own an apartment and have all your books out of storage and have time to write. These are not unreasonable demands; they're not corrupt." Wylie arranged a four-book deal with Farrar, Straus, whose executives no doubt swallowed hard when she won the MacArthur Foundation's don't-call-it-genius award the following year, bringing her $340,000 over five years.

They're cheering now, of course. And Sontag is feeling quite cheerful herself. "I think I'm a slow developer," she says. "I ask myself this all the time—why did it take me so long?" Her answer: "I didn't have access to this kind of expressiveness, of inner freedom. . . . One blushes to use such well-worn phrases as 'maturity,' but I think it is. . . . I think I will do, now, my best work."

One of the disadvantages of being classically well educated is that one's standards of literary merit are exceedingly high, causing a certain weakness in the knees when undertaking new projects. Another is that one knows things like this: "The passage of time does not always work in a writer's favor," Sontag says. "It's common for a painter or composer to do his best work in the later years; it's not common for writers."

How it feels to turn 60, then, as Sontag will in January, is one of the questions an interviewer fears to pose; it seems insufficiently intellectual. But Sontag is not dismissive of her looming milestone, acknowledging that "it's very haunting—how can it not be? It's scary. Turning 60, you think it's like the other side of the moon."

Still, 59 hasn't turned out to be a bad year, has it? "It doesn't feel like what I've dreaded," Sontag says. "It doesn't feel like what other people have described. It just shows you there are more options than we've been told."

Besides, she points out, "I haven't lived my life in the right order." Precocious and in a hurry, she did all the grown-up things at startling ages: She entered college at 15, married a University of Chicago sociology professor at 17, had a son (author David Rieff) at 19. When she was divorced at 26, "my adolescence began," she says. "I had a very enjoyable adolescence from the age of 27 to about 35, which coincided with the '60s—I enjoyed them in a way people much younger experienced them."

It may be oddly appropriate, therefore, that in her late fifties, Sontag figured out how to write a novel. "I learned to dance," she says, "when I was 26."

The Twentyfirst Century Will Begin in Sarajevo

Alfonso Armada / 1993

From *El Pais* (July 25, 1993), p. 23. An English version of the interview was published in *The Guardian* (July 29, 1993), supplement pp. 8–9. Reprinted by permission.

At the age of 60, Susan Sontag, one of this century's most influential critics, has decided to turn herself for five weeks into part of the scenery in Sarajevo, in Bosnia-Herzegovina—a country that has been subjected to an implacable assault from Serbian forces for more than 500 days.

Sontag's moral courage has now brought her to Sarajevo to stage a play. The choice of the piece and the decision to return to Sarajevo for the second time amid the bombing were both Sontag's. The play that is to be staged is *Waiting for Godot*. Sontag's production of Samuel Beckett's play can be seen in a theatre at the end of August in Sarajevo, a city which Sontag says "began and will end the 20th century."

What was behind your visits to Sarajevo since the war began?

The first time that I came to Sarajevo was in April. That visit was initiated by my son, David Rieff, who is writing a book about the war in Bosnia. Before that, I had already felt involved in what was going on here, through my own sense of horror and indignation. I have to say that I had never thought of coming to Sarajevo because I did not know what to do here. What can you do in Sarajevo if you are not a journalist or a worker with a humanitarian organisation? And I had never had fantasies of becoming a "Blue Helmet" for the United Nations.

Then, I spent two weeks here and it was an extraordinary experience. What really makes an impression on you in Sarajevo—apart from the suffering of the people—is that here you can establish a very strong link with the Bosnians and the Bosnian ideals, that Bosnia should be able to be a country. Afterwards, I searched for a way to

267

come back to Sarajevo and spend some time doing something morally decent. During my first visit, I met up with some theatre people and I asked them if they would like me to come back and work with them for a while. They said "Yes." The play itself occurred to me without thinking about it too much; *Waiting for Godot*.

Why Waiting for Godot?

Because it has an obvious resonance, which does not need to be explained. Everyone smiles when you relate it; the people moving towards death while, day after day, they wait for something that never arrives. People who, with a savage humour, talk about life and the situation that they find themselves in without any hope, but who, in spite of that, keep going. It would be difficult to find a piece with more resonance. And not just because of its symbolic value. The second reason for staging *Waiting for Godot* is that it is a chamber piece.

I would really like to put on a work of Shakespeare's but it is impossible to do Shakespeare on a tiny stage, in candlelight and in a theatre which could be bombed at any minute. In fact, I am going to put the public in the stage area because it is safer than in the yard with seats. The theatre has felt some impacts in the roof and, when I was there the other day, a missile landed next to the building and the walls shook. So, I am not going to put the people who come to watch in any danger.

What is the significance of Sarajevo towards the end of this century?

I believe that the 20th century began here and that the 21st century will also begin here. This has been a short century. The first world war began in this city. Centuries do not begin numerically with two noughts. The 19th century really began in 1815, with the restoration of the old order after the fall of Napoleon. I suppose the 21st century really began in 1989 with the suicide of the Soviet Union, but you could also say—in a more ironic way—that it began with Sarajevo because now we have a total picture of what the 20th century was.

What is the sensation of time like in Sarajevo?

One day in Sarajevo is like a week in New York. Each day is so full that, when I spend a week here, it seems as if I have been here for a month. Each day is full of new and terrible impressions. But not only terrible because what takes place here only happens in very extreme circumstances. Here, you are witness to the most terrible acts that man is capable of, but at the same time you can meet the best and the bravest people you are likely to meet in the course of your life. Extreme situations of disaster, of war, in a certain place, attract the best and the worst people.

Do you think that history can still teach us something, or has the world forgotten Auschwitz?

I believe that history teaches us continuously. What happens is that people do not want to listen. There is no doubt that, in two or three years maximum, the official version of what has happened here will be that the western nations have made big mistakes, which they are still making. We are talking about the third major incident of genocide during this century; in 1915, the Armenians, at the end of the 1930s and the beginning of the 1940s, the Jews and Gypsies, and now, the Bosnian Muslims.

What is the fear like here?

A person would be mad if he or she were not afraid. You have to be afraid. There are different levels of danger. There is no safe place but some places are safer than others. Last night, I had dinner with the director of the newspaper *Oslobodenje*, Kemal Kursaphic. He lives 50 metres away from the Serbian lines, and can show you bullet holes from snipers in his living room. His neighbor on the fifth floor—he lives on the second floor—died last Saturday of a gunshot. If you ask him where the Serbs are, he says: "In that building."

Here, people do extraordinary things. Some 350,000 people live in Sarajevo. Ten or 15 people die every day and around 20 get wounded. I have a one in a thousand chance. But people are killed in the place where you were just an hour before or an hour later. But the marvellous thing is that many people try to preserve all the aspects of normality that they can.

Are you going to write about your experiences and your impressions?

I am writing a kind of diary called "Waiting for Godot in Sarajevo."

Do you think that Europe and the West are going to pay a high price for their policy?

Of course. I believe that the Serbs want to have all of the former Yugoslavia. I usually opt for the worst scenario, as in the old saying from Gramsci: "The optimism of barbarity and the pessimism of intelligence." I think that the worst is yet to come. I think that the Bosnians are going to be completely defeated, that Sarajevo will be occupied, divided and destroyed. Even if this pathetic government signs the partition of the country—which is unthinkable—it will bring enormous suffering to its people. I think that we are going to find ourselves in a situation—on a smaller scale—similar to that of Hitler. The war also presupposes that Europe will be totally discredited.

What do you think of the behaviour of the United Nations, Europe, the intellectuals and Left regarding Bosnia?

I deplore it, I am critical of and I regret the refusal of my own government to intervene. But I think that the biggest and the most shameful responsibility lies with the governments of Britain, Germany and France. My government should intervene because it sees itself as a superpower.

The European governments have the moral and political obligation to intervene because this is Europe. Sarajevo was the San Francisco of eastern Europe, it was a cosmopolitan and sophisticated city, much more so than Belgrade and Zagreb. And perhaps it is because of this that people want to destroy it. Without the United Nations, it is perfectly clear that Sarajevo would not have survived. In this sense, I feel very grateful to the United Nations High Commission for Refugees.

But the United Nations security force is not carrying out the orders of the Security Council. The Serbs commit violations every day. Sarajevo ought to be a safe city, and you can see just how safe it is. [*At that moment a grenade exploded not far from the hotel.*] As for the attitude of intellectuals, I find it painful. When I came back from here in April, I suggested to everyone I met that they come to Sarajevo. Out of the long list of famous people I spoke to, only two responded; one has just left, Juan Goytisolo, whom I admire from the heart; the other is Annie Leibovitz, a very famous photographer, who is still here. Many people said to me "it's very dangerous," or "you must be mad," or "it's very sad."

And the Left?

There isn't any Left now. It's a joke.

A Gluttonous Reader:
Susan Sontag

Molly McQuade / 1993

Published by permission of Molly McQuade. *An Unsentimental Education: Writers and Chicago*, University of Chicago Press, 1995.

Susan Sontag earned a B.A. in 1951 from the University of Chicago, where she studied English, philosophy, and much else. The critic, novelist, dramatist, and short story writer received the National Book Critics Circle award for criticism in 1978 for On Photography *(Farrar, Straus & Giroux, 1977).*

In her large, light-filled Manhattan home, books and papers were stacked up everywhere, and Sontag's assistant cudgeled a computer in a lilting Southern accent. Sontag's signature white streak in her mane of black hair seemed to hyphenate one part of her mind with another. Informality and warmth marked the conversation.

Her books include Against Interpretation *(Farrar, Straus & Giroux, 1966);* Styles of Radical Will *(FSG, 1969);* Illness as Metaphor *(FSG, 1978); the novels* The Benefactor *(FSG, 1963);* Death Kit *(FSG, 1967), and* The Volcano Lover *(FSG, 1992), as well as* I, etcetera, *a collection of short stories (FSG, 1978).*

What led me to Chicago? It was reading an article in, I believe, *Collier's* magazine in 1946 or 1947. It was either by Robert Hutchins, explaining the aims and curriculum of the College, or it was an article about this eccentric place, which didn't have a football team, where all people did was study, and where they talked about Plato and Aristotle and Aquinas day and night. I thought, that's for me.

Not only did I determine I would go there, but I persuaded my three closest friends in high school to apply as well.

I chose Chicago because I understood the College to be different from any other college in the country (except for St. John's, a clone of the "Hutchins" College). What drew me was the idea of the fixed curriculum—*that* curriculum.

Going to Chicago was like finding home, the place where I would finally meet people who were interested in what I cared about.

I'd learned to read when I was about three, so that when I entered first grade able to read and write, I was immediately put into third grade. I had a very mobile childhood, and went to many elementary schools. Because I was skipped at another point, I graduated from high school just before I turned sixteen.

When I graduated, my mother and her second husband were living in southern California, and she was hoping I would not follow my dream. Her fantasy about the university had nothing to do with the curriculum. She'd become a California patriot, and Chicago was "back East"—very dirty and very cold. She insisted that I try Berkeley. Since I was graduating in January, I agreed to go to Berkeley for the spring term while applying to the University of Chicago for fall admission. Her hope was that I would like Berkeley so much that I would give up Chicago.

And I did like Berkeley a lot. I took some terrific courses in that first semester. I realized I could get a very good education at Berkeley. But I had been accepted into the College, as had my friends, who were graduating from high school in June. I thought, "It's going to be even better at Chicago."

And Chicago was exactly what I expected it to be.

At Chicago, in September, I took the placement exams given every entering student, which determined how many of the fourteen year-long courses one was required to take. (Students took four courses a year. In the fourth, or senior year, one was allowed to take some electives from the graduate divisions.) Since I had already found my way to many of the books which were required reading in the College, I placed out of all but six courses, which meant that I had less than two years of work for a B.A. I was actually quite disappointed that I would be finished so soon.

I still have all of the syllabi—the mimeographed "Selected Readings"—for my courses in the College. They're compilations of the assigned literary and philosophical texts and historical documents. I've carried them with me through twenty moves.

I don't think I would have been any different if I hadn't gone to Chicago. Yet it was a pleasure to be in a place where there was nothing to ignore. This was a place where all one was *supposed* to do was study.

Until Chicago, I'd been a gluttonous reader. But the kind of intellectual work I was doing until I came to Chicago was simply *taking in*; I didn't have a method. The method practiced at Chicago was comparative, and basically ahistorical. Let's say you started with Plato—in the College, we invariably started with Plato—and you examined Plato's views on this or that, and then you went on to Aristotle, and then you compared Plato's and Aristotle's views, and then you added Aquinas, and then you compared Aquinas and Plato. There was a constant dialogue of texts; and the method of comparing them, which I learned at Chicago, is one I still practice in my essay writing.

A Chicago student was not taught to situate the idea or the spirit of a text in the time in which it emerged. You could be comparing John Stuart Mill with Aristotle, and you didn't think about the difference between fifth-century B.C. Greece and nineteenth-century England. So if there was any *defect* in the education, which I've spent, now, a lifetime correcting, it was the absence of attention to or respect for the historical context of ideas. It took me a long, long time to understand what could be learned by seeing how ideas emerged out of their historical and social context. These texts were ideal models in an ahistorical space.

We were taught to be reasoners. We were encouraged to participate in class discussion, and one's contribution to discussion was judged by a very high standard. We were expected not to "answer" a question, but to present an argument. You would be asked to compare Aristotle's and Aquinas's ideas of virtue. You'd raise your hand and deliver a reasoned exposition that would go on for several minutes. The professor would listen and say, "How would you consider the following?" You were expected to be able to develop an argument orally and, when it was questioned, defend it with precision.

We were taught to be very close readers. We were taught incredible reading skills: to be able to examine a text thoughtfully word by word. (One might spend three class hours on two sentences.) It was the best education for learning how to read that one could imagine. But we were not taught to write. At Chicago, no attention was paid to writing skills. Of course, some of us became writers anyway, because the kind of people who are attracted to that sort of education often are very articulate.

I was writing—stories, poems, plays—from the age of about seven.

But during the time I was so sated and happy a student at Chicago, writing was postponed. One couldn't give oneself to this exhilarating education and then go back to the dormitory and write stories. Creative writing is a different way of thinking. (Writing comes from a kind of restlessness and dissatisfaction. And I was so satisfied at Chicago.) Besides, participating in the courses in the College was a full-time job—not to mention the classes in the divisions I was not enrolled in but auditing, concerts on campus and screenings at Doc Films, and occasional forays to the Art Institute and the opera. I had no creative powers at all during that period. The university annihilated them.

I had been writing stories in high school, and I started writing again when I left Chicago. But the university was a total situation, a benevolent dictatorship. Which was fine with me.

The single greatest teacher in the College, and the most important teacher I ever had, was a man named Joseph Schwab. He was a genius teacher, the best embodiment of Chicago's version of the Socratic method. All I ever learned about him is that he came from a small town in Louisiana (he had a deep Southern accent) and had been trained as a zoologist (he'd done his Ph.D. thesis on fruit flies). And then he had come to the University of Chicago and begun teaching in the College. He was electrifying. Schwab taught several sections of Observation, Interpretation, Integration ("OII"). This was the master course, the philosophy course. In the second year, I audited the whole course with him again. I still think with tools I learned from Schwab.

Kenneth Burke was another great influence on me. I studied with him during my first year at Chicago, 1949–50, when he was a visiting professor and was teaching a section of Humanities III. That was one of the courses I was required to take (I had placed out of Humanities I and II, though I was auditing them), and it was sheer luck that I was assigned to the section he taught.

I remember the first day. The man standing in front of the class looked ancient to me; he was probably all of forty-five. I was sixteen. He wrote "Mr. Burke" on the blackboard. Then he began talking about the approach to literary texts he would be using. I thought, "This sounds familiar."

I'd already been reading Kenneth Burke on my own for several years—I read a lot of criticism and literary quarterlies. After class I went up to him and said, "Excuse me, Mr. Burke"—I was very shy, and didn't approach a teacher easily—"I hope you don't mind my asking, but could you please tell me your first name?"

"Why do you ask?" he said. I have to explain that at that time Kenneth Burke was not famous. I mean, he was famous to a tiny literary coterie, but he certainly didn't expect any undergraduate to know who he was.

I said, "Because I wondered if you might be Kenneth Burke."

He said, "How do you know who I am?"

And I said, "Well, I've read *Permanence and Change* and *Philosophy of Literary Form* and *A Grammar of Motives*, and I've read . . ."

He said, "You *have*?"

Another miracle.

Burke was not a Chicago product—in fact, he'd never even gotten a B.A. But his approach confirmed the Chicago method of close reading. I remember we spent three months on one shortish novel of Conrad's, *Victory*, reading and discussing it line by line.

I had other wonderful teachers, too. There was Ned Rosenheim, who taught Humanities III, and Christian Mackauer, a Hitler refugee, who taught History of Western Civilization.

Who else? At Chicago, I also audited courses from the beginning. I remember auditing English 203, a course given by the poet Elder Olson on the classic texts of literary criticism from Plato to Matthew Arnold, and several courses with R. S. Crane. And most impressive of all were the philosophy seminars given by Richard McKeon and Leo Strauss. I remember (indeed I still have my notes for) McKeon's seminar on Aristotle and Strauss's seminars on Machiavelli and on Nietzsche's *Beyond Good and Evil*.

I revered McKeon. But he also made me, and I think not only me, cringe. He might put a question to the class, a student would dare to say something, and if it were less than brilliant, McKeon often replied, "That is a very stupid answer." Or someone would be huddled in class in his or her coat—Chicago has very cold winters—and in the middle of a sentence McKeon would stop dead, and say, " 'Miss So-and-So' or 'Mr. So-and-So,' I'll wait until you take off your coat."

I was only auditing, so I never spoke in class.

This was a time when one never called teachers by their first names; of course, they didn't address you by your first name either. It's hard now to imagine this kind of formality in the classroom. The idea of being disrespectful to a teacher, or talking back, was unthinkable. Our professors were gods, and we couldn't imagine that we could have a social relation with them.

My attitude was that if a teacher was warm, like Ned Rosenheim, great. But if he wasn't, I could live with it—just as you shouldn't choose the doctor because the doctor is nice but because the doctor is competent. I was shocked and frightened by McKeon's manner, but I wouldn't have allowed it to stop me from going to his class and learning from him.

I didn't think, and do not now think, that the main job of an education is to teach the student to be independent. The point was to learn; you have your whole life to be independent. I thought *life* should teach you to be independent.

We still understand this with the hard sciences, or medicine. But with the humanities or social sciences, we think that all kinds of psychological elements should come into play, that studying should be a "growth" experience, that there should be "personal interaction," and that students should learn to be independent. Yet there's so much to be taught, and so much to learn, that if the teacher is teaching, and a student brings an attitude of respect to learning, then the issue of independence doesn't arise.

How can I say it? Since everything that was taught was praised, you learned all kinds of things were interesting that you hadn't *known* were interesting. You were always being stretched.

Of course, I disagreed with my teachers from time to time. But I thought the point was to get whatever I could from them. I *wanted* to be changed by them. I wasn't interested in showing that I was smarter, I was interested in learning as much as I could.

My main friends the first year I was at the university were my fellow high–school students who'd come with me from southern California. They were the people I spent most of my time with, plus some new friends I made at the university. One was Mike Nichols, who was a boarding-school friend of one of my friends from high school. My friends and I were effortlessly high-minded. We talked with one another incessantly, until all hours of the night, about our readings. We didn't have gym, we didn't have sports. (At one time, there were intramural football teams called the Platonists and the Aristotelians.) We were students, and we were studying.

Allan Bloom was a brilliant, real—enrolled—student in the seminars of Strauss and McKeon that I audited, and I remember him well. I deplore the vindictiveness in his popular book and the lament for lost (largely imaginary) privilege. I disagree with much of his use of Plato. I don't hate the young, and I'm not interested in promoting the fortunes of some establishment, educational or political, in this country. I don't have the agenda that he had. But like Bloom—and like George Steiner—I am absolutely a defender of the mandatory curriculum, shaped by philosophical inquiry, and beginning with, yes, Plato and Aristotle and the Greek dramatists and Herodotus and Thucydides. I expect to continue to reread the books on this list for the rest of my life.

At the beginning of my second and last year in the College, I had been auditing a section (I forget whose) of Social Science II (which I'd placed out of) for several months, when one of my friends who was enrolled in another section recommended hers. It was taught by an instructor named Philip Rieff, who, she said, was very good on Freud. And Social Science II had just reached the two assigned texts by Freud, *Civilization and Its Discontents* and *Moses and Monotheism.* So I dropped in on that section one day, and Philip Rieff and I married two weeks later. We were both eccentric, intense people. That changed my social life. And it eventually took me away from Chicago. The following year, after I received my B.A., my husband was offered an instructorship at Brandeis, and the year after that, after our son was born, I was admitted as a graduate student at Harvard.

Harvard was a superb university, but still, an ordinary university, with a big menu and no "right way."

At Chicago, we learned to read, to reason, and to debate. But we didn't write papers—we weren't expected to turn in papers any more than Socrates's students were expected to turn in papers. And our end-of-quarter exams were all multiple-choice, which means they were read by machines. The way I interpreted it was, "Well, these people don't care about tests. They're so high-minded that they don't take the grading situation seriously."

But I discovered in graduate school a whole dimension of teaching I had missed: doing a long paper and having your professor give you a close and careful reading with comments.

If my husband had continued to teach at Chicago, I would have been happy to continue there. I would have gone into the Committee on Social Thought and studied with Strauss and McKeon.

At Chicago I was handed an invaluable set of tools, and my enthusiasm and my natural respect for seriousness and for learning were confirmed. The University of Chicago was the single most important part of my education. My entire life has been a development of and a debate with the education that I received there. I think anybody who knows about Chicago and knows my work would make the connection.

Index

DATE DUE